Landscape of Discontent

Landscape of Discontent

Urban Sustainability in Immigrant Paris

ANDREW NEWMAN

A Quadrant Book

UNIVERSITY OF MINNESOTA PRESS
MINNEAPOLIS · LONDON

QUADRANT

Quadrant, a joint initiative of the University of Minnesota Press and the Institute for Advanced Study at the University of Minnesota, provides support for interdisciplinary scholarship within a new, more collaborative model of research and publication.

http://quadrant.umn.edu.

Sponsored by Quadrant's Global Cultures group (advisory board: Evelyn Davidheiser, Michael Goldman, Helga Leitner, and Margaret Werry) and by the Institute for Global Studies at the University of Minnesota.

Quadrant is generously funded by the Andrew W. Mellon Foundation.

The University of Minnesota Press gratefully acknowledges financial assistance for the publication of this book from Wayne State University.

Portions of chapter 4 were published in "Contested Ecologies: Environmental Activism and Urban Space in Immigrant Paris," *City and Society* 23, no. 2 (2011): 192–209. A different version of chapter 5 and portions of chapter 6 were published in "Gatekeepers of the Urban Commons: Vigilant Citizenship and Neoliberal Space in Multiethnic Paris," *Antipode: A Radical Journal of Geography* 45, no. 4 (2012): 947–64; copyright 2012 Antipode Foundation Ltd.

All photographs were taken by the author unless credited otherwise.

Published by the University of Minnesota Press
111 Third Avenue South, Suite 290
Minneapolis, MN 55401–2520
http://www.upress.umn.edu

Library of Congress Cataloging-in-Publication Data
Newman, Andrew.
    Landscape of discontent : urban sustainability in immigrant Paris / Andrew Newman.
    Includes bibliographical references and index.
    ISBN 978-0-8166-8962-0 (hc) — ISBN 978-0-8166-8963-7 (pb)
    1. Urban ecology (Sociology)—France—Paris. 2. Urban parks—Social aspects—France—Paris. 3. Sustainable urban development—France—Paris. 4. City planning—Environmental aspects—France—Paris. 5. Environmentalism—Political aspects—France—Paris. 6. Immigrants—France—Paris—Social conditions. 7. Immigrants—Political activity—France—Paris. 8. Paris (France)—Environmental conditions. 9. Paris (France)—Ethnic relations. 10. Paris (France)—Politics and government. I. Title.
    HT243.F72P377 2015
    307.760944'361—dc23   2014049429

Printed in the United States of America on acid-free paper

The University of Minnesota is an equal-opportunity educator and employer.

22 21 20 19 18 17 16 15   10 9 8 7 6 5 4 3 2 1

For
Shane Ali and Shaira

CONTENTS

ABBREVIATIONS

AAS   Agents d'Accueil et de Surveillance: welcoming and surveillance agents under the employ of the Paris Parks Department

AIRPARIF Association Interdépartementale pour la Gestion du Réseau Automatique de Surveillance de la Pollution Atmosphérique et d'Alerte en Région d'Île-de-France: a regional nongovernmental organization officially tasked with monitoring air pollution and publishing air-quality alerts in the Île-de-France region, which includes Paris and its suburbs

APUR   Atelier Parisien d'Urbanisme: a publicly funded organization tasked with producing maps and spatial analyses of Paris and the Île-de-France region; an important source of data for urbanists, urban planners, and architects

BGA   Braves Garçons d'Afrique, Brave Boys of Africa: an organization founded in 2001 by a group of northeast Paris youths of African and Antillean origins

CCTV   closed-circuit television

CRS   Compagnies Républicaines de Sécurité: a national law-enforcement agency (frequently refers to riot police)

CUCS   Contrat Urbain de Cohésion Sociale: zone-based strategy emphasizing social cohesion in neighborhoods

DAL	Droit au Logement: the right-to-housing movement
DEVE	Direction des Espaces Verts et de l'Environnement, the City of Paris Parks and Environment Department
EU	European Union
FN	Front National, National Front: a far-right political party widely associated with anti-immigrant sentiment in France
GPRU	Grand Projet de Renouvellement Urbain: large urban-renewal plan focused on the peripheral areas of the city of Paris
HLM	*habitation à loyer modéré*: publicly subsidized, rent-controlled housing
ICLEI	International Council for Local Environmental Initiatives: a global policy network that focuses on the diffusion of urban sustainability expertise and knowledge between cities
IUP	Institut d'Urbanisme de Paris: urban planning school at the University of Paris XII
MRAP	Mouvement contre le Racisme et pour l'Amitié entre les Peuples: nongovernmental organization associated with the antiracism movement in France
NGO	nongovernmental organization
OPAH	Opération Programmée d'Amélioration de l'Habitat: urban-rehabilitation programs
PCF	Parti Communiste Français, French Communist Party
POS	Plan d'Occupation des Sols: land-use plan
PS	Parti Socialiste, Socialist Party
RER	Réseau Express Régional: commuter railroad network serving the Île-de-France region
RPR	Rassemblement pour la République, Rally for the Republic: France's dominant right-wing political party until the early 2000s; superseded by the UMP
SEMAEST	Société d'Économie Mixte d'Aménagement de l'Est de Paris, Corporation for the Mixed Economic Development of Eastern Paris: a quasi-public development authority
SNCF	Société Nationale des Chemins de Fer Français, National Railroad Company of France

SYCTOM	Syndicat Intercommunal pour le Traitement des Ordures Ménagères: a regional garbage collection and disposal authority

UMP	Union pour un Mouvement Populaire, Union for a Popular Movement: France's dominant right-wing political party since the early 2000s; it grew out of the RPR

UNCED	United Nations Conference on Environment and Development: widely known as the "Earth Summit," this 1992 meeting of UN member states and NGOs gave rise to Agenda 21 and shaped policies on urban sustainability into the twenty-first century

ZAC	Zone d'Aménagement Concerté: urban zone of concentrated development

ZRU	Zone de Redynamisation Urbaine: zone of urban redynamization

ZSP	Zone de Sécurité Prioritaire: priority security urban zone

ZUS	Zone Urbaine Sensible: "sensitive" ("at risk") urban zone

INTRODUCTION

On a rainy day in May 2007, the mayor of Paris held an inauguration ceremony for the Jardins d'Éole, a new park billed as the first sustainable addition to the capital's internationally renowned system of green spaces and
public gardens. It was to be an auspicious occasion: two years before, the
design was featured at the Museum of Modern Art in New York City in an
exhibition touting innovative "palliative spaces" for "abused and polluted
sites" in postindustrial cities.[1] In keeping with these transformative aims, the
onetime railroad freight depot-turned-park is a far cry from famous Parisian
gardens such as the Jardin du Luxembourg or Jardin des Tuileries. Sited in a
postindustrial district of the capital where public housing towers vie for
space with railroad tracks and empty factories, the park's wide-open spaces
have a stark quality that is exaggerated by still fledgling trees and an overall
aesthetic of austere minimalism. Concrete stairways and aluminum catwalks
bridge artificial knolls and dales of unnatural symmetry. Instead of delicate
flowerbeds and hedges, one finds brushed metal surfaces, gravel, asphalt,
and a chemical-free lawn that appears almost boastful of its heretical irregu-
larities. In many respects, the landscape of the Jardins d'Éole is a material
expression of a polemic on the political and social meaning of urban park-
lands as much as it is an amenity for a neighborhood whose residents have
long lacked access to green space.

Fittingly, contestation and debate would even mark the inauguration day
itself. The highlight of the ceremony was expected to be a dedication speech

delivered by Bertrand Delanoë, who was elected as the first Socialist Party mayor of Paris, serving between 2001 and 2014. Delanoë, who was only half-jokingly referred to by many as the first Left-wing leader of Paris since the Commune of 1871, took to a podium in a tent that had been hastily set up in the park's center as a shelter from the ubiquitous springtime rain. His speech described the green space as created not only for the people of the neighborhood but *by* them, as the "fruit of local democracy and participative urbanism." He spoke directly to the front rows of the crowd—largely made up of local activists—who had, as he mentioned, been part of a successful grassroots campaign to construct the park in an area of the capital that has long suffered the consequences of political, economic, and environmental inequalities. There were waves of applause.

But Delanoë's normally suave manner was decidedly flustered on this particular day; indeed, the mayor was shouting at the audience, and he (along with many others in the front rows) wore looks of deep consternation. This was because his dedication was barely audible over the ongoing sounds of women's voices, chanting, shouting, and clapping deep in the back of the audience. Just outside of the inauguration tent, and unperturbed by the springtime downpour, a crowd of protesters—composed mainly of women of West African and Maghrebi descent—clothed in either traditional West African wraps or *hijab,* and in some cases carrying infants, had gathered. Chanting "Hey, hey, Delanoë! Nous sommes les *mal-logés!*" (a French neologism meaning the "poorly housed"), the women came from a protest group that has been increasingly active in northeastern Paris because of rising rents and forced evictions accompanying urban redevelopment. A group of CRS (Compagnies Républicaines de Sécurité: national riot police) formed a barrier between the women and the rest of the audience, but they could not prevent the protesters from trying to drown out the mayor.

The mayor, his entourage, and the other invited guests were clearly caught off guard by the protest, especially because it occurred in a neighborhood long viewed as friendly territory for Socialist Party politicians in Paris. After a brief pause in the ceremony to consult with aides and the police, it was decided to proceed with the hope of not encouraging further disruption. And so Delanoë and the other speakers continued as planned with their speeches touting the importance of community input, sustainability, and public space, all the while pretending that the crowd of angry, shouting immigrant-origin women gathered in front of them was simply not there.

The Jardins d'Éole is an example of an urban form that is becoming increasingly common in cities around the world: the postindustrial "brownfield" repurposed as a sustainable landscape. Sites such as the Jardins d'Éole materialize a green turn in urban policy, planning, and design that is swiftly becoming ensconced as a global orthodoxy guiding the ways cities are being built, reimagined, and inhabited. This ethnography has been written in response to this shift, which is at once urban, social, and political.

This book argues that this turn toward ecological urbanism is not merely a design trend, but part of a broader reimagining of what nature, the city, its citizens, and political contestation mean at a fundamental level. A great deal of this book addresses this reimagining of the city and its inhabitants by way of the contentious politics of cultural belonging in France. In contrast to those who seize upon events such as the heinous *Charlie Hebdo* shootings to highlight a supposed clash between Islam and France's republican values, I highlight the stories of several immigrant-origin activists and residents who embrace and even rework republicanism to tease out its humanistic and pluralistic potential to a greater extent than the "official" versions endorsed by the state (ironically, a few of these individuals come from the same public housing

View of the Jardins d'Éole, looking north.

projects where the *Charlie Hebdo* perpetrators lived as children, on the Rue d'Aubervilliers, up the block from the Jardins d'Éole). At the same time, there are aspects of Paris's urban political economy—namely, the fact that it is a rapidly gentrifying, postindustrial city whose policy elite struggle to assert their place in global interurban competition—that make my argument about the relationship between politics, ecology, and the city relevant far beyond the borders of France itself.

Put otherwise, this ethnography explores the political and social implications of what happens when environmentalists and their allies gain some control of the production of space in a major global city fraught with disparities that are at once economic, ethnoracial, gendered, and environmental.[2] The Jardins d'Éole was built at the demand of a multiethnic, neighborhood-based protest movement. However, the mobilization's agenda was also congruent with an ongoing reinvention of northeast Paris's multiethnic, predominately West African and Maghrebi neighborhoods along the lines of sustainable urban design. Indeed, the changing identity of the site is itself revealing of these social paradoxes. Originally, a postindustrial *terrain vague* (wasteland) known as the Cour du Maroc (the Moroccan Court), the site was eventually renamed the Jardins d'Éole during the late stages of the design project.[3] The new name invokes Éole (Aeolus), the Greek god of wind, and thus the mythological roots of European civilization, the primordial, elemental strength of nature, wind as a sustainable energy source, and most recognizably to locals, the RER ÉOLE—a commuter train that roars along the neighborhood's railway tracks linking central Paris to the surrounding *banlieue* (suburbs).

The Jardins d'Éole and other ecologically inspired urban projects described in this book materialize the political contradictions between "movement environmentalisms," multiethnic neighborhood mobilizations of various types, and ostensibly progressive urban planners and policy makers focused on creating a more sustainable (and economically competitive) Paris.[4] As a result, this is not a tale that features neat battle lines drawn between categories such as "residents," "activists," "the state," or "capital." In everyday life, such entities are internally differentiated and stratified by a variety of individuals and groups with diverse and conflicting interests. As I observed while doing ethnographic research in and around Paris, political struggle is multidimensional, and often not a simple tug-of-war between diametrically opposed entities. Frequently, urban politics plays out as a war of position,[5] or the careful courting of allies and cornering of adversaries through conscious choices of language, style, and symbolism, which I describe in chapter 2 as the spatial strategy of urban politics.

As a result, this book is not as much a study of the Jardins d'Éole itself as it is an ethnography that examines the park as a highly political assemblage, revealing connections between environmentalism, invocations of nature, urban politics, and the remaking of Paris and its peripheries into what former President Nicolas Sarkozy called the "post-Kyoto city."[6] For Éole activists as well as Paris's urban policy elite, the Jardins d'Éole is a means for a broader social and political project, and not merely an end in itself. My analysis of these strategies, which often incorporate and rework the materiality of the city itself, ranging from urban gardening to housing rights activism, demonstrates that such practices amount to often conflicting attempts by people of varying sociopolitical positions to realize what Lefebvre called "the right to the city."[7] The stakes behind these practices are simultaneously ecological and urban, while also being about more than the city itself: as David Harvey has written, "the right to the city is far more than the individual liberty to access urban resources: it is a right to change ourselves by changing the city."[8] Indeed, like the Jardins d'Éole itself, the "right to the city" is best understood as a means for broader social transformation, and not an end it itself.

As I will demonstrate, however, there is something about everyday life in heterogeneous, unruly places such as northeast Paris that appears to defy many attempts to "fix" these spaces according to the static vision or ideal of many different types of urban projects, whether mobilized by urban planners or by residents. Upon only brief examination, such sites appear to be suspended—if ever so tenuously—in a continual state of becoming and possibility.[9] This quality of indeterminacy is no accident; nor is it a mystical quality emanating from some imagined essence of the city itself (even in such a thoroughly mythical place as Paris). It is the city as a *commons* and it is the result of the creativity, struggle, and labor of people in ways that are quotidian at times, and, in other moments, spectacular and historic. Thus, while outwardly focused on a newly dominant trend in urban design, this book ultimately concerns itself with a time-honored, but still poorly understood, question (especially in today's era of neoliberal urban governance):

how do people—from residents to planners—create "vibrant" urban spaces, and how are such places reproduced in everyday life, and for what political end?

Landscaping Discontent: Rethinking the Politics of Urban Design from the Ground Up

Over the course of my research with residents, activists, and urban planners in northeast Paris, I realized that I was not merely observing contestation over the city; I was witness to a churning, unresolved process that is central to the making of the urban landscape itself, defined by confrontation, negotiation, and creativity. As the infrastructure and neighborhoods that make up the city are forever in a state of construction, deterioration, maintenance, and reconstruction, I paid special attention to how the discontents, visions, and aspirations of numerous individuals (not only urban planners) are constantly being built into the landscape. This book is therefore an anthropology *of the* city[10]—not merely *in the* city. It combines an ethnographic focus on the material infrastructure[11] of the city (parks and green spaces are understood by planners to be part of a system in much the same way as streets, railways, pipes, and the electrical grid), with an emphasis on how such assemblages are integrated into the production of space under global capitalism. Most important, this ethnography privileges the everyday practices, lives, and stories of people who with their own creative agency rarely follow the logic of the designs accorded to them by architects, planners, or, for that matter, social theorists.

The Jardins d'Éole is provocative in this regard. On the one hand, it is explicitly envisioned as part of Paris's infrastructure, and in particular the repurposing of an obsolete part of an industrial revolution–era rail system into a network of "regional ecological continuity" that channels flows of "biodiversity" through the city.[12] Indeed, parks pose interesting questions for the anthropology of infrastructure because these spaces invert the process that Ashley Carse has aptly described as the transformation of "nature into infrastructure";[13] urban park design and management accomplishes the opposite feat by transforming infrastructure into nature. In effect, parks aspire to naturalize the city—and the production of space under capitalism—itself. As a result, the Jardins d'Éole is an important asset for a Paris reimagined as a global capital of urban sustainability, a place where nonhuman forms of life are recast as biodiversity and hence transformed into a form of capital. On the other hand, the Jardins d'Éole is also the outcome and continued site of everyday political practices that can fit somewhat awkwardly with such grand visions. It was the focal point of an environmental justice mobilization that was transformed into an urban planning project because of an apparent political success. The park therefore blurs the distinction between "planners" and "users" that is often the premise of many designs. While this mixing of roles was certainly resisted by some members of the city planning establishment, it was embraced and promoted by the newly elected socialist mayoral administration as a hallmark of its democratic and participatory approach to urban governance and sustainability. Since the electoral swing to socialist mayoral administrations began in 2001, the city government's much touted affinity for environmentalists has been oriented toward building not only a more sustainable Paris but a more globally competitive Paris as well. Paris's écologistes now find themselves to be a newly important element of a far greater project: Paris's becoming a distinctly green global center of politics, finance, and culture.

The work of Henri Lefebvre—and in particular, *The Production of Space*—illuminates the complex, interrelated dynamic between built, social, and political environments, as imagined designs and material sites. For Lefebvre, to understand and correctly read the city as a process is to understand the political, creative, and humane potential of its inhabitants. Thus, Lefebvre's reading of the city weaves together urban planning, architecture, design, and a range of other "specialists of space" as varied as artists and ethnographers.[14] Lefebvre elaborates a theory of capitalist urbanization by exploring the relationship between knowledge, creativity, expertise, and political practice. Indeed, the book's relevance to urban politics was informed by his direct engagement with many of the same postwar era battles over urban development that gave birth to Paris's écologiste movement.[15]

However, projects such as the Jardins d'Éole reveal the problems with Lefebvre's approach, which become apparent when one examines the stark contrast he draws between the powerful and the weak, and domination and resistance. Lefebvre's use of the language of passivity to refer to the social reality of "space as lived" and the space of "inhabitants" and "users" is starkly different from the "dominant space" of planners, scientists, and other experts.[16] The deep gulf between the powerful and powerless, and the determinism undergirding this framework, mangle Lefebvre's own approach and any analysis that naively draws from his work. Indeed, the problems of such determinism plague Lefebvre himself at times, who seems frustrated when writing about

> the space of those who are referred to by means of such clumsy and pejorative labels as "users" and "inhabitants." No well-defined terms with clear connotations have ever been found to designate these groups. Their marginalization by spatial practice thus extends even to language.[17]

Lefebvre seems to blame this difficulty writing about "users" (a term he criticizes and yet feels compelled to employ throughout *The Production of Space*) on "their marginalization by spatial practice." Could it be, however, that it is actually Lefebvre's own theoretical framework that marginalizes, resulting in a "silence of users" whose defining social position is that they are "planned for" as opposed to being planners themselves?[18] If analytic constructs such as "the user" seem enigmatic, silent, and one-dimensional, it is because they are theorized as such, in order to exist merely as the opposite of an often better elaborated theoretical figure, in this case, "the planner." Even when people choose to shed their role as mere "users," organize, and engage in explicit political activity, the role of social movements is envisioned in a reactive and resistant, simplistic zero-sum game vis-à-vis the state, planners, elites, and others in power.

Indeed, my focus on decidedly nonexpert residents who seek to transform their urban surroundings is meant to draw attention to the urban designs of people who are not necessarily architects and urban planners. In this regard, my understanding of who might be termed a designer is parallel to and directly informed by Gramsci's definition of an intellectual: he famously compared intellectuals to cooks and tailors, pointing out that although "it can happen that everyone at some time fries a couple of eggs or sews up a tear in a jacket" only a few people in society had a recognized social function pertaining to this work.[19] In a similar fashion, while there are only a few people in society who have developed the professional and technical experience to legitimately work as urban designers, numerous people observe the rhythms and flows of the city around them in everyday life, develop readings of what they see, and frequently attempt to intervene. At times, such interventions might seem to exist in the domain of practice, such as carefully watching a street corner for suspicious activity, and in other moments the designs of residents may have more material outcomes, such as urban gardens or the Jardins d'Éole itself. However, I argue that even everyday forms of sidewalk territoriality amount to design as practice (here the usage of *design* as a verb is especially important).[20] People envision and analyze infrastructure, parks, streets, city blocks, and neighborhoods in terms of movements and flows that may or may not correspond to the understandings of planning authorities; they also attempt to redirect, fix, shift, or even maintain the movements within and across these spaces by reimagining these sites and even materially reshaping and reworking places and infrastructure. Many aspects of these processes contain elements of design; not only do style and aesthetics come into play (especially in urban gardening) but, at a fundamental level, spaces are conceived and envisioned, and lines are drawn between them, as people "connect the dots" between their positions and broader historical and political processes shaping society, with the city itself serving as the medium of change. Such designs form the basis for many residents' claim for a right to the city, and frequently, as I will show, these efforts directly engage with and modify the work of the "legitimate" architects and designers, occasionally with transformative consequences.

To return to Lefebvre, my motive for unsettling the distinction between the categories of dominant planners and silenced users is intended to humanize and nuance this framework, not dismiss it outright. The relationship between environmental activism and the green turn in urban design provides an ideal context in which to revise Lefebvre's approach—despite his claim that the city is a space where "nature is emptied out."[21] Ironically, however, as this book will demonstrate, Lefebvre's approach allows us to comprehend articulations of "urban nature" as part of a highly productive process involving a wide range of actors, from architects, policy makers, activists, and even outwardly apolitical urban gardeners. A nuanced and revised understanding of Lefebvre's framework is of vital importance to understanding the profound ways that cities are being transformed as part of a turn toward ecological urbanism.

Nature as Urban System

As ethnographers work toward blurring the distinctions between urban and environmental anthropologies, an urban/nature dichotomy that factored heavily in the discipline's history is disappearing.[22] Historically, the relative lack of anthropological attention to the socially constructed boundaries between the natural and built environments is surprising, given the amount of attention that has been lavished on overturning this age-old binary in fields as varied as history, geography, architecture, and urban planning.[23] Even though the nature/culture and rural/urban binaries have been a topic of analysis in anthropology, the production of urban nature—which is now embedded in the hegemonic policy discourse of urban sustainability—raises a new set of political, spatial, and urban questions that ethnographers are uniquely equipped to address.

This book is based on a political approach to ecology that does not reify nature as an object of study, but rather analyzes the production of nature as part of broader processes of political contestation.[24] As Maria Kaika and Erik Swyngedouw have pointed out, "there is no such thing as a singular nature around which an environmental policy or an environmentally sensitive intervention can be constructed . . . Rather there is a multitude of urban natures and a multitude of existing, possible, or practicable socionatural relations."[25] This ethnography draws on a rich and varied tradition of political ecology in anthropology and other disciplines to understand how multiple urban natures are produced—and rendered productive—in city politics and in the context of the nation.[26] My approach seeks to understand the political motivations, stakes, and social practices underlying the production of multiple—at times competing—urban natures. In northeast Paris, for example, many struggles sparked by highly gendered, ethnoracial, and class-based inequalities related to toxic-waste dumping and air pollution, as well as housing rights, child care, and immigrant rights, were connected in the mobilization for the Jardins d'Éole; the park (and multiple invocations of nature) became a viable symbol to unite and "landscape" all of these strands of discontent, though the park later become a symbol of gentrification and the "reconquest" of the city by way of sustainable urban planning (based on yet another notion of nature). This book therefore represents an effort to contribute an ethnographically grounded approach to the interdisciplinary field of urban political ecology.[27]

Indeed, the Jardins d'Éole represents an example of a broad-based strategy to rebuild (and re-brand) cities through sustainable landscape urbanism in the twenty-first century. This concept of sustainability has evolved a great deal since being popularized by *Limits to Growth* (1972) and *Our Common Future* (the so-called Brundtland Report) in 1987, the former of which suggested that "the future course of human society, perhaps even the survival of human society" was dependent on global cooperation to urgently address a host of issues, including population explosion and finite resources.[28] By 1992, many of the core values of the Brundtland Report were adapted to cities in the Agenda 21 Declaration that was developed at the 1992 United Nations Conference on Environment and Development (the so-called Earth Summit). Agenda 21 helped to define cities as important sites to materialize the sustainability principles embraced by the United Nations, member states, and allied NGOs. At a conceptual level, sustainability has, of course, been a subject of debate for a long time, with the neo-Malthusian overtones of sustainability discourse having drawn particular ire from those who otherwise welcome calls for increased environmental protections.[29]

More than a decade into the twenty-first century, however, sustainability is increasingly enshrined in the techno-managerial logic of accumulation and efficiency;[30] two writers in the *Harvard Business Review* went so far as to compare sustainability to "electrification" and "mass production" for its transformative implications for capitalism.[31] Increasingly, for a range of institutions from businesses, to universities, to NGOs and governments at all scales, a focus on sustainability is equated not just with taking steps toward environmental responsibility, but with a corresponding display of worldwide awareness, global insight, and ultimately competitiveness. Indeed, from the time of the *Limits to Growth* to the more overtly neoliberal incarnations of the concept, sustainability has always been oriented toward a particularly important form of capitalist spatial practice: the reimagining of scale.

The naturalization of scale has been of special significance in European environmental and urban discourse. In the early 1990s, at the same time that heads of state were formulating the political and geographic limits of the new European Union, leaders from cities across the Continent focused on Agenda 21 principles as a way to redefine the meaning of European identity at the urban scale. The Aalborg Charter, ratified in 1994, adapted Agenda 21 to the context of "European Towns and Cities" and served to produce, reify, and naturalize the category of the European city as a space that is synonymous with sustainability and ecologically oriented urban planning. As chapter 4 discusses, this pan-European approach has provided an important theme for the celebrated revitalization of cities such as Barcelona, where the embrace of European identity enabled the foregrounding of a Catalan identity over that of Spain,[32] but it also offers a new way to rearticulate and reinforce the nation in capitals such as Paris. This form of globally oriented, self-consciously fashioned European green urbanism reaches its apex in neoliberal projects such as Sweden's Hammarby Sjöstad, a self-contained green neighborhood plan designed to be exported as a model overseas.[33] Europe's relationship to sustainable urbanism is a highly Lefebvrian tale: the globally important green turn in urban planning has largely been innovated by European cities, while the "new European city" (in an imaginary and material sense) is partially an invention of the green turn in urban planning and design.

The resulting ubiquity and policy preeminence of the sustainability concept has elevated (or, as some would say, degraded) the idea to the status of a buzzword, and more than a few environmentalists suggest abandoning the term altogether. But despite the elastic-to-the-point-of-ethereal quality that often accompanies the meaning of sustainability, urban design, planning, and architecture (and in particular landscape design) have done more to operationalize sustainability through ecological design than many other fields. For all of the greenwashing that accompanies development programs and urban boosterism today—indeed, it has grown difficult to find a major urban project that is *not* touted as sustainable now—the last two decades have seen a tremendous increase in the sophistication and degree of specialization in the technique, know-how, and philosophy of building ecologically low-impact urban spaces. Pioneering works such as Anne Spirn's *The Granite Garden,* which declared the city to be "a granite garden, composed of many smaller gardens, set in a garden world," celebrated and resuscitated the long-standing "city as organism" metaphor and placed biological processes at the center of how urban spaces were imagined, conceived, and designed.[34] At the same time, a range of professional urbanists as diverse as traffic engineers, hydrologists, and landscape architects have become, in effect, specialists of sustainability and have been hard at work consciously blurring the lines between ecosystems and urban networks. Urban ecological systems, often understood in terms of "natural cycles" or "metabolic" processes, have become central to the ways that cities are being rethought and rebuilt.[35] Often sustainable spaces emphasize the importance of a "rediscovery," "return," or "reclamation" of nature, or natural cycles, to cities alongside increasing concerns for urban biodiversity that invert the traditional "city as organism" metaphor: animal and plant life are now understood as part of the urban environment. As notions of global interurban competition have become a hegemonic fixture in the way cities are branded and reinvented, so has urban sustainability: it is increasingly described as a survival adaptation in an innovation-driven neoliberal world that is equal parts Malthusian and social Darwinist. At the same time, and in a testament to the contradictory nature of sustainability as "myth and practice," many sustainability initiatives—such as the Jardins d'Éole—are a product of democratic and grassroots-led efforts to build more just cities.[36]

This ethnography shows that projects such as the Jardins d'Éole are not merely a green gloss for business as usual but represent a new way in which the city is rendered both productive and political by way of invoking nature. Previous innovations in the way cities are built and designed, ranging from Haussmann's boulevards to the high modernism of Brasília, have also been accompanied by new ways of inhabiting cities, new forms of belonging and exclusions alike, and new routes toward political and social transformation. This ethnography is therefore an attempt to begin to chart out the social and political life of ecological urbanism and sustainable design not only as a new urban form, but as a broader social and ecological vision that is being adapted differently in cities around the world.

Paris on the Boundary Line

There is a taken-for-granted story that social scientists always tell about Paris. The capital is where one finds the Louvre, the Eiffel Tower, and throngs of tourists on the Champs-Élysées, it is a playground for tourists and a bastion

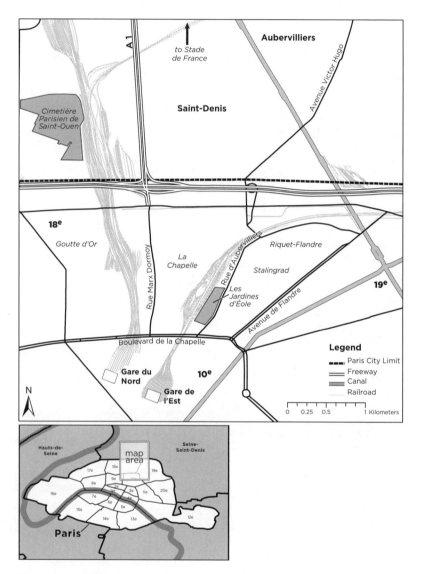

The Paris metropolitan area; northeast Paris and adjacent municipalities. Map by Olivia Dobbs and Tim Stallmann.

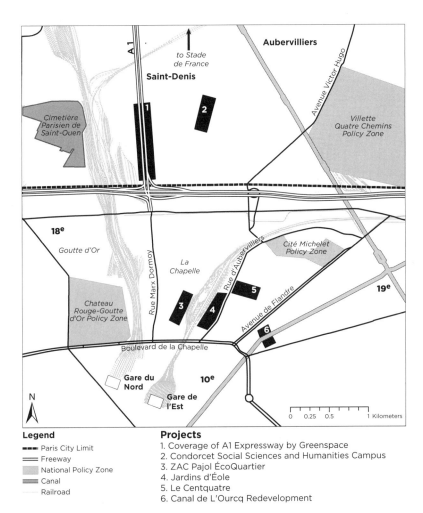

Legend

- ▪▪▪ Paris City Limit
- ═══ Freeway
- ▬ National Policy Zone
- ▬ Canal
- ··· Railroad

Projects

1. Coverage of A1 Expressway by Greenspace
2. Condorcet Social Sciences and Humanities Campus
3. ZAC Pajol ÉcoQuartier
4. Jardins d'Éole
5. Le Centquatre
6. Canal de L'Ourcq Redevelopment

The Jardins d'Éole and other redevelopment projects and urban policy zones. Much of the area included in the upper (northern) half of this map is covered by a large-scale project known as Paris Nord-Est. Moreover, a vertical axis originating from the railroad terminals and moving northward is an important component of an even larger project, the Grand Paris plan. Map by Olivia Dobbs and Tim Stallmann.

for the elite. The *banlieue* is where one finds the social housing projects (termed HLM—*habitations à loyer modéré*—rent-controlled housing) where the immigrants and the poor live; it is imagined as a kind of "zone of social abandonment" where people cast as the failure of something called the "French model" are condemned to live.[37] The capital is French and secular; the *banlieue* is immigrant (usually Arab or African) and Muslim. The capital is rich; the *banlieue* is poor. The capital has a voice; the *banlieue* is silenced, except for occasional outbreaks of unrest, as in 2005. The capital—and France itself—is the victim; the *banlieue* is the threat. Like any good myth, this tale of two cities is not only self-evident and a self-fulfilling prophecy, but generative: an entire cultural (and scholarly) edifice, including years of social and urban policy, has been built upon this dichotomy.

As with all binaries, the Paris/*banlieue* dichotomy conceals as much as it reveals, and when one looks more closely, the messiness of everyday experience starts to challenge such abstract simplicity. Obviously, the differences between an elite block in Paris's eighth arrondissement and a crumbling public-housing complex in Clichy-sous-Bois, outside of the city, represent near opposite ends of a profoundly important geography of political and economic inequality.[38] But the *banlieues* are anything but uniformly poor, immigrant, or even working-class, and Paris itself is not as "museumized" in everyday life as it is in a great deal of social science. It is a dynamic and contested global city that reproduces its own internal divisions and dichotomies (notably, a long-standing politically and economically meaningful east/west divide), and, in particular, numerous outlying *quartiers populaires* that house large numbers of impoverished residents of diverse immigrant origins (many of whom are excluded from the social housing system while at the same time being subject to the displacing effects of gentrification that are distinct to the capital). The birth of the *sans-papiers* (undocumented migrants) movement is highly symbolic in this regard, as it began with a vigil to seek shelter at the Église Saint-Bernard de la Chapelle directly at the foot of the popular tourist destination of Montmartre, in the eighteenth arrondissement. Why? While the political symbolism of the capital is important, many undocumented migrants struggle to find space in Paris itself to avoid the cost (and especially the surveillance) of the rail-based commute to the often-distant *banlieue* communities. In fact, despite a half century of efforts by urban planners, large and often overcrowded neighborhoods populated by multiple generations of immigrants are present throughout the city, and in such areas apartment buildings that lack running water are far from difficult to find.

This last point deserves special emphasis, as the severe spatial inequalities within Paris continue to be reproduced despite more than a half century of efforts by policy makers to push so-called *quartiers difficiles* outside of the capital. How? Such internal differentiation is the geography of Paris's (and France's) politically fraught, on-again, off-again flirtation with neoliberal doxa. Nevertheless, France's resilient statist tradition has made Paris a decidedly square peg in the global cities framework and as a result the city is absent from most scholarship in the neoliberalization of space.[39] It has undergone the same neoliberal urban strategies of gentrification and consumption-driven redevelopment seen in cities throughout the world.[40]

For example, many former working-class districts were redeveloped around tourism and culture, such as the Beaubourg area with the building of the Centre Pompidou during the 1970s, and the art industry–related gentrification of the Marais neighborhood in the 1980s. The 1990s and 2000s

No running water in the City of Light: pump used by residents who reside in nearby abandoned buildings. Paris's northeastern neighborhoods have long had the city's highest numbers of "insalubrious" residences; many such buildings function as squats that house diverse, newly arriving groups of undocumented immigrants and refugees.

have seen the eastern neighborhoods of Belleville and Ménilmontant shift away from being working-class and immigrant enclaves as more artists and young professionals move in. Yet, such transformations have occurred in a highly particular fashion, with the state playing the paradoxical role of channeling and focusing neoliberal forms, not rejecting them outright. Paris's financial district, La Défense, provides a case in point. Despite being a globally important bastion of finance and Europe's largest American-style "central business district," it was built *outside* of the urban core (technically in the *banlieue*) and was planned with a great degree of state involvement, which defies common expectations of neoliberal projects, what the "private" and "public" do, and therefore whose agency is presumed to underpin such projects. The Paris region's urban form, and in particular the divisions within the capital, are a material expression of the uneven efforts by elites to assimilate a globally hegemonic policy discourse and produce what has been termed a "néo-libéralisme à la française" through urban space.[41]

The built environment of northeast Paris: a mix of modernist *cité* (public housing neighborhoods) and nineteenth-century apartment buildings. The bridge in the foreground is one of only a few places to traverse the railway tracks that divide the neighborhood between east and west.

This state-centered assimilation of neoliberal urbanism has transformed metropolitan Paris's geography of inequality in two important ways: the increasingly uneven reach of the welfare state and the mobilization of the state's repressive powers in the form of militaristic policing and surveillance.[42] Both strategies have played an important role in the production of northeast Paris as a liminal borderland between the capital and the *banlieue*. Northeast Paris illustrates the relationship between Paris's development as a global, capital city and national politics. Processes of gentrification, as well as the planned *mixité sociale* of public housing, have led to a situation in which economic and cultural difference and diversity must be articulated and addressed for cooperation, organizing, and mobilization and coalition building. Beth Epstein's examination of how ethnic diversity is lived in everyday life through *mixité sociale* in Cergy–St. Christophe demonstrates that the powerful Paris–*banlieue* border narrative conceals remarkable differences of class and ethnicity within the *banlieue* as well.[43] In similar fashion, this ethnography calls attention to the class-based, ethnic, urban, and environmental inequalities that mark a city that often plays the part of an affluent narrative foil against the spectral figure of the *banlieue*. I argue that the sociospatial topography of the city plays a fundamental role in the process by which diversity is politicized in everyday life. To build on Epstein's analysis, northeast Paris therefore provides a window into the way that diversity is not only lived in contemporary France but made politically meaningful (and productive) through politics that constructs the nation at the scale of the neighborhood.

The horrific *Charlie Hebdo* shootings of 2015 (including the anti-Semitic violence that accompanied it and the subsequent Islamophobic backlash) have placed these fraught questions of cultural diversity in France under a global spotlight. The terrorist attack itself led to the recycling of a well-worn, bigoted narrative that claims that Islam is incommensurable with (or at war against) France's core republican values. As this book shows, such dangerous rhetoric belies the fact that many of France's immigrants and Muslims (as well as generations who were raised in France by immigrant parents) have been organizing and protesting for access to the rights enshrined by France's core republican values, not against them. Indeed, demands for equality were the basis for the protest marches that led to the October 17th Massacre in Paris of 1961, protests over social conditions at workers' residences in the

1970s, the SOS Racisme mobilization of the 1980s, and the *sans-papiers* of the 1990s and 2000s. Ethnographic research in France has also illustrated the multitude of lesser noticed but highly significant ways in which residents from throughout the former colonies assert belonging in contemporary France.[44] Much of this literature has focused on a "double bind" facing France's postcolonial minorities, where an ideology of assimilationist republicanism is hegemonic: any identity politics is viewed as illegitimate, corrosive to national solidarity, and even antihumanist,[45] though the Sarkozy era saw none other than the president himself crack the facade of state-guaranteed secularism (*laïcité*), as well as moments of racialization in the everyday life of Paris as a global city.[46] Nevertheless, in a self-fulfilling prophecy, activists who demand rights for those who are the victims of ethnoracial processes of marginalization are frequently delegitimated with the accusation of invoking sectarian ideas of "community," and are therefore cast as corrosive to the Republic.

This book demonstrates the ways these legacies of empire are both evident and being reworked in Paris's urban ecology. The spaces, networks, and infrastructure of the city, especially when integrated with nature and the environment, are an important way through which difference is articulated in everyday life in Paris. Through activities as varied as urban gardening, environmental activism, and the everyday appropriation of disused land by youth, residents express alternative idioms of difference focused on the city's infrastructure and nature. These visions of pluralistic belonging are neither utopian dreams nor imported versions of so-called Anglo-Saxon multiculturalism (a criticism often leveled by proponents of an assimilationist republicanism). Instead, the politics of difference in northeast Paris constitutes a reworking of republicanism that is often more humanistic than hegemonic assimilationism espoused as it "actually exists" to function in the in the context of globalized, multiethnic city.[47] As I show, grassroots politics—and even municipal-level initiatives—quietly embrace a pluralism that is at times inconsistent with the national-level rhetoric of any of the major political parties. In northeast Paris, republicanism has many natures.

These alternative visions of the French republic are far from aberrations embraced by fringe activists and renegade elected officials. Indeed, Paris's eighteenth and nineteenth arrondissements play a prominent role in the national-level Socialist Party establishment that overturned the Sarkozy presidency. I therefore demonstrate how cross-cultural coalition building and electoral politics embracing a subtle pluralism are integral to the reproduction of France's political power structure at the highest level, despite a commonly stated official disdain for multiculturalism. Ironically, in France's current climate of assimilationist politics, the exception doesn't merely prove the rule, it is needed to maintain the rule.

These struggles unfold against a backdrop of dramatic global and urban shifts, which have economic and ecological implications. Northeast Paris has gone through a seismic process of deindustrialization in which industrial jobs declined from 575,000 to 134,000 between 1962 and 1999.[48] One in four households are now officially listed as "low income" (*à bas revenus*), a figure twice the Paris average.[49] The downward mobility facing the area's largely immigrant-descended working class (most residents are of West African and Maghrebi descent who arrived to work in manufacturing starting in the 1950s) has been coupled with the complete rebuilding of the district. A quarter of all the industrial sites razed in the city were torn down in Paris's northeastern neighborhoods.[50] Today, in some neighborhoods, as little as 25 percent of the building stock is of pre-1948 origin, in a city famous for its preserved Haussmann-era cityscape.[51] These transformations leave behind a legacy of toxic-waste dumping and garbage-strewn lots alongside apartments with lead-contaminated paint and air pollution caused by the diesel trucks and trains that continue to use the area's main transit arteries. In many cases, it is this ecological component of urban restructuring that has given rise to activism and other forms of reimaging the urban future in Paris's northeastern neighborhoods.

A wave of reinvestment, much of which is related to the sustainable reinvention of the capital, is now reshaping this flexible landscape in a new fashion. Demolition and construction projects are visible at every level: city-block and district-level projects include the razing and redevelopment of individual apartment buildings, projects such as the Jardins d'Éole, the ZAC Pajol ÉcoQuartier (econeighborhood), the tourism- and consumption-oriented redevelopment of a former industrial canal (the Canal de l'Ourcq), and the creation of a contemporary art center, Le Centquatre, in a building formerly used by the municipal undertakers. On a truly vast scale, however, the area is witnessing redevelopment of substantial portions of the city and suburbs, such as the Paris Nord-Est project (a complete demolition and rebuilding of the city/suburb boundary) and the Plaine Saint-Denis Regeneration (a five-hundred-hectare megaproject that included a national soccer stadium—the "Stade de France"), a new university campus for the humanities and social sciences, and the covering of a major expressway by green space. Since the mid-2000s, these projects, along with more than six hundred others in the metropolitan area, have fallen under the umbrella of the Grand Paris concept—a nationally led project (commenced by Sarkozy and continued under Hollande) to remake the capital in a fashion that is both sustainable and globally competitive.[52] Indeed, if these areas are socially distant (if just a few kilometers away) from the Paris of grand monuments, this landscape is still viewed by policy makers as an important site for the reproduction of the nation.

Northeast Paris once represented a final frontier in Paris's geography of gentrification, but redevelopment has driven a steep increase in real-estate

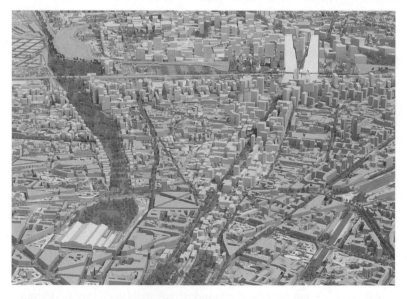

Urban nature as renewal strategy: the Atelier Christian de Portzamparc's proposed reimagining of the area's railways as "ecological corridors" for the Grand Paris plan. Grand Paris copyright AECDP.

prices compared to the rest of city, and resulted in mass demolitions in precisely the same areas where the largest proportions of immigrants reside.[53] While much of the new redevelopment in northeast Paris is public housing, housing activists and some residents have indicated to me that middle-income residents appear to be moving into the new units in disproportionately large numbers.[54] For this reason, and the inability of many immigrant families to access public housing, many families are increasingly forced into a "shadow" economy of long-stay hotels, squats, or, most commonly, extremely crowded room shares in apartments lacking running water and proper ventilation.[55] Moreover, journalists and policy makers commonly use the term *reconquête* (reconquest) to describe these renovations—a term that, despite being normalized and apolitically deployed in planning and media discourse, appears to underline the idea that these often nationally led projects entail retaking the city from an other.[56]

While a number of issues related to these urban transformations have spawned protest movements in Paris, the Éole moblization is striking because it represents a highly material, tangible effort by residents to transform the political and ecological predicament facing a postindustrial neighborhood. The demand for a park was articulated as providing relief for families with children living in crowded apartments and a symbolic cultural space of belonging for groups whose membership in the French nation is increasingly under attack. Indeed, the vision of the park was a form of political-ecology analysis of urban inequality in the area; had the residents not mobilized, a diesel-truck depot or garbage-processing facility was planned for the area instead, despite the fact that the neighborhood has among the highest proportion of children in its population of any area of the city.[57] And yet, the park merged with the Grand Paris plan, and in fact predated its focus on sustainable urbanism. The building of the park therefore sets the stage for a conflict between ecological visions of Paris's urban future.

The Everyday Life of the Urban Commons

The second decade of the twenty-first century opened with a wave of protests across the world in which urban public spaces have played iconic roles, from Syntagma Square in Athens, to Cairo's Tahrir Square, to Zucotti Park in New York City, to Gezi Park in Istanbul, to Dataran Merdeka in Kuala

Lumpur. While such historical events have rekindled the interest of many observers in the importance of urban space as a practical and symbolic means of sociopolitical transformation, the example of the Jardins d'Éole is a reminder that protest is a normal—not exceptional—part of urban life (and the urban process).[58] Indeed, the meaning-laden terrain of city squares, parks, and buildings is continuously being appropriated—and at times physically remade—as part of movements for sociopolitical transformation. In this sense, the urban commons exists is an undetermined state of contested becoming.

This ethnography engages a long-standing, interdisciplinary body of work that addresses the relationship between social and political contestation and the built environment.[59] In many such discussions, public space is held up as a symbolic arena of urban contestation at the level of particular squares and parks while urban space as a whole is subject to privatization and increasingly racial and class-exclusive definitions of public space. However, I prefer to use the term "urban commons" to describe the political potential of urban space as a site of democratic protest and social transformation, and use the term "public space" exclusively as an architectural classification to refer to squares, plazas, and parks built for "public" use (whatever the hegemonic definition of the public may be). Notions of public and private are, as I will show in the case of contemporary Paris, historically contingent and subject to constant redefinition and negotiation on the ground. Struggles over urban space as a commons are less characterized by a conflict between public and private than by the strategic use of each concept by different groups as part of a larger strategy to "fix" often unruly urban space according to a specific social image.

My use of the term "urban commons" draws from various sources, including "insurgent citizenship," the "open city," and the "right to the city."[60] My fusion of these admittedly diverse ideas represents an attempt to conceptualize an ethnographic approach to what I call the "political life of small urban spaces." I use this expression as both a nod to and a profound critique of the influential work of William H. Whyte.[61] By highlighting the relationship between broad historical and political processes and the everyday life of streets and parks, my goal is to engage his largely apolitical, ahistorical concern with urban vibrancy by foregrounding politics and the production of space (as we shall see, a small park can be understood by many people to occupy a global space). My main concern with Whyte lies with matters of contestation and scale (a topic to which I will return in chapter 6), though I concur with his and Jane Jacobs's general emphasis on the broader social importance of everyday street life. Thus, while I agree with Jacobs's evaluation of the importance of "eyes upon streets," I ask: What larger political projects shape the reasons residents watch (and whom they are watching)? And though I concur with Whyte that "social diversity" is an important criterion for a "successful" urban space, I ask: Successful for whom, and for what purpose?

As already stated, this does not mean that my focus in the ethnography is limited to the Jardins d'Éole; for me (as well as for many of the actors in this ethnography), the park serves primarily as means to intervene in a global problematic related to politics in the city. Rather, my focus on the political life of the Jardins d'Éole and street life in general is meant to understand the urban commons as an everyday site of vibrant creativity and even political possibility. Urban commons do not have to be explicitly revolutionary spaces such as the Tahrir Square of 2011. In fact, one can argue that the commons are an essential part of enjoying everyday life in the city, what Harvey describes as "the sensibility that arises out of the streets around us," Sharon Zukin analyzes as "the yearning for authenticity," Jacobs calls the "ballet of the good city sidewalk," and Lefebvre calls the city as "*fête*."[62] Above all, urban commons are sites identified with, and often informally controlled by, residents, but the question of *which* residents is always the subject of ongoing contention—a commons does not always imply a harmonious place. Indeed, as chapters 5 and 6 demonstrate, despite the best intentions of public servants and even residents to play an ambiguous role as "gatekeepers," a commons often belongs to everyone and no one (much to the frustration of many). It is, therefore, always in a contested state of becoming. Architects and city officials can design a "public space," but only residents, artists, and activists can create an urban commons through inhabiting it, imbuing it with meaning, and using it for their own projects. When the various practices of negotiation, contestation, and territoriality observed by me and other ethnographers of northeast Paris that reproduce the city as an urban commons are shut down by either social homogenization (often brought about by intense gentrification) or aggressive policing and surveillance, the commons are enclosed as well (even in an ostensibly public space).[63]

Negotiating Networks and Crossing Spaces: Between Embedded Participant Observation and Ethnographic Drifting

Ethnographic research in a contested neighborhood is a delicate affair. In my efforts to convey multiple positions and perspectives, I was constantly pulled between the poles of being fully incorporated into various associations and mobilizations and the loose position of drifting autonomously between networks. In this environment, and after months of carefully building ethnographic rapport with people from a variety of positions, I found that my preferred role was never entirely within (as much as anthropological doxa stresses the merits of being adopted) or outside, but somewhat in between. Indeed, the most fitting way to negotiate this contested political terrain as an ethnographer appeared to be lingering among different groups for a while before drifting between networks. I never felt comfortable letting one group's perspective shape this ethnography in its entirety, and in representing each I have attempted to upset (rather than simply invert) the social and political asymmetries that normally structure who is represented and who is not. My goal as an ethnographer is to illustrate how people inhabit and negotiate contradictory political positions, rather than smooth them out of the narrative or conceal them altogether. In this regard, my aim is to convey a view of a complex political field rather than an "embedded" perspective from a single mobilization.

I began to gravitate toward this approach after my first conversation with one leader of the Éole mobilization, Rachel. During an introductory conversation, as ethnographers are prone to do, I emphasized how important it was to me that my work contributed to the activists' project, listed potential ways I could help, and stated that I was open to her ideas on how my ethnographic fieldwork could be "useful" for her. Rachel, who was a veteran of several grassroots campaigns, including a particularly difficult battle over the rights of undocumented students (*sans-papiers*) in schools, addressed my earnest statement with a smile: "Don't worry," she said, "we'll find a use for you." The comment reminded me how anthropologists—in their important efforts to preserve the agency of their informants and help them—often display a tendency to take their own agency as ethnographers for granted, perhaps naively so.

While I was broadly sympathetic to the Éole activists, the political and intellectual significance of the dilemma between writing as an embedded voice of a particular mobilization versus a more free-floating approach should not be understated. Even if an ethnographer is content to blur the boundary between one's project and that of one's informants, the potential to miss the broader "political field" in which contentious politics operates has already been identified as a problem of ethnographic research on social movements.[64] Such blindness raises potential issues for anthropological scholarship on contentious politics *and* the movements with which we work (even more so when we agree with them).

It was no small irony that my reservations about "being adopted" came after weeks of difficulty seeking out the Éole mobilization. A few months prior, my initial entry into Paris had been as part of a CNRS research group based at the Institut d'Urbanisme de Paris (IUP).[65] This experience with colleagues was invaluable for its intellectual richness and logistical support, and introduced me to staff at municipal agencies such as the DEVE (Direction des Espaces Verts et de l'Environnement—the city of Paris Parks and Environment Department), as well as to the discipline of urban planning and design in France. In sharp contrast to the typical gaze of the ethnographer, this involved learning to see the city as a series of lines, spaces, forms, flows, and uses, and gaining an understanding of design as a set of interventions in a system that was as aesthetic as it was social.[66] I was also able to participate in a workshop on the Jardins d'Éole itself, and several of my colleagues were involved in the design process of the park. As a result, I expected that fieldwork would be unusually easy, and indeed, within days of my arrival the project seemed well under way and likely to unfold seamlessly.

However, my efforts to forge connections with activists via this network of planners and policy makers proved far more difficult than expected. The silence of the activists was frustrating and mysterious. As I speculated on possible causes or grudges that formed its basis, I could not help but dwell on Lefebvre's observation about the supposed "silence" of those who are often described in urban planning parlance as not "planners" but the "planned for."[67] The first weeks became an increasingly stressful period of waiting.

Days were spent taking the crowded buses along the bottlenecked Parisian ring road (the Boulevard Périphérique) and passing through cafés on the bustling *portes* that formalize the boundary between the city and its *banlieues*. I began to know the daily rhythms and movements of people that distinguish Paris's northern peripheries from its resplendent center. At times, I found northeast Paris and its surroundings to be less a set of neighborhoods than a transitional zone—a concentration of infrastructure with some residential areas in between—linking the edges of the metropolitan area to its center. At the same time, the area can appear dehumanizing. It is a place of wide expressways, vast tracts of unused land strewn with garbage, and what can feel like relentless frenetic motion: loud truck traffic at night, ever-passing freight and passenger trains, and hurried crowds filing in and out of buses and train stations. Thanks in no small part to the constant activity of yard locomotives and the ever-present flow of buses and delivery trucks, the air is often pungent with diesel exhaust. And yet, and in contrast to many of the gentrified or affluent neighborhoods in the capital, one sees a full age range of individuals living their lives on the sidewalks, from newborns swaddled by parents to the elderly gathered on sidewalk benches. Silence has indeed its virtues for an ethnographer, and my initial weeks of fieldwork gave me ample opportunity to learn to watch, hear, and smell the city. There is some value to drifting, as long as such periods stay brief, and within a few weeks I managed to meet a few members of the Éole mobilization in no less surprising a place than the park itself.

Even after I built up a sense of rapport, I never lost an appreciation for the ethnographic value of being somewhat detached. I built a close and enduring relationship with a variety of people who were involved in the Éole mobilization, from founding leaders to neighbors who could best be described as "fellow travelers." At the same time, I strategically drifted between other groups of activists involved with environmental justice-related projects, tenants' and housing rights, and youth "prevention" organizations. Beyond those who fit the messy category of "activists" (I encountered people whose political and civic practice ran the gamut from traditional organizing and letter writing to outwardly apolitical hobbies such as gardening; even hanging out on a street corner in northeast Paris can be an intense engagement in urban politics), I worked with individuals whose professional focus tied together urbanism with nature and ecology: these included DEVE staff at various levels (especially gardeners and park security guards) as well as the members of the design team of the Jardins d'Éole itself. Finally, I built relationships with a diverse group of individuals whose approach to nature, urban ecology, and space was often more casual, but no less political. These residents included a few people who could be described as "fixtures" or "public figures" in and around the Jardins d'Éole, including a clique of young men who spent time on one of the more contested parts of the park (the esplanade). Despite this immense variety of social positions, I sought these individuals and groups out because of their involvement with claiming the right to the city, often in a manner that incorporated nature and the environment into their demands.

Strategic drifting between networks (as well as more concrete spaces) became a central method of my fieldwork, and appeared a practicable way for me to map out a set of social relationships that are only visible or legible upon entry within the network itself.[68] I find this approach especially appropriate for an urban context in which ethnographers must choose between a de-spatializing approach (in which ethnographers confine themselves to social networks) and reifying space (the "urban village" approach based on ahistorical and geographically bounded notions of culture and, ultimately, ethnographic analysis as well). My approach emphasized the importance of space as process while utilizing multiple social networks that occupied either side of (and crossed) fault lines of ethnoracial difference, gender, and class. Ultimately, the "field" revealed itself to me as neither a geographic space nor a set of social networks, but as an assemblage of actors, spaces, and infrastructure that extended well beyond the Jardins d'Éole itself.

Of course, every approach has its distinct advantage and shortcomings. Although I often developed a warm rapport with many of the groups and individuals with whom I worked, I never developed the kind of immersive depth gained by more focused ethnographic approaches to urban spaces that only privilege small cliques or even single subjects.[69] In return, however, I have been able to show a diverse set of ways in which people "landscape" their political discontents and dreams. This juxtaposition of different voices is crucial to render the politics of northeast Paris's ecology in ways that capture the complexity of struggles that do not unfold around a dichotomous oppression/resistance dynamic, but are multidimensional.

Finally, I have built this ethnography around the situational analysis of several extended case studies that allow me to expose not only the linkages between the microlevel actions of individuals and much larger, global-level processes, but, more important, the fashion by which categories of local and global are produced and emerge in the "field" (in both the political and the ethnographic sense of the word).[70] Such case studies and situations—which include events such a protest sparked by a fire in a single-room occupancy hotel and a public debate over whether motor scooters (and their riders) are environmental menaces—demonstrate how struggles to remake the urban and national fabric are intertwined in northeast Paris. Ultimately, the most difficult part of fieldwork can be fully grasping the substance of the "field" itself: my approach is based on the idea of the field as neither a geographic space nor a set of social networks, but an intertwined, mutually constitutive network combining actors *and* spaces, and the "built" and "natural" environments alike.

Plan of This Book

This book is structured around six chapters that interweave the themes of urban political ecology, national belonging in France, and the political importance of urban space and street life.

The first two chapters trace the linked process of urban transformation and the emergence of social movements through the perspective of individual residents and activists. In both chapters, I demonstrate the importance of nature and the environment as a political idiom in varying (and often contradictory) projects to reshape city and society alike. Chapter 1 focuses on the political and ecological making of northeast Paris as a distinct "hinterland" that is neither city center nor *banlieue.* The neighborhood's history of environmental injustice and grassroots movements is situated at the confluence of empire, immigration, housing, and deindustrialization. In chapter 2, I place special emphasis on the Éole mobilization to examine the importance of the politics of nature and the aesthetic self-fashioning of mobilizations in grassroots strategies to transform the city. Chapter 3 engages with debates on political belonging in France by introducing the idea of republicanism's nature. It examines how a range of actors—from urban gardeners and youth activists to the DEVE—articulate a humanist vision of political belonging that is arguably so republican that it refuses to even reify the French nation.[71] Chapter 4 examines how the late-twentieth-century/early-twenty-first-century green turn in urban design and policy is reshaping the way cities are imagined as "global" and is providing a new "natural" logic for capital accumulation. Chapter 5 offers a critical view of Jane Jacobs's "eyes upon the street" idea to show the numerous and contradictory ways that residents not only watch each other, but enact a neoliberal and republican mode of citizenship by doing so. Chapter 6 examines the importance of the public/private dichotomy for movements, residents, and actors from the DEVE, whose professional role consists of managing urban parks as sites of social control and governance. I show how a variety of movements plays with the boundaries of public and private (rather than simply resisting the enclosure of public space) to strategically deploy both types of space in their efforts to claim the right to the city.

I conclude by suggesting a way forward for an anthropology of the city that integrates conceptions of nature with an emphasis on the politics of the urban design process. Urban anthropology (insofar as it is imagined to be the study of a fetish object called the city that is oppositional to the rural or natural) increasingly appears a thing of the past. However, an integrative anthropology of the urban process, which focuses on the creativity of people who reshape the built/natural environment around them, is both relevant and urgently needed. This effort to focus on the nature of grassroots politics is an attempt to realize how such an anthropology of the urban might appear going forward.

1 Poets and Locomotives

Ecology and Politics on the Margins of Paris

The design, use, and meaning of urban space involves the
transformation of nature into a new synthesis.

—Matthew Gandy, *Concrete and Clay*

On a beautiful spring afternoon I took a stroll with Mamadou, who would
later become one of my most trusted interlocutors in northeast Paris. Mamadou, who at that time was just embarking on a fruitful career in activism and
Parisian politics, had invited me for a walk through the high-rise *cité* and
the surrounding neighborhoods where he grew up. A native of Burkina Faso,
and onetime aspiring rapper turned activist and advocate for immigrant
youth, Mamadou shifted the conversation seamlessly between his adoles-
cence in the neighborhood, the immense scale of urban redevelopment evident on nearly every street, and the evolution of French hip-hop since his
youth in the 1980s.

Eventually, we wandered to a crossroads where Mamadou's autobiographi-
cal account and the path of our afternoon *dérive* intersected, the street corner where the short Rue Caillié meets Rue du Département at the Jardins
d'Éole. At this spot, we stood astride several different transitional spaces that
marked the intersection between Mamadou's life, the history of northeast
Paris, and the cultural makeup of the French nation. Below us, a bullet train
roared and screeched through a canyon of tangled railroad tracks linking
Paris to the *banlieue* and ultimately to the border city of Strasbourg and des-
tinations in Eastern Europe. Beyond us lay the towering *Cité Michelet* where
Mamadou was raised and which *Le Monde* had recently described as a "Tower
of Babel" for its multiethnic, supposedly fractious immigrant-origin tenants

1

whose compatibility with the secular values of the Republic was seen as suspect.[1] Behind us, along the full length of the short Rue Caillié, stood a line of collapsing nineteenth-century apartment buildings lacking running water that would soon be razed, and which were used as an informal refuge by undocumented migrants from across West Africa. Finally, immediately before us stood the recently completed Jardins d'Éole itself. With its newly poured concrete, verdant lawns, and MoMA-endorsed design, it appeared to have been dropped here from a different world. Indeed, elites in France's urban policy establishment have targeted this area for the creation of a so-called *écoquartier* or "econeighborhood" that would not only point the way toward a more sustainable, globalized Paris but change the relationship between the city center and the surrounding *banlieue.*

Mamadou turned the subject to his family, starting with his father, who immigrated in the 1960s to work in the Renault and Peugeot plants, and his

Blues du Nord? Mamadou took me to this spot, at the corner of Rue Caillié and Rue du Département, and presented it as a temporal juncture, where a past defined by "insalubrious" apartments and *hôtels meublés* (single-room-occupancy or long-stay hotels) collided with a future of sustainable renewal and redevelopment. The trees of the Jardins d'Éole are visible in the background.

mother and siblings (including him), who arrived in the 1970s to join him. The story was in many respects the classic narrative of guest-worker migrants from the former colonies and their children, who are often described as *jeunes issus de l'immigration,* a liminal category that implicitly marks a generation of young people raised in France as outside of the nation without ascribing them a specific ethnic or foreign identity per se.

In discussing these themes, Mamadou began to link the neighborhood itself with the plight of "the first wave of young kids who were *issus de l'immigration*":

> What happened was that it was a generation who was completely lost, who posed the question, where did I come from? I live in this neighborhood, but I have nothing to go back to. There is no structure, it is a neighborhood that is completely abandoned.

As he spoke, he beckoned across Jardins d'Éole and the landscape of railway tracks and high-rise *cité* that lay beyond: "We called it the La Chapelle wasteland *[terrain vague]* then. All the artists used to go down there, dancers, rappers, taggers. It was a kind of a revolution in the *cité,* in the neighborhood, because the artists, the rappers, dancers, and taggers appropriated their environment, the walls, the trains, the rooftops." Gesturing excitedly toward spectral abandoned industrial spaces that were now green lawns, he continued: "That's where hip-hop was born in France, there, in those old warehouses." Mamadou's contention that this site was the origin of French hip-hop is by no means accepted by other residents or scholars of hip-hop, but the comment made it clear that the place was special as a generative site of creativity and global sociocultural connection.

Mamadou and his adolescent friends' fascination with this *terrain vague* of abandoned buildings and overgrown plants (then known as the Cour du Maroc—or Moroccan Court) paralleled a broader urban studies and art-world obsession with such derelict zones of urban nature.[2] For the youth, this former wasteland of overgrown weeds and empty buildings was a landmark: a site that once provided the raw material for a "lost generation" to appropriate a landscape that was seemingly abandoned and yet a space of possibility and becoming. "Through appropriating their environment" the youth transformed the site into a locus of creativity that remains beloved by Mamadou long after its disappearance. In Mamadou's words, it was a place where "a kind of revolution" came in the form of dance, graffiti, rap, and "socially conscious" hip-hop. Despite being a vacant lot, it was nonetheless a point of convergence of varying global connections that helped to change the alienating, marginalizing aspects of liminal identity into an empowering sense of possibility and becoming. Mamadou credited this crucible of insurgent and artistic energy as launching his career into activism and politics.

Mamadou and his peers' attempts to make sense of (and transform) their place in society by way of the urban spaces in which they came of age highlights a central tension in this chapter: the relationship between political acts of reappropriation by residents (or claiming the right to the city) and the historical production of northeast Paris as a space with distinct social, cultural, and ecological qualities. In some respects, Mamadou's narrative is archetypical of *jeunes issus de l'immigration,* caught between his homeland of Burkina Faso (to which he has never returned) and a France that offers neither cultural acceptance nor economic security. However, his story is also about the importance of the city's spaces and infrastructure for the process of imagining alternative futures. Northeast Paris has long been fertile ground for people to seek to change themselves by changing the city, to paraphrase David Harvey.[3] The history of northeast Paris is one of urbanization defined by the struggle over the right to the city: that is, conflict between and among varying groups of city dwellers (as well as large institutions, landowners, and political elites) to control the rich economic, social, cultural, and imaginative value of urban space.

As this chapter demonstrates, ecology plays a central—though frequently overlooked—role in such struggles, and thus the urban process itself. My ethnographic approach to urban political ecology is, at one level, an attempt to better understand the relationship between the production of urban spaces and infrastructure on the one hand, and ecological processes on the other. This is not, however, a neat and tidy story of capitalism's impact on nature. Northeast Paris has developed over time as a result of the total imbrication of nature and the city to the point that urban processes are impossible to separate from ecological ones. In sum, I see the urban landscape as a complex assemblage that combines power and political struggle with the city's built environment and infrastructure, as well as the biophysical processes of ecology and geomorphology (and even meteorological patterns, as we shall see). This ensemble of processes shapes—and is shaped by—contestation over the right to the city.

At a second level, my approach builds on Rademacher's attention to the ways that people produce their own political ecology analyses of the city.[4] Some of these perspectives are quite oppositional to the theoretical-political positions advocated by what might be termed a canonical political ecology, but I describe them as such because each presents a way of making sense of urban contestation that is fundamentally intertwined with nature and the environment. Indeed, as twenty-first-century trends in urban policy indicate, social theorists are not the only ones thinking about "urban ecology" in a political sense anymore: ecology is an important idiom embraced by planners and policy makers as well as environmental activists. These multiple and at times conflicting ecologies are nonetheless "grounded" by the fact that each represents an environmentally focused way to make sense of northeast Paris's past, present, and aspirational future.

In northeast Paris, notions of liminality, becoming, and borderlands are a common theme in these ecological understandings of the city.[5] Implicitly or explicitly, ecological injustice has long been a—if not the—defining feature of this area throughout its history of urbanization. An ethnographic approach that takes urban ecology as a starting point therefore provides an important insight on the myriad ways that residents, as well as members of the urban policy establishment, contest the right to the city, while also demonstrating how the biophysical character of the urban landscape shapes (and is shaped by) political action.

Zones in Transition

Northeast Paris is not a well-defined place. The area is best described as space in between more "known" places. This quality has proved troubling for a host of actors, ranging from urban planners to neighborhood activists, who long struggled to name and define the area. Once, an activist from the mobilization for Jardins d'Éole aptly described it to me as a "frontier between Paris and the *banlieue*." This makes northeast Paris somewhat of a paradox: it is peripheral not only to the capital's core, but to the area that is generally recognized as the urban periphery itself. It has, in many respects, been constituted as a hinterland similar to the classic usage (the term "hinterland" originates from the German term for "land behind"), which refers to areas immediately beyond coastal ports. Indeed, northeast Paris's neighborhoods lie just beyond and are largely defined by their proximity to the city's well-defined "ports" or openings to the *banlieue* to the northeast (specifically, the Porte de Clignancourt, Porte de la Chapelle, and Porte d'Aubervilliers), as well as the train terminals linking the city to the *banlieue* and beyond (the Gare du Nord and the Gare de l'Est). Moreover, the area is marginal within Paris's socially charged geography of outer neighborhoods, lying between Montmartre (the mythical, now Disneyfied Paris of Impressionist painting and Moulin Rouge fame), the Goutte d'Or (often known as Little Africa), and Belleville: a storied, rough-and-tumble neighborhood of Paris's blue-collar past, birthplace of Édith Piaf, and now home to one of Paris's largest Chinatowns. For many Parisians and tourists alike, northeast Paris is merely the place "behind" the railroad terminals, experienced on a regular, if not unconscious, basis as a postindustrial valley of ashes seen from commuter train windows en route between Paris, the *banlieue,* and Charles de Gaulle international airport. It is viewed as an interstitial domain largely created by the city's railroad infrastructure.

It is therefore fitting that the inhabitants of northeast Paris—like Mamadou—are often understood as inhabiting a transitory social and cultural space of their own. More than many other neighborhoods in the capital, northeast Paris is frequently identified with immigration from the former French colonies in the Maghreb and West Africa. France's thirty-year postwar economic expansion, the Trente Glorieuses, depended on the cheap and often nonunionized labor of guest workers. Labor migration to the area accompanied the geopolitical decline of France's colonial empire: Maghrebi immigration in France reached its height toward the end of the Algerian war in the late 1960s, and many found refuge in a still-existing semiformal "shadow economy" of *hôtels meublés,* which are often operated by migrants from an earlier, more established group.[6] Others from the former colonies, especially the West African nations of Senegal, the Ivory Coast, Gabon, Mali, and Burkina Faso, followed. Paul Silverstein points out that during the postwar period more than 350,000 Algerians worked in the construction industry alone, and by the 1990s, the Algerian population in France had grown to as many as 1.5 million men, women, and children.[7] Although many versions of the generational narrative of immigration are of a "patrilineal" nature, a significant portion of immigration has long been both female and focused on the decidedly precarious and impermanent domain of domestic labor (especially housekeepers and nannies).[8] As a result, more than a third of the residents in northeast Paris today were born abroad; in this regard, the district more closely resembles the *banlieues* to the north and east of Paris than the capital itself.[9]

France's shift from *dirigisme* to a hybrid, state-centered neoliberalism *à la française* has exacerbated this transitory quality for Mamadou's "lost" generation of youths, and for the district as a whole. *Dirigisme* was centered on a strong state as "gatekeeper of capital" leading the way in economic development.[10] Under this system, state funds first fed industrialization and reconstruction after World War II, particularly with regard to public housing and infrastructure projects, as part of an effort to modernize the French economy in the wake of the war and produce an urbanized French middle class (with the guest-worker program providing the low-cost labor to undergird the transformation). Gradually, under the presidencies of Valéry Giscard d'Estaing (1974–81) and François Mitterrand (1981–95), the state's role in moderating the cycles of unemployment caused by deindustrialization and capital flight was reduced—precipitating the downturn of many of France's working-class neighborhoods (a process that began anew under the administration of François Hollande and the European financial crisis). After the onset of the 1973 OPEC crisis, the guest-worker program was effectively ended, and France began hemorrhaging jobs in the very sectors that employed most migrant laborers.[11] Guest workers and other immigrant laborers were among the first to feel the dislocating effects of the county's shift toward a postindustrial, service, and finance-driven economy.

Many aspects of French statism have been preserved, but this does not mean the neoliberal French welfare state has much to offer the low-income residents of northeast Paris, especially those who are foreign-born or even of foreign descent.[12] Immigrant-origin workers have been less likely to be unionized than their French counterparts, and are far more likely to be employed on temporary contracts, with the generation of youths born to immigrant parents being especially vulnerable and facing unemployment rates from 20 percent to more than 30 percent in some cases.[13] The predicament leading to what Mamadou described as a generation "lost" is not only a product of their postcolonial, immigrant origin; they were also orphaned by France's shift from *dirigiste* statism to hybridized, state-centered neoliberalization, which began in the 1970s.[14]

For Mamadou and his friends, these struggles were not only existential and economic but fraught with physical violence as well. During our walk, he took me along the Canal de l'Ourcq, part of a Napoleonic system of waterways designed to facilitate the flow of goods and freshwater to and from the capital. By the 1990s, it formed a polluted boundary (ecologically and symbolically) where groups of skinheads would violently clash with Maghrebi and African-origin youth. In a bizarre show of nostalgia for urban wars of the past, the teenagers would often meet at night at the nearby Place de la Bataille de Stalingrad for their dangerous encounters. These confrontations took place in the context of a concentrated campaign by the right-wing National Front party (FN) directed against northeast Paris in the mid-1990s, and in particular the expansion of the second-largest mosque in the Île-de-France region, Adda'wa.

The spatial politics of the mosque resonates with many struggles faced by France's Muslims at a national level. Adda'wa was established in 1979 and was headed by Larbi Kechat, an Algerian-born theologian who frequently used the secular title of rector instead of imam. Despite his demonstrated propensity for interfaith dialogue, he was arrested but subsequently released in an antiterrorism dragnet led by then interior minister Charles Pasqua, a key sponsor of legislative crackdowns (the Pasqua laws) on immigration in the 1980s and 1990s. In addition to Kechat's difficulties, the mosque faced continual obstructions from the city of Paris (then led by the right-leaning Tiberi administration) as it sought to expand its facilities during the 1990s. Thanks in small part to the support of Roger Madec, the Socialist Party (PS) mayor of the nineteenth arrondissement, it ultimately prevailed (prompting the National Front to descend on northeast Paris for a series of protests in the late 1990s).

After a series of confrontations between the FN and activists from the national antiracist movement SOS Racisme, a pipe bomb was detonated in front of the mosque on March 17, 1997. The blast wounded one person and led to the eventual demolition of Adda'wa; no perpetrators were ever caught or identified. Since that time, efforts have been under way to rebuild the mosque and ground was broken on an ambitious cultural center and prayer space that would be a transformative addition to religious life in northeast Paris. Despite receiving public support from Madec and Mayor Bertrand Delanoë in the 2000s, Adda'wa has been subjected to continual criticism and scrutiny by journalists hungry for stories on radical Islamists in Paris, and the construction project has been slowed to a halt by financial problems.[15] At the time of this writing, the congregants gather for prayers at a provisional site near Porte de la Villette in the shadow of an abandoned, elevated railway known as La Petite Ceinture, on the boundary line between Paris and the surrounding *banlieues* of Aubervilliers and Pantin.

Taken together, Mamadou's experience and its intertwining with the story of the Adda'wa mosque reveal the degree of symbolic, social, and physical violence that underlie the creation (and reproduction) of such liminal sites. This strife is the outcome of both an Islamophobic facet of France's crisis of national identity and global economic restructuring as it is realized in the terrain of northeast Paris (the original Adda'wa mosque was built on a postindustrial site where many of its congregants might well have labored in an earlier time). The spatial politics of France's struggles of national belonging therefore reveals the importance of the urban process in forming the contours of this struggle, which results in the creation of places (and people) embroiled in an uncertain and often painful process of becoming. This liminality, as we shall see, is fundamentally connected with the ecology of northeast Paris.

Vertical Ecologies

It's a neighborhood of poets and locomotives.

—Léon-Paul Fargue, "Mon quartier"

Sergio was one of the first residents of northeast Paris I met, at a reception hosted by the local office of a national association serving low-income neighborhoods (the Régie de Quartier). Other than a little work for the Régie as a handyman, Sergio depends entirely on public assistance (RMI—Revenu

Minimum d'Insertion) for survival, though, as an Italian-born transplant, he represents somewhat of an oddity, if not an anachronism from a previous era, considering France's changing demographics of immigration. I was immediately struck by the enthusiasm and warmth he showed the first time we met and he learned of my project. He quickly and excitedly led me away from the group where we were mingling to a corner of the Régie's office where a large map of Paris's northern half was hanging on the wall. "People often ask me where I want to travel outside of France," he said, "and I say 'nowhere' because the whole world lives right around me." He pointed to various streets that he identified as "Chinese," "Jewish," "Maghrebi," "Indian," and "African." The streets making up La Chapelle, he explained, were like a set of worlds in themselves, "isolated" by two massive chasms of railroad tracks, which terminated at the Gare du Nord and the Gare de l'Est, respectively. We both stared at the map for moment and then he ran both hands down the map, one along each set of tracks, making a swooshing sound as if physically cutting the map. "This is a form of oppression," he said.

Sergio is far from the only one to make such an observation. The railroads have long been a defining feature of northeast Paris at a political and ecological level, nourishing the center with metabolic flows of resources, commodities, and people.[16] The railroads figure prominently in residents' "on-the-ground" political ecologies of northeast Paris and planners' visions for a sustainable city, albeit in multiple and conflicting ways. The lines are variously viewed as life-carrying arteries that connect the city to global flows of capital or as cutting through and dividing neighborhoods, creating, as Sergio described it, the cultural equivalent of isolated ecological niche communities (indeed, the relationship between the railroads, biodiversity, and ethnic diversity would become an important theme in politics of cultural belonging in the area). Moreover, the vacant land that almost invariably abuts railroad tracks often becomes a site for illegal dumping, and is therefore symbolic of the environmental injustice endured by those who live nearby. At the same time, the bundles of infrastructure and the places that become associated with it are appropriated by residents who transform the landscape in a variety of ways, ranging from graffiti drawing to urban gardening.

Nevertheless, what one of the principal architects of the Jardins d'Éole once described to me as northeast Paris's "verticality" is part of a political and ecological configuration that vastly predates, and even prefigures, the development of the railroads in the 1840s. This is partially owing to the topography of Paris's northern sections. The north/south axis arguably has its origins as far back as the Roman conquest under Caesar. The eastern portion of the eighteenth and much of the nineteenth arrondissements lies in a relatively flat valley called Le col de la Chapelle between the largest hills in the city, Montmartre and Belleville. The Celtic inhabitants of the region, known as the Parisii, had relied primarily on the Seine for transportation, food, and trade, but the Roman rulers solidified their conquest by famously cutting roads overland to support military expeditions. The current Avenue de Flandre, the first major piece of infrastructure in the area, began as one such road, connecting Lutetia (the Roman city centered on Paris's Île de la Cité) with the provinces of Belgica and the imperial frontier in Germania Inferior. The villages of La Chapelle and La Villette, which would develop into the neighborhoods of the same name, grew over the next millennium around an economy based on carriage repairers, wheel makers, blacksmiths, inns, and inexpensive taverns and dance halls located just outside the city limits called *guinguettes,* all of which served to maintain the growing city of Paris's flows of goods, travelers, and military expeditions in and out of the city, along the north–south (vertical) axis.[17]

In addition to road construction, the Romans left another "vertical" legacy that would directly shape northeast Paris's ecology: gypsum mining. The areas that would later become the eighteenth and nineteenth arrondissements became a principal site of gypsum extraction until the latter half of the nineteenth century. These quarries, at the time outside of the city, were the source of plaster of Paris, which contributed directly to the facades and construction of the capital through the centuries and was eventually a lucrative export. Many gypsum mines were massive open-air operations (in the nineteenth century, one of the largest would be transformed into the Parc des Buttes-Chaumont in order to lure the center-city bourgeoisie into the city's western districts). By the 1800s, the landscape north and east of the capital, though outside of the city itself, was far from bucolic in that it was riven by quarries and windmills that processed the gypsum.

This evisceration of the landscape proved to be only part of the environmental problem posed by gypsum extraction. Gypsum's water solubility makes it a useful primary ingredient for plaster walls but a menace when quarries are located in densely built urban environments. From the medieval period on, increasing urbanization in the Seine Valley intensified a long-standing pattern of regular winter and spring flooding; catastrophic inundations became a nearly once-a-century occurrence starting in the thirteenth century. Spring and winter rains combined with the poorly drained urban environment to channel floodwaters into the quarries, dissolving the subterranean gypsum deposits. The resulting erosion caused significant problems with instability and subsidence that were so great that buildings were limited to just one or two floors until the nineteenth century.[18] The instability and environmental degradation caused by gypsum extraction had a double effect: most dramatically, is has led to building collapses that are still a focus of northeast Paris's écologistes. However, the fear of instability and presence of such socionatural limits on construction set the northern sections of the city on a path of underdevelopment for years to come.

Increasingly, the center of the capital became associated with governance, finance, and elegant consumption. Other areas outside the city walls (the Mur des Fermiers Généraux) became either bourgeois retreats or teeming working-class neighborhoods. Northeast Paris, however, was given over to the infrastructure supporting the capital's expanding metabolic needs for goods and materials. Roads and gypsum quarries were followed by the ninety-six-kilometer Canal de l'Ourcq, established to bring freshwater to the capital, and to support the logistical demands of France's imperial pursuits under the reign of Emperor Napoleon Bonaparte. By 1841, the Canal de l'Ourcq nourished an industrial boom so great that barge traffic in the nineteenth arrondissement was equal to ship traffic at Le Havre, France's English Channel port.[19] Canal building effectively transformed northeast Paris into both a center of industry and infrastructure and a border area within the capital itself.

The coming of the railroads intensified this spatial logic and the urban inequalities that accompanied it. Northeast Paris was forever changed by the construction of the Gare du Nord in 1846, the Gare de l'Est in 1849, and the "gare de marchandises" (freight terminal) in 1847—the latter would later become the Jardins d'Éole. Under the direction of Seine Prefect Georges-Eugène Haussmann (who preferred to be known as "Baron" despite his lack of a noble title) and Napoleon III, the center of the capital south of the rail stations was rebuilt in grandiose fashion, with wide boulevards connecting the rail stations with spectacular icons of bourgeois urbanism such the Opéra Garnier and the Place de la République. The villages of La Chapelle and La Villette north of (or "behind") the terminals underwent a rapid transformation from semirural *faubourgs* to railway service quarters made up of switching yards, locomotive turntables, engine shops. At the site of the current ZAC Pajol, a customs facility was built that officially marked the area as a "borderland." Railroad-centered development would accelerate after the area was annexed under the orders of Haussmann in 1860, and reformed as the eighteenth and nineteenth arrondissements with the Rue d'Aubervilliers forming the boundary between the two districts. The railroads would henceforth become a defining feature of northeast Paris's landscape in an economic, symbolic, visual, and environmental sense.

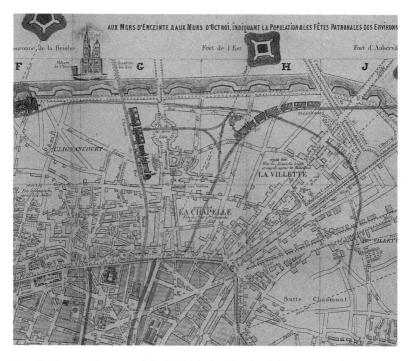

A section from an 1855 map of "Paris with its fortifications" demonstrates the importance of the railroads to the identity of the area before it was incorporated into the city itself. Copyright BHVP / Roger-Viollet.

Together, this intricate meshwork of canals, roads, and rails formed the underside of Walter Benjamin's (1969) famously named "capital of the nineteenth century." The areas north of the railroad stations became host to noxious, polluting processes of production and destruction that sustained the glamorous and sensual consumerism for which Paris became legendary. By order of Haussmann, sections of railway track far wider than the grandest boulevards were slashed through the neighborhoods of La Chapelle and the adjacent Goutte d'Or (a newly constructed neighborhood named for the vineyards it replaced) for steam engines to carry migrants into the city from the French countryside as well as goods to be sold in the new *grands magasins* and arcades. Other trains carried in modern breeds of cattle, such as the popular Charolais, which arrived from the countryside to new slaughterhouse districts such as La Villette, immortalized in Georges Franju's documentary masterpiece *Le sang des bêtes* (the blood of the beasts), before gracing the tables of the city's famous bistros, brasseries, and cafés. Around the corner from La Villette (in a flair of irony that Franju would surely appreciate), a large site on the Rue d'Aubervilliers became yet another important node in the urban "metabolism": a massive *pompes funèbres* (the municipal undertaker's depot for hearses), which coordinated the movements of the deceased to cemeteries, many of which were outside of the city in the *banlieue* (the building would also be called upon to serve as a funeral home for the Second World War and the conflicts in Indochina and Algeria).[20] Liminal spaces such as northeast Paris function as more than mere border zones: they are sites where the otherwise hidden transformation and redefinition of goods, materials, commodities, and life itself take place.

Thus, the area behind the grand facade of the train terminals operated as a "backstage" hinterland to the spectacle of modernity that was Haussmann's Paris. It was neither working-class *banlieue* nor bourgeois City of Light; and the uses for the district (slaughterhouses, funeral homes, and, for a short period, gallows) suggest that a profane quality was attached to its sociospatial liminality. Despite being formerly located within the administrative zone of the city itself, and in fact being integral to the capital accumulation driving urbanization, it is a distinctly separated entity from the Paris that is a capital both of France and of modernity itself.

The combined urban, political, and ecological nature of these transformations did not go unnoticed or uncommented upon. Marcel Aymé's short story "Rue de l'Évangile" offers a fictional, albeit vivid, rendering of northeast Paris in the literary-ecological imagination of the time. Appearing more than fifty years before the onset of many of France's national debates about the impact of immigration on French society, Aymé's racist narrative depicts La Chapelle from the point of view of an animalized migrant worker from the Maghreb named Abdel (he is described as "flea-ridden").[21] Abdel inhabits a nightmarish, polluted corner of the city "veiled by a mist dirtied with smoke."[22] Cast onto the sidewalk by a xenophobic café owner, the solitary, rejected, but always optimistic Abdel wanders from street to street, seemingly lost and yet transfixed by the city around him. An introductory paragraph uses the ecological spectacle of La Chapelle to set the somber, yet surreal tone:

> The northern part of the La Chapelle quarter is enclosed within bare walls concealing factories, goods stations, railway lines, gasometers, grimy trains and wandering locomotives. The smoke of the eastern and northern railway systems, mingling with that of the factories, blackens apartment houses built with an eye to economy, and the sparsely frequented streets have the aspect of a drab corner of the provinces surrounded by a desert of rust and coal. It is, in short, a literary landscape where the sensitive pedestrian, hearing the trains whistle in the murk, may find himself murmuring a prayer to God that life shall not last unduly long.[23]

Despite being firmly situated in the cultural context of interwar France, "Rue de l'Évangile" focuses on the same themes, urban/ecological imagery, and even language that would grip northeast Paris residents of the 1990s and 2000s, and in particular environmental activists. The landscape, at once urban and provincial, is a "desert of rust and coal," where the soot of locomotives and factories "blackens" apartment buildings in a place "enclosed" from the rest the city (the original French expression used by Aymé is the more organic verb *resserré*, meaning "squeezed or tightened," implying constant pressure, and even choking).[24] This violent separation, materialized by walls and railroad track, is the basis for its peculiar landscape with "trains [whistling] in the murk" (again, *murk* has been glossed from Aymé's original, more organic choice of words: *brume souillée*, which literally means "soiled mist" or "contaminated mist," implying a corrupted or dirtied nature).[25] All

of this coal-fired movement and production underlines the transitory, indeterminacy of the area, which is given over to "wandering" and thus lacks
a fixed identity (being neither country nor city). La Chapelle itself, like
Abdel, is in a "grimy" transitional state, between the rural and the urban,
nature and culture.

Activism, Air Pollution, and the Production of a Neighborhood

Although steam-belching locomotives may be a thing of the past, the environmental impact of the SNCF (the French railway system) has not only
provoked outrage by residents but has itself provided an example of how
ecology can define a historically "incoherent" neighborhood. Rail transit is
often discussed as an environmentally friendly alternative to automobile
and air travel, but this has not been the view of many northeast Paris residents. The railroads have consistently been depicted as an environmental
menace, both during the era of steam-powered locomotives and in the present, because large numbers of diesel engines continued to be employed

Railroad tracks and tunnels in northeast Paris.

behind the rail terminals for scheduled service as well as "dead mileage" uses such as the assembly of passenger trains.

One resident who led the charge against the SNCF was Fabrice, who lives in a boxy 1970s-era HLM building perched above the Gare de l'Est tracks. Fabrice is a regular at public meetings and has a reputation as a confrontational, even cantankerous opponent of the national railroad, which frequently strikes many environmentalists who are unfamiliar with northeast Paris as counterintuitive. Despite his thorny public persona, he never failed to impress me with his hospitality when I visited his apartment, where a glass of pastis, ice, and a carafe of water often greeted my arrival. Fabrice was raised in the Antilles to a French-origin family. For most of his life, he says, "I had my opinions, but the idea of being political never passed through my head." France's general strikes of 1995, which were sparked by Prime Minister Alain Juppé's aggressive plan to reform the French welfare state, changed that for Fabrice. The strikes, which were largely led by the railroad workers and were France's largest since 1968, had a particularly transformative effect for life in northeast Paris. For the first time in recent memory the trains stopped running for weeks on end. When life returned to normal, he and other neighbors saw their surroundings through different eyes.

"We become conscious of something," he said, "a horror in the neighborhood. Every day, I found myself noticing dozens of engines, rolling down the tracks, warming up." Fabrice and other residents began closely monitoring many of the SNCF's diesel locomotives from their windows, which, prior to making their journeys, would go through a warming-up cycle during which thick, acrid clouds of diesel exhaust would be expelled above the tracks and blow down the surrounding neighborhood streets. Many residents began to grow alarmed at the potential dangers posed by the diesel fumes (especially given the proximity of the tracks to local schools). Fabrice was one of many residents who began to organize. They formed a neighborhood association with the goal of confronting the SNCF over the diesel emissions. Alliances were formed with a regional association called Île-de-France Environnement (part of the first wave of Parisian écologistes who organized against an expressway in central Paris in the 1970s) and a small global network known as the Union Environnement sans Frontières (Union Environment without Borders) that included environmentalists in the United States and Eastern

Europe. France's battle over welfare-state reform (itself a response to the 1993 Maastricht Treaty that created the European Union) had, in effect, rendered northeast Paris's unjust political ecology visible to residents. When the activists had difficulties in obtaining responses to their concerns from what he called the "SNCF's administrative monarchy," Fabrice proved skilled in pressuring the city of Paris and regional government (Île-de-France) via television stations and newspapers in depictions of "neighborhoods poisoned" by the SNCF and other nearby industrial interests. Reports and articles often showed images of smoke-belching locomotives and the ashen postindustrial landscape surrounding many of the area's apartment buildings and schools.[26] By the start of the 2000s, Fabrice and his allies had succeeded in persuading local and regional governments to underwrite environmental scientists to conduct an air-quality study. Northeast Paris residents' "on-the-ground" political ecology now yielded a new and powerful form of spatial practice, the scientific construction of the neighborhood as ecosystem.

The publicly sponsored study, coordinated by AIRPARIF (an air-pollution monitoring association focused on Paris and the Île-de-France), entailed two primary elements: a surveillance system consisting of approximately thirty air-quality sensors and a complex computer rendering of the neighborhood to model the movement of air pollutants through the built enviroment. The six-week surveillance "campaign" began with the establishment of a "perimeter" around the railroad stations followed by the installation of two mobile laboratories (for real-time air monitoring) and the positioning of air-monitoring sensors on the streets, public squares, bridges above the railroad tracks, and in the rail terminals themselves.[27]

The subsequent air-quality analysis found, first and foremost, what the researchers termed the "omnipresent" mixture of dangerous contaminants that are the "signature" of road traffic—nitrogen oxide compounds and benzene—in concentrations that are comparable to metropolitan Paris as a whole (2). However, on the tracks behind the Gare de l'Est, the analysis also revealed levels of nitrogen oxides, carbon monoxide, and particulate matter at levels averaging 20 percent greater than usual in metropolitan Paris (ibid.). Real-time analysis also revealed the presence of brief, intense, and highly localized "plumes" of nitrogen oxides at concentrations five times the normal levels on the surrounding streets; these observations appeared to be associated with varying types of locomotive activity (ibid.). As a result, researchers—and environmental activists—were able to make scientifically credible claims of increased levels of harmful contaminants in the air in northeast Paris.

The creation of a computer model of the neighborhood was vital to this aspect of the project, as it allowed the researchers to postulate a strong and quantifiable linkage between air contamination and specific locomotive activity because the nearby streets already generated high levels of emissions; indeed, an estimated fifty-one thousand vehicles per day made their way down the congested Boulevard de Magenta (ibid.). The result was a virtual neighborhood that, when viewed from the top down, resembled a kind of video game or architecture model in which every building, alley, and street was rendered in 3D mesh for the purposes of modeling airflows. The system included a "vertical" model as well, identifying different airflow layers from the level of the railroad tracks, to the streets, and finally to the tops of buildings, in order to create a meteorological rendering of the neighborhood.[28] Finally, the warm-up and heating phases of a specific model of SNCF locomotive—the Alstom CC72000 series—were incorporated into the simulation because it is the most common type in use at the Gare de l'Est, as well the most polluting SNCF locomotive.[29] The model allowed researchers to bolster their observed data with a dynamic mechanism explaining, as the study's title suggests, the process of "the dispersion of polluting emissions in the neighborhood."[30] The virtual neighborhood model provided a vivid and arresting demonstration of the ways that color-coded plumes of nitrogen oxides and other contaminants drifted through the streets from a point of origin in the train terminal, with meteorological variables included in the calculation.

As an outcome of the study, the SNCF decreased the use of CC7200 models at the Gare de l'Est while also becoming more vulnerable to accusations of environmental injustice by activists (this would be an important factor in the mobilization for the Jardins d'Éole). Indeed, activists and environmental scientists had in effect created an authoritative and coherent identity for the neighborhood as a zone scientifically defined by spatial and ecological injustice vis-à-vis the railways.

In this sense, activists and environmental scientists jointly contributed to the production of space in ways that resonated with tropes from the past and the present. There was, of course, a long history of linking northeast Paris's "soiled fog" with social inequality. Moreover, the relationship between train stations and "pollutants of different origins"[31] has a long history that resonates with old anxieties over "insalubrious" housing and long-stay hotels in the context of immigration, as well as more recent concerns over youths from the *banlieue* congregating in rail terminals and the surrounding public spaces.[32] Thus, the work of Fabrice and his fellow activists, as well as the scientists with AIRPARIF, demonstrated the ways that a political ecology–based critique and environmental science could successfully confront sources of inequality while reinforcing long-running themes relating the area's status as a transitional zone with liminality and dangerous public spaces.

A 2012 report by APUR (Atelier Parisien d'Urbanisme), arguably Paris's most important and influential producers of spatial knowledge, demonstrates how influential the railroad-centered concept of northeast Paris as a distinct ecological niche has become. The document, titled "Quartier des gares du Nord et de l'Est" (neighborhood of the North and East train stations), describes itself as a "prospective diagnosis" of the area.[33] It was assembled in the midst of ongoing efforts, and in particular Nicolas Sarkozy's vaunted Grand Paris plan, that posit the rebuilding of the Paris–*banlieue* boundary as a key element in a neoliberal strategy focused on interurban competition against other global finance capitals, and in particular London, New York, and Tokyo (see chapter 4). As is often the case, APUR, which could be described as having refined the Lefebvrian notion of "representations of space" to that of a high aesthetic, creates a veritable carnival of 3D computer-generated models and cartographic fireworks that provide in lavish detail an urban planner's version of the neighborhood as an ecological niche community.[34]

The train stations provide both a namesake (and metaphor) to literally envision the neighborhood as a distinct entity. According to APUR, the train stations provide more than a place-based identity, and are a master optic to "render these neighborhoods visible," along with the movements of people within it.[35] Nearly every form of traffic circulation is mapped from trains, trams, and automobiles to bicycle routes and even preferred pedestrian paths between train stations; the location of "innovative" small businesses is carefully plotted to trace centers of growth, as are varying concentrations of urban forest and green space (even variable levels of tree height across the area do not escape being mapped). The APUR report is a masterful demonstration of the planners' surveillance apparatus for gathering a variety of data, coupled with an equally impressive display of spatial information. At a conceptual level, the APUR report redefines the neighborhood by introducing the scale of the global. Many representations in this neighborhood study trace flows and circulatory patterns far beyond Paris itself, defining northeast Paris as a "first point of connection" between France, Europe, and the world. The maps of the neighborhood are therefore contiguous with those tracing connections to London, Brussels, and beyond, though in this perspective on globalization, little about the enduring connections and flows to points in the former colonies is mentioned. More than 120 million travelers pass through the stations every year, we are reminded, and with more international high-speed trains and increases in Paris–banlieue rail service, APUR predicts that the number will rise to more than 160 million by 2020 (13). It draws special attention to the fact that six of the design proposals submitted for the original Grand Paris project targeted the neighborhood for redevelopment or special emphasis, with celebrity architect Jean Nouvel's plan describing the space as a "new urban landmark" precisely because of its value as a nodal connection between other places (8).

At the same time, however, an ecological sensibility permeates the report. Interestingly, the discussion is less oriented toward biophysical ecology (i.e., the relationship between air, soil, and inhabitants' health) and instead naturalizes and reifies the neighborhood in terms one might use for a threatened rain forest. While "they [the neighborhoods] still know many difficulties," the report states, it places special emphasis on the "rich complexity of the neighborhoods" and their "essential diversity" (5). The report maps centers of heritage (these include the Église St. Bernard as well as the ZAC Pajol, Le Centquatre, and Jardins d'Éole), including points in the neighborhood that provide vistas of the "great landscape" (65) of railway tracks in the neighborhood, recodifying the most infamous aspect of the neighborhood's ecology as both an attraction and a form of heritage.

Interestingly, in a representation that tests the republican political taboo against reifying ethnic difference, the report also plots the area's "multiethnic mosaic." Explicitly commodifying several areas as part of the area's "cultural and tourist potential," the report charts districts of the Goutte d'Or as "North African" and "West African" along with the "Asian" district of Marx Dormoy and a "Tamil" district near the Gare du Nord itself, citing the need to "preserve" these areas, though many immigrant neighborhoods consisting of modernist social housing are omitted (ibid.). These discussions of the imperative need to retain diversity amount to an ecologically friendly variation of the urban "frontier" narrative;[36] northeast Paris is talked about much as one might describe a threatened ecozone that requires careful planning so that its social and ethnic diversity is preserved.

This metaphorical intertwining of the area's liminal, railroad-based identity with ecological imagery reaches its zenith in several architects' proposals for the Grand Paris plan. Grand Paris, which has been described as a twenty-first-century Haussmannization of the Île-de-France region with a focus on global interurban competition, consists of approximately 650 projects across the Paris metropolitan area.[37] Northeast Paris plays a central role in the vision, and many architects target the area for intensive transformation precisely because it is where the rail networks connect the city to some of its most socially precarious suburbs, many of which are also the targets of ambitious redevelopment plans.

Two master plans submitted by internationally reputed architectural firms—Atelier Christian de Portzamparc and Rogers, Harbour, Stirk and Partners—propose to transform the railroad tracks themselves into large greenbelts (termed "green armatures" in the latter plan and "ecological corridors" in the former).[38] Both plans bury the railroad tracks for a considerable length below the greenbelts, which are in turn viewed not simply as ornamentation or "green space" per se but as part of an elaborate system intended to transform the metropolitan region as an ecosystem. There are considerable differences between the two visions: the Rogers, Harbour, Stirk and Partners plan views the armatures as a circulatory system for a variety of the city's metabolic needs (ranging from public transport to energy and waste), while the Portzamparc plan proposes "ecological corridors" in terms of air, soil quality, water circulation and biodiversity (i.e., the circulation of seeds, pollen, and animal life). In both schemes, however, the infrastructural connections between neighborhood, region, and the global are reimagined to constitute an ecological or "natural" zone. Ecology, therefore, does the important conceptual work of reimagining and naturalizing scale for a global neighborhood. The line between urban ecology as metaphor and reality is completely blurred in such visions.

Ecologies at Odds

Lilian is a well-known personality in northeast Paris's sphere of redevelopment politics. A veteran activist of the city's *écologiste* movement and resident of La Chapelle for nearly thirty years, I met her soon after arriving in the field as she appeared to be at every planning and urban policy–related meeting or event. When we finally had a chance to sit together for an interview, she had recently left a meeting over the development of the ZAC Pajol: a project to transform an abandoned mail collections and customs house across the tracks from the Jardins d'Éole into an *écoquartier*.

The gender politics of urban planning and architecture had significantly shaped her style of intervention. "I'm always the only woman there," she said of the planning meetings with a wry chuckle about the "boys" (by whom she meant architects, urban designers, and city officials) who were involved in reshaping the neighborhood through megaprojects. Lilian was one of the few activists from northeast Paris with formal training in urban planning, and I noticed her attending not only planning events in northeast Paris but presentations by urbanists in universities and professional contexts. She was therefore fairly unique among the residents for her fluency in the parlance, terminology, and conventions shared by policy and design professionals. On many occasions I noticed that she often surprised and even intimidated presenters (who tended to be male) with her pointed questions. She described her role to me as a "translator" for her neighbors.

Lilian, who had spent much of her life outside of France in Belgium and the United Kingdom, was part of a middle-class, university-educated stratum of environmental/urban activists. She named her association Cactus, she said, because it could thrive in the neighborhood of La Chapelle, which she likened to a "desert." After pointing out that the association survived without a subsidy, she jokingly added another rationale for her organization's name: "a cactus has both a sting and flowers."[39] The metaphor, rooted in a gendered politics of urban nature, conveyed the notion of a thriving

object of desire that is both a survivor of a harsh environment and well pro-
tected against outsiders.

Cactus focused on multiple environmental justice issues facing the neighborhood. It had been an ally of Fabrice's struggles against the SNCF's diesel
locomotive pollution and had mounted a campaign against lead poisoning
that targeted landlords: northeast Paris's poorly maintained housing stock
combined with its sheer number of children had led to infant lead poisoning
rates that are among the highest in the Île-de-France.[40] Cactus exemplifies
the degree to which the *écologiste* movement in Paris views political ecology
as a way to confront broader urban inequalities. Increasingly, such movements are not merely environmentalisms in the city; rather, ecology is a
political idiom through which urban inequality is imagined, discussed, and
confronted that often intentionally blurs the boundaries between the built
and natural environments.

The dominant issue faced by Cactus between the 1990s and the 2000s
was the ZAC Pajol project. A ZAC (Zone d'Aménagement Concerté) is one
of the main instruments of France's national postwar urban renewal policy.
ZACs were originally envisioned as a way to facilitate redevelopment projects in carefully delimited geographic zones when multiple developers and
local governments were involved. ZACs are synonymous with the development of modernist public housing in Paris's suburbs as well as large-scale
urban renewal in the city itself; Henri Lefebvre's *The Production of Space*
was written as a direct response to such "zone"-oriented development. The
ZAC Pajol project was originally launched in the early 1990s to create more
than six hundred public-housing units. The transformation of postindustrial
sites into *cités* had been the dominant form of urban development in northeast Paris since the 1960s. As a result, 35 percent to 58 percent of northeast
Paris's housing stock is social housing, compared to a Paris average of 16
percent, and the area is among the city's most densely populated neighborhoods.[41] For all intents and purposes, the ZAC Pajol represented a continu-
ation of this trend.

By the mid-1990s, however, a network of organizations had assembled
with the goal of shifting this pattern of urbanization. Cactus and roughly
a dozen other neighborhood organizations and associations formed a coalition to oppose the project. The alliance treaded a delicate political line

in discussions with officials from the eighteenth arrondissement and the city of Paris: the associations—which were made up disproportionately of middle-class environmentalists—adamantly maintained that they were not opposed to public housing per se, and therefore attempted to avoid appearing to be classist and possibly anti-immigrant. Rather, the coalition demanded that housing construction be halted unless other types of public facilities (especially schools, community recreation centers, and child-care facilities) were built as well. As Lilian told me: "There's no school. There's no playground for children . . . There are no facilities. What do you do with kids? There's no nursery school. There's no day care. How do you live?"

While the opposition to the ZAC Pajol project was ideologically heterogeneous, Lilian's primary point of emphasis was intensely ecological, with a focus on "life" itself, and frequently the politics of raising children and social reproduction in an urban environment deemed inhospitable to survival at a basic level. This approach would set the broader tone of neighborhood politics in the following decades, and opposition along these lines led by Lilian grew so intense that plans for the development were initially called off. One Green Party official would later afford the debates (held in both public meetings and behind closed-door sessions) a mythic quality in the annals of Parisian politics, describing the ZAC Pajol as "a place of Homeric battles" between environmentalists and urban planners representing the city and regional development authorities.[42]

But in true mythic fashion, the death of the ZAC Pajol would be followed shortly by its resurrection and metamorphosis. In the early 2000s, the quasi-public developer SEMAEST (Société d'Économie Mixte d'Aménagement de l'Est de Paris—the Corporation for the Mixed Economic Development of Eastern Paris) relaunched the project in an entirely new guise: ZAC Pajol as ecological urbanism. SEMAEST still built additional social-housing units in the neighborhood, albeit in more dispersed, low-density projects, but housing was no longer part of the ZAC Pajol. The reborn ZAC Pajol would instead be home to private offices as well as a youth center, a shelter for displaced youth, an athletic facility, and a library, high school, and technical school.

From an environmental point of view, the ZAC Pajol is an exemplary piece of sustainable urban design; one architect stated in a 2013 planning meeting that "such a building would have been unthinkable a decade ago."[43] The roof of the ZAC Pajol complex is covered with 3,500 square meters of solar panels, the buildings' innards and basement contain equipment designed to capture and recycle rainwater, and the construction project itself used enough recycled materials from the previous site to avoid thirty equivalent tons of carbon emissions in unneeded truck miles.[44] Not only do such innovations point to a clear path forward in ecological urbanism, but it has an important political meaning: since the election of Socialist President François Hollande (and the appointment of Cécile Duflot of the Green Party as minister of territorial equality and housing), the ZAC Pajol was adopted as part of the first wave of France's newest zone-based instrument of national urban policy, the ÉcoQuartier. The ZAC Pajol can therefore be said to represent the largesse of ecology's political capital, as well as its "cultural capital": owing to the preservation of the old mail and customs terminal, the neighborhood's liminal status as a "borderland" is now touted as a form of national heritage.

Despite often being identified as an *écolo*, however, Lilian has continued to contest numerous aspects of the ZAC Pajol project (and has been instrumental in adding further "socially" sustainable elements to the design, such as a youth shelter). For her and many other residents of northeast Paris, the resource-focused interests of green architecture and the highly symbolic elements of sustainable urbanism seemed distant, if not wholly divorced from, the immediate life-or-death struggles facing the neighborhood's inhabitants on a regular basis, leading to her to describe the ZAC Pajol as a "green cathedral" built by the "boys." Such projects, she argued, contribute to this dehumanizing reality by amounting to a "redo of Haussmann's boulevards," evoking the image of an autocratic megaproject resulting in the demolition of a working-class neighborhood and the displacement of its residents. Lilian's (and many of her compatriots') critique was that sustainable urbanism prioritized concerns with the city's metabolic process or environmental footprint over what might be termed the fundamental need of ensuring survival for vulnerable residents. In many respects, the continuing debates over the ZAC Pajol had resulted in Lilian and her allies developing their own political ecology-based critique of sustainable urbanism.

Another example of the way in which the development of the ZAC Pajol highlights contestation among ecologies is illustrated by the case of an urban gardening group called Écobox, which was displaced by the ZAC Pajol project in the mid-2000s. In a manner reminiscent of Mamadou and his friends, the members of Écobox appropriated their own space of creativity along the interstitial "wastelands" where the railroad tracks meet the rest of northeast Paris's urban fabric. By the time I met the members of Écobox, they had already been displaced from the ZAC Pajol site and had found a new site overlooking the Gare du Nord tracks, in a vacant lot behind a collection of twenty-story HLM towers. Most of the Écobox members lived in the surrounding public-housing towers and represented a diverse swath of the area's residents in terms of age (garden participants ranged from their mid-twenties to their seventies) and ethnicity (gardeners were of French, Maghrebi, West African, and Antillean origins).

In some respects, Écobox arguably represents political ecology as a form of gardening practice. As its name implies, Écobox can be distinguished from other urban garden groups by its modular approach: all cultivation took place in hundreds of artfully arranged boxes; thus nothing is planted in the ground. The use of small portable boxes eliminated the persistent problem of soil contamination faced by many urban gardeners. The *écoboxes* themselves consisted of nearly every type of plant container imaginable, with repurposed objects scavenged from the nearby vacant lots being especially well represented, ranging from baskets, buckets, and crates to lost shoes. From all of this urban flotsam spilled an immense variety of flowering plants, garden vegetables, and herbs. Each gardener was typically given an old warehouse pallet to garden upon, an approach that intensified the notion of gardening as a creative and productive process. Like the city around it, the gardens typically grew upward by using stacks of boxes, trusses, and homemade arbors. This gave Écobox a feeling of enclosure—though the garden itself was neither gated nor locked—and thus a sense of being a distinct social world unto itself that nonetheless mirrored the vertical density of the surrounding HLM towers.

This configuration was also a statement about the spatial politics of gardening in the city. One of the gardeners, Luc, a man of French-origin in his thirties, was stoic and accepted as a near inevitability the eventual departure of Écobox from the site: "In Paris, every square meter of land is of importance for the economy and real-estate market." Indeed, he and the rest already knew what would soon arrive in the site: the Chapelle International

project, a component of the Paris Nord-Est plan to reestablish Paris's competitiveness as a global city (see chapter 4). All of the gardeners at Écobox
were quite matter-of-fact about their eventual displacement. After all, the
concept itself was designed to be somewhat nomadic, even if the overflow-
ing verdure of the garden had begun to take on a semipermanent quality.
Although the members of Écobox could have joined more official "permanent" gardens such as those created as Paris's Main Verte program, which
established community gardens in the city's parks, something about the
project's ephemeral quality appeared to draw in many residents.

As an elderly gardener named Hervé explained, "This a public space" but
"there are no opening and closing hours" (unlike a city park) and it is "not
one where we are customers or spectators." Being a member of Écobox was
about expressing creativity through gardening, and it epitomized the notion
of the city being reappropriated as a site of generative creativity and cultural
possibility. However, like many such "urban commons," Écobox's status as a
space of freedom was inseparable from its transient qualities. Moreover, the
irony of Écobox's nomadism was clear: this would be the second time the
gardeners would be displaced by a sustainable architecture project touted
for its commitment to environmentally friendly design and its generous proportion of surface area given over to publicly accessible green space.

Perhaps this irony is why Luc, the closest person the horizontally organized group had to a leader, so adamantly distanced himself from environmentalism. Sitting across from me at a picnic table surrounded by planted
boxes, he explained: "I hold the point of view that environmentalism is a
bit of an epiphenomenon." With a wry smile on his face, he spoke very slowly
and deliberately into my recorder: "The fact that we are gardening here leads
some to think we are écolos, but that's not true. We are not écolos. We are,
well, 'sociolos.'" Of course, given the surroundings, the name of Luc's organization, and even his general appearance (long hair, slightly unshaven, wearing a hoodie underneath a workman's jacket and jeans), he was well within
the style favored by many self-described écolos; one could not have been
blamed for assuming otherwise. The term sociolo, a spontaneous neologism
and rather untranslatable pun, comes closest to sounding like "sociologist"
but was meant to refocus the political meaning of gardening in an over-
whelmingly social direction: this was "social gardening," or the cultivation

of forms that were social as well as organic. But what precisely did this idea mean?

The richest explanations can be found in the words and actions of the gardeners themselves. On one occasion, while speaking with Hervé, along with Philippe (a man of Antillean origin) and Martine (a woman in her forties), Martine described the garden as a kind of a "space to take a breath," unlike the world "out there" where one is "always bothered." As she tended some basil and tomato plants growing atop a discarded wooden wire reel, she explained: "Over time, you see that something in the culture has been lost—the fact that you can cultivate something." Her fellow gardeners suggested that "cultivation" referred to something beyond the domain of flora. Phillipe, whose plot was continually praised for its imaginative and fanciful creativity by the other gardeners, made this clear: "For me, everyone here is kind of family," he said as I admired an intricate assemblage of wicker baskets housing purple and pink flowers and pea plants, intermingled with children's toys, and presided over by a now skeletonized umbrella, which he had painted purple.[45]

Écobox, a modular (and hence mobile) urban gardening project located along a railway edge, at the base of HLM buildings.

Philippe's garden at Écobox.

"The other night, "I came out late. It was actually early in the morning, and everyone was out here," Philippe said. "It's a place of equilibrium, exchange, and flows." He described the garden as a dynamic—albeit idealized—social ecology in itself. Beside him, Hervé (standing in front of his row of shoes and boots repurposed as an herb garden) picked up on this thought: Écobox is a place where "you encounter different people, often unexpected, each time you come."

Martine chimed in that such spontaneity was "indispensable" for understanding the appeal that Écobox held for its members; the social space, like nature itself, seemed to hold a certain degree of spontaneity that one could never quite predict. Hervé, who spoke with the detached confidence of an elder, situated the garden in the context of his own urban lifeworld.

"This is a place that is not quite the city," he explained. "It's between work and the home. Between the store and the, uh—"

"Television," finished Philippe.

I was struck by the parallels between the gardeners' description of Écobox and the themes of imagination, creativity, and circulation that characterized urban planners such as APUR's understanding of urban ecology.

Écobox itself was talked about as if it were either a form of infrastructure, a social world outside of the city, or both. At the same time, however, the gardeners spoke primarily about such exchange and circulation at a level of human sociality and creativity. Listening to them, I was often reminded of Lefebvre's description of spatial practice as the "daily life" of a "tenant in a government-subsidized high-rise" and I could not help but think of the vibrant and inspiring collection of plantings as contradicting the presumptions of the tenant's passivity and lack of imagination inherent in Lefebvre's quote.[46] In contrast, as both a site of social and political convergence and a built/natural environment, Écobox is a creative response to urban life. In both its verticality and its density, the gardeners' work appeared to be congruent with the spatial organization of the HLM complexes where the vast majority resided; Écobox appeared like a green parody of the modernist city around, complete with toys, knickknacks, and playful bric-a-brac. But as all of the gardeners made clear, the garden was not merely a floral critique of modernism but was a broader commentary on the relationship between culture and creativity. Gardening is about regaining control over "cultivation" and reappropriating not only the material space of the city but the imagination itself. In this sense, it is similar to myriad other interventions in the city by planners and residents alike.

Conclusion

The historical production of northeast Paris as a distinctly liminal territory or "hinterland" in the city reveals the close relationship between urbanization and struggles over the "right to the city." The urban process is not only spatial, economic, and political, but fundamentally ecological as well. Northeastern Paris's landscape of inequality is the product of geomorphological processes combined with the creation of roads, quarries, canals, and rail connections to undergird military expansion and economic accumulation. The resulting liminal and often polluted landscape, home to multiple generations of different newcomers to France, is a site of convergence and contestation, seemingly caught in a perpetual state of becoming.

Such indeterminacy carries with it the potential for transformative politics, but instability should not be romanticized. As the experience of Mamadou and the Adda'wa mosque demonstrate, this liminal experience can be one of violence and suffering, even if it also offers promise. While part of this transformation might include "healing" (recall that the Jardins d'Éole was described as "palliative space"),[47] the liminal qualities of northeast Paris have given rise to efforts by immigrant youths and urban gardeners to transform brownfields into spaces of insurgent cultural expression and community building. Mamadou's reminiscence of his youth is especially pertinent to the story of the neighborhood's development as a whole: the railroad's historical primacy in the area has led to a political and ecological situation in which the tracks (and interstitial land among the rails) are both a symbol of social and environmental injustice and a site for creative, politically meaningful acts of reappropriation.

As part of this process, ecology, nature, and the environment form an important, if continually shifting and indeterminate, idiom of struggle over the right to the city. As a diverse array of perspectives ranging from that of urban gardeners to environmental scientists, activists, and planners shows, urban ecology is not simply one type of politics, nor is it just an environmental aspect of urban contestation. Rather, urban ecology is a political prism through which the city (and the social inequalities within it) are materialized, made visible, knowable, and, in some cases, changeable. It provides an idiom for speaking about aspirations and plans for urban and social change.

At the same time, ecology explains and naturalizes the value of the city (in economic and social terms). It therefore plays a central role in capitalist logics of urban-based accumulation *and* the ways residents can reimagine and rework their surroundings in an effort to claim the right to the city, making it the domain of both locomotives and poets.

2 Space, Style, and Grassroots Strategy in the Éole Mobilization

> You must never go to the politicians' place; you always have to get them to come to you.
>
> —Tomi, Éole mobilization leader

As I spent time with residents and activists in northeast Paris, I became aware of an irony about the politics of urban parks: places where people supposedly go to "do nothing" reveal a great deal and even amplify the contradictions present in the surrounding city. Scholars, planners, and even many city dwellers often display a remarkable tendency to consider parks and green spaces as apolitical places of leisure and escape, or mere decoration. However, it is telling that the majority of people who use the Jardins d'Éole—and many neighborhood parks—are parents (and more often than not, women) with children. Urban parks have tremendous importance in forming an infrastructure for the everyday work of social reproduction, which, despite being gendered, hidden, and even devalued, is nonetheless vital for the continuity of capitalist social relations, and life itself.[1] Urban green space is therefore not merely about ornate landscaping and *flânerie*, even if such a thoroughly bourgeois, frequently male conception has historically been the predominant viewpoint.[2] In places like northeast Paris, which are densely populated with large numbers of low-income families who reside in crowded, substandard housing conditions with children, the politics of green space is far from being a simple a matter of beautification. When people mobilize for access to green space in such cases, they are confronting urban inequalities that are at once gendered, class-based, ecological, and often ethnoracial as well. Put differently, the demand for a park is a grassroots articulation of an urban political ecology.

For some city dwellers, such as Nassima, a native of Algeria and a sympathetic "fellow traveler" with the Éole mobilization, the completion of the park was the defining temporal and spatial marker of an important transformation of the world around her. It meant the end of a period in which the area had been "a cold neighborhood, an austere neighborhood, where people were afraid." The construction of the park itself was important for multiple reasons, not the least of which was providing Nassima with access to outdoor space for her then infant son.

In other respects, however, Nassima was worried. The arrival of the park was accompanied by ominous changes. She noticed that her rent and that of her friends was rising. Newcomers, "people with the means," as she put it, were coming to the neighborhood and renovating apartments. The shuttered site of the municipal undertakers' depot at 104 Rue d'Aubervilliers was renovated by the city of Paris and transformed into a contemporary art center, Le Centquatre. Even a local bakery was swept up in the changes, augmenting its usual selection of North African pastries with some "classic" French offerings in hopes of catering to the taste of newcomers and, now, even a few tourists who were newly visible on the sidewalks outside.

Many residents' views of the new park drifted along a continuum of urban and environmental justice versus gentrification, while others felt disconnected from the entire debate, and their relationship to Paris could be viewed as diametrically opposite to Nassima's. Tashia was a woman from Mali in her mid-twenties who had been in France for only five years and worked at a grocery store directly across the street from the esplanade of the Jardins d'Éole; like many recently arrived immigrants, she lived in a crowded, deteriorating apartment with several roommates. While always gregarious and friendly, Tashia never minced words about her own predicament. I clearly remember what she told me the first time I met her and explained that my research project related to the new park across the street. "I don't have time to go to a garden!" she said. "I only go to work and home, every day. I'm just trying to save money and get out of Paris." Like many recent immigrants, Tashia's survival was predicated on working in a low-wage job for so many hours each week that spatial access to the park was a moot point:

her economic position largely deprived her of the temporal space, and she was not alone.

The experience of Nassima and Tashia raises important contradictions surrounding the politics of green space. Some scholars who focus on the very significant process of "green gentrification" have a tendency to over-look the social importance of parks themselves because of the prominent historical role played by green spaces in real-estate speculation and gentrification.[3] However, a view of parks as urban "greenwash" and mere ornamentation is frequently disconnected from the reality of people who depend on them. As with many "public" goods, parks and public spaces have a tendency to be more important for people who are excluded from private access to things as basic as open space, clean air, and other shared facilities (e.g., education, health care, child care). This is not to deny that there are too many people, including Tashia, who find themselves unable to access the space even though they live and work literally across the street. Rather, one must avoid the assumption that parks and green space are merely other spaces of consumption appearing alongside upscale shops and restaurants composing a landscape of gentrification. Parks, as it turns out, can be both, and therefore expose a strict division between production and consumption as a false binary.

The mobilization for the Jardins d'Éole provides an effective way to grasp the complex and contradictory politics of urban green spaces. Indeed, when one talks about what people do in parks, one speaks in an idiom that is at once personal and exceptionally political, productive and consumerist, by invoking ideas such as child rearing, encountering neighbors, or even "enjoying nature" (and thus defining what is natural and what is not). To demand a park as a solution for urban inequalities, is therefore, to articulate a vision that politicizes these varied but interconnected elements.

The mobilization to create the Jardins d'Éole used the politics of green space as a spatial strategy to confront a wide range of urban inequalities. I argue that the objective of the mobilization—the park—is as important for being a political idiom for broader social issues as it is a goal in itself. The idiom of park politics is *spatial* in a manner following Lefebvre's notion of the "right to the city"; it entails the reappropriation of the function and meaning of urban spaces as a strategy for enacting broader social and political change.

In this regard, I demonstrate how the Jardins d'Éole itself is—like the "right to the city"—a means, and not an end.

As this chapter demonstrates, this strategy of grassroots politics has a *style* that relies on symbolic visual and verbal cues employed by activists. My focus on the style of protest politics is informed by Graeber's analysis of the class connotations of "activist culture."[4] Stylistic recognition is of crucial political importance for perceptions of the movement's legitimacy; it signals the class politics of the mobilization (despite its economically and socially heterogeneous constituency), situating it in the context of France's *soixante-huitards'* (the "May '68" generation or the sixty-eighters) role in the remaking of Paris's politics and neighborhoods.[5] The spatial strategy mobilizes the idiom of *nature* in multiple ways: the demand for a park echoes environmental justice interventions as a remedy for unjust toxic-waste dumping and issues pertaining to diesel emissions; it is also an effort to forge a "civic ecology."[6] Nature—often in conjunction with the built environment and the infrastructure of the city—provides a meaning-laden framework for activists engaged in "park politics" to make sense of social inequality by envisioning alternative urban and social futures that are materialized in the form of parks. Each of these aspects of the strategy explains the ways in which Éole activists were successful in their bid to transform northeast Paris's largest brownfield into the Jardins d'Éole. Moreover, by chronicling the mobilization to build the park, I am able to demonstrate how park politics operates as a means to the broader end of transforming the social, political, and environmental landscape of the city.

A Fertile Wasteland

The Jardins d'Éole—as both a park and a spatial strategy—was born amid the intermingling of nature fetishism and electoral politics. In 1993, France's minister of the environment, Ségolène Royal, plunged a symbolic shovel into the earth of the Cour du Maroc, which at the time was a vacant railroad facility. Royal had come to northeast Paris to help promote fellow Socialist Party politician Daniel Vaillant in his reelection campaign for the nineteenth legislative district in Paris. As children from the neighborhood looked on, Vaillant planted a symbolic tree in the Cour du Maroc and the politicians outlined a vision to transform six hectares of abandoned SNCF warehouses, switching yards, and turntables into a vast public garden. The fruit of this vision would be called the Jardins d'Éole, to be named after the RER E or Éole, then the newest addition to the Réseaux Express Régional (RER), a regional commuter railway network that would tunnel under the site. (Éole itself stood for Est-Ouest Liaison Express.) Royal, who was then the partner of the future president François Hollande, would go on to become one of the stars of the national political scene: the first woman to be nominated for the presidential election, she was defeated by Nicolas Sarkozy in 2007. Vaillant, meanwhile, would lose the 1993 election (but take office anyway because of an annulment of the results) and soon after become the mayor of the eighteenth arrondissement (a post he would hold between 2003 and 2014) and, for a crucial period in the early 2000s, the minister of the interior. The plans for the park, on the other hand, remained forgotten by everyone except residents and activists in northeast Paris, leaving the Cour du Maroc not only a vacant lot but a memorial to a potent factor in electoral politics: the broken campaign promise.

In a public ceremony, Daniel Vaillant and Ségolène Royal plant a symbolic tree at the Cour du Maroc, 1993. Photograph by Daniel Keller.

Of course, this space, one the largest "available" parcels in Paris, also had tremendous value for the accumulation of profits—a fact that was not lost on several commercial interests in the area. The Tafanel corporation, a tenant of the SNCF and a beverage distributor employing some four hundred employees on property adjacent to the Cour du Maroc, aimed to expand onto the site for warehouse space. SYCTOM (the Syndicat Intercommunal pour le Traitement des Ordures Ménagères—the regional garbage collection and disposal authority) also had its eyes on the site as a potential processing and storage facility, and in fact a number of businesses had been using the site for illegal dumping of construction materials and even toxic waste. The value of the land was not lost on the SNCF either; the railroad began formulating plans for the reindustrialization of the site for freight services almost immediately after the completion of RER line E.

Thus, even before becoming a park, the Cour du Maroc was the focus of a diverse array of projects and strategies. It was an important site for the creative reappropriations of Mamadou and his friends (described in chapter 1), the dreams articulated and offered to the public by politicians, and, of course,

By the late 1990s, the Cour du Maroc was used as a dumping site for construction waste and industrial refuse (some of which was later discovered to be toxic). Photograph by Daniel Keller.

expectations of future profit. The presence of such interests only served to increase the intensity of the "land rush" that would take place in 1998. At this point, the tunneling project for the commuter rail project ended and the future of the Cour du Maroc was open to contestation among various parties, each of whom had a different vision of the site's value in symbolic, political, and economic terms.

For one group of residents, the vacant tract appeared to symbolize the neighborhood itself, or, more precisely, the ability of residents to realize their own vision of what the urban future should hold. Tomi and his partner Monique have lived in the neighborhood since the early 1980s and over time became the informal leaders of a group of activists who became fixated on what one described as the "betrayal" of the residents by the politicians. Although of French origin, Tomi held a strong attachment to the eastern border region of Alsace (famous for its connection to Germany) where he was born; indeed, many "French-origin" activists I met in northeast Paris often seemed to resist a hegemonic French identity by explicitly self-identifying with their home region in the provinces.

The Cour du Maroc, early 2000s. Here, the site is being utilized by a traveling circus troupe, the Cirque Électrique. Photograph copyright Vianney Prouvost.

Tomi and Monique live in a small apartment overlooking the Jardins d'Éole that he had purchased twenty years earlier in a slightly dilapidated nineteenth-century building.[7] Éole activist meetings are often held there over potluck dinners where one could find anything from couscous and homemade yogurts to rhubarb confiture and homemade eau-de-vie: sharing food became one of the most important ways the members of the group asserted national and regional identities. The couple are particularly noted for serving guests salad greens that have been culled from the dumpsters of high-end restaurants in Paris's wealthy western arrondissements (the first time I ate at their house, Tomi felt the need to justify this to me, saying, "those people over there, they are a different social category than you and me, and they'll throw it out if it's more than one day old!"). Although not affluent by the broader standards of Paris, Tomi and Monique, like many other middle-income residents in northeast Paris, had managed to live comfortably in the neighborhood on their modest salaries.

The Éole mobilization, in which the couple play a leading role, is relatively small, counting roughly three hundred members. It is entirely member-supported; in order to maintain its independence, it collects no subsidy from the state. The core leadership is made up of middle-income, primarily public-sector workers such as teachers and city, regional, and government employees of French (nonimmigrant) and Maghrebi origin, though the wider membership includes residents from a more recent wave of West African immigration. Women play a visible role in the group's leadership, and, in particular, parents with children have been an important presence in the group's public events and protests. The broader membership varies in class composition from neighborhood merchants and professionals to unemployed residents wholly dependent on public support for their income. In spite of the social differences, members were united by a common urban predicament with deep historical roots in Paris's spatial structuring of land-use and environmental inequality.

Tomi and many other activists sensed that the future of the neighborhood would be determined by fate of the Cour du Maroc. If it was transformed into space of "collective or educational usage," Tomi claimed, the "four-hectare area could be a issue with which to leverage a better a life for the neighborhood." Thus the large, undeveloped tract of land (which Rachel, another of the Éole mobilization's leaders, once described as one of the "last free spaces in the city") appeared symbolic of both the neighborhood's current state and its potential for an alternative future. To dictate the development of the SNCF-controlled site would be to claim control over a territory and a set of social conditions beyond the actual boundaries of a single lot. The Éole mobilization was undertaken, then, with a mission that was not only "to create a great park on the SNCF land (la Cour du Maroc)" but "to contribute to the defense and improvement of urban conditions—the conditions of life, the environment." Given the vaguely identified hinterland that is northeast Paris, however, no neighborhood name was articulated, and instead was defined only through an extensive list of streets and boundaries ("the perimeter of Boulevard de la Villette, Boulevard de la Chapelle, Rue Philippe de Girard, Rue Pajol, Rue de l'Évangile, Rue d'Aubervilliers, Boulevard MacDonald, Avenue Corentin-Cariou, Avenue de Flandre"). Activists would therefore have to construct a neighborhood identity as well as mobilize if they wished to have a neighborhood-based movement.

A diverse array of questions, but especially the increasingly public selling and consumption of illegal drugs (heroin and crack cocaine in particular), as well as residents' worries over the dilapidated state of housing, were central to the movement. A flood of problems related to poor-quality housing was particularly urgent for immigrant (and especially undocumented) families, who often rented in a "shadow market" of unregulated, apartment buildings that were poorly maintained, unsafe, and frequently lacking running water and private bathrooms.[8] A high proportion of these renters (as well as a number of squatters) consisted of large families living in overcrowded conditions in apartments without proper ventilation and in a poor state of repair. Yet, many families also lived in constant worry of housing demolitions by the public authorities, who frequently condemned the structures, and in some cases these spaces were shared with drug users who also squatted in the buildings or used hallways to smoke crack cocaine and inject heroin. Even those who lived in newer modernist social housing often found themselves having to organize into tenants' associations to demand repairs and improvements from HLM operators. For these residents, the question of the park was less related to "public space" than to the need for more safe open space, particularly for children, who make up a higher proportion of the area's population compared to most Paris neighborhoods.[9]

While green space fulfilled a profound social need for families and children, it was also important for aging residents. The experience of Odile, an eighty-eight-year-old woman who had moved to France from Martinique in the 1960s, exemplifies the importance of "park politics" for the aging. The mobilization became an important site of social interaction and intergenerational movement politics.[10] Odile was (and continues to be) a "public character" in a Jacobsian sense as well as a political firebrand of sorts, as she embraces (and invokes) radical antiracist politics to a greater degree than many younger activists.[11]

Odile can often be found at the benches or picnic tables of the Jardins d'Éole, or just inside the window of her nearby apartment, which is on the first floor. It has long been a common practice for her to keep watch on the street from her nearby window. At the same time, Odile lived alone, and the mobilization members functioned as a fictive kin group for her; when many longtime residents (including most of the principal Éole activists) passed her window, it was common practice to give a knock and call her name, "just to check on her and say hello," as Tomi liked to say.

However, in contrast to the ageist assumption that intergenerational movement politics merely provides a way to keep the aged occupied, Odile played the role of an informal but persistent ideological mentor to the younger leadership of the activist group.[12] Tomi and the other leaders espoused an ecological perspective that focused on questions of equity (e.g., lack of access to resources or disproportionate exposure to toxic waste and pollution) that tended to dovetail with a dominant republican ideology that legitimizes protest against discrimination while avoiding any appeal to the rights of a particular minority group. Odile, on the other hand, often spoke to me (and mobilization activists) about the particular form of discrimination she experienced as an Antillean of Afro-Caribbean descent, despite being a French citizen.[13] She stressed the importance of a politics focused on justice for those who were the victims of racist oppression, and once described France's embrace of republican ideals as "hypocrisy" over a dinner with me and several Éole activists. Odile's influential perspective was the result of her political coming of age in the era of decolonization and the globalization of the Black Power movement (upon first meeting me and learning I was American, she immediately expressed her affinity for the writings of Angela Davis). In this regard, Odile's interventions created a productive point of ideological tension: Tomi, Rachel, Paul, and other key Éole strategists sometimes found her arguments counterintuitive but never disregarded her opinions entirely, and they always afforded her the respect due to an "elder." As a result of such discussions, the ideology of the Éole mobilization would remain broadly compatible with republican values and yet hint at various times toward an incipient "justice" politics focused on the social and environmental predicament of immigrant-origin residents in particular.

The Game Begins

By the late 1990s, an array of powerful but competing interests was already in the process of assuring that the Cour du Maroc would remain in private hands for the sake of profit accumulation. Upon completion of the RER line in 1998, the SNCF announced that the Cour du Maroc would be split between the Tafanel corporation and its own freight operations, with the potential for "a small neighborhood garden" on 10 percent of the site. According to Paul, another Éole activist who played the role of informal strategist for the group, neighborhood meetings in the late 1990s were marked by feelings of "deception and worry by inhabitants who had heard of a possible return of freight activities at the Cour du Maroc." However, the Éole activists were able to find open ears early on with local mayors. The group appealed forcefully to Daniel Vaillant as a member of the neighborhood ("The people here know you are a 'neighborhood guy,'" Tomi wrote him) and to Roger Madec, mayor of the nineteenth arrondissement. Although the latter lacked jurisdiction over the territory itself (Rue d'Aubervilliers is the boundary between the arrondissements with the Cour du Maroc lying just inside the eighteenth arrondissement), most of the affected citizens lived in the nineteenth arrondissement.

The SNCF, like many railroads throughout Europe, had already sold off vast tracts of its valuable urban land because of redevelopment in postindustrial areas; in Paris it had recently let go of major rail yards in the twelfth and seventeenth arrondissements (both of which had been redeveloped as parks). However, it had no intention of abandoning the Cour du Maroc as it now stood poised to sign a lucrative lease with the Tafanel corporation, which in turn planned to expand its warehouse operations onto the site. In line for access to the Cour du Maroc behind Tafanel was SYCTOM, the sanitation and garbage collection authority, which had the explicit support of Paris's mayor Jean Tiberi (a protégé of former Paris mayor and then president Jacques Chirac), and of the dominant center-right party at the time, the RPR (Rassemblement pour la Républque—Rally for the Republic).

At the same time, the Tafanel corporation (and by extension the SNCF) also enjoyed the public support of the Communist Party (PCF), which had strong union ties to the railroad and favored the reindustrialization of the area, which it still viewed as its home territory (despite having lost an electoral majority there, the PCF national headquarters lay just a kilometer away). Meanwhile, Daniel Vaillant, by then the Socialist Party (PS) mayor of the eighteenth arrondissement, held negotiations between Tafanel and the SNCF. However, despite privately reassuring the activists of his support through written correspondence, Vaillant did not invite them or any other residents to the earliest discussions of the site's future. Only Roger Madec (PS), the mayor of the nineteenth arrondissement, who by virtue of ward boundaries represented the residents near the Cour du Maroc (but not the site itself), publicly expressed support for the Éole activists from the outset.

Thus, a broad discursive project was undertaken by the Éole activists to demonstrate how the presence of the new park would satisfy the needs of the population, with public gatherings, parties, and demonstrations serving as a setting where an idealized vision of the neighborhood could be manifested. The struggle over the development of the Cour du Maroc was part of a larger vision of urban change. A flier for a protest made the following appeal to residents:

> Everyone knows that a family of seven can't live in a two-bedroom and that the overburdened classes and their children's future are threatened by the problems of this country ... To fight for a four-hectare park with cultural, athletic, and community facilities is to make a bet that a bit of "living space" [espace de vie] in the area from La Chapelle to Stalingrad, Château Landon to Crimée, could give these neighborhoods—and the people who live there—

more unity and identity. It is urgent that we respond to the suffering of the residents.

Invoking images of "overburdened classes" and overcrowded apartments, the Éole activists linked broader issues of class and housing to issues of family and the need for athletic and cultural facilities. Not only would a park offer a space for low-income families living in crowded conditions, but it would create a "neighborhood space" for local identity and solidarity as a response to the "suffering" of inhabitants.

Just as important, the prospect of a new public park was viewed as a means to create a shared identity around the theme of a renewed neighborhood center. The disparate places listed in the flier have strong and conflicting identities, though all are populated by residents of diverse immigrant origins. La Chapelle, for example, has a built environment that retains a quaint village character and is populated by West African and North African residents, as well as a growing Chinese community. Stalingrad refers—without irony—to a contested, plaza-like public square known as the Place de la Bataille-de-Stalingrad that is popularly associated with the illegal drug economy and youth delinquency. Crimée is associated with the monumental *grands ensembles,* whose large multiethnic population includes a spectrum of income levels. The built environment, social space, and neighborhood were thus merged with social-cultural difference.

In this regard, a defining architectural feature of the Cour du Maroc—a large wall running the length of the site—gained particular symbolic importance in the eyes of activists. The wall came to symbolize a variety of divisions within the neighborhood beyond the very real and often inconvenient physical division between La Chapelle and Flandre-Stalingrad. At one rally in support for the Jardins d'Éole, Albert, an environmental activist of Polish descent, announced that bridging this divide was part of a struggle to make sure that a "multicultural society was not a vain word." In his view, a respect for "nature in the city" appeared to be the best solution for the "aggressive poisoning by urbanization" of the residents. He concluded his speech with a reading from Rabindranath Tagore's *Sadhana,* which provided a cogent analysis of the metaphor of the walled city as a tool to "divide and conquer" while decrying exploitative relationships with nature. The Jardins d'Éole, it appeared, would be the material outcome of such a critique, which sought to tear down walls, figuratively and literally.

Despite this effort to "unify" the neighborhood's areas, the cultural implications of this new identity were frequently left ambiguous. In one respect, the notion that a public garden "could give these neighborhoods—and the people who live there—more unity and identity" suggested that the park could function as a microcosm of national assimilation. However, despite a demand for "cultural facilities," the Éole activists were reticent to mention any particular cultural identity in relation to a public garden—French or otherwise. For the mobilization's discourse, the most common normative category for the constituency was "the neighborhood" or "the people of this neighborhood" (les gens du quartier). In essence, the use of this spatial referent allowed activists to claim unequal, discriminatory treatment without appealing to any particular cultural identity. This spatialization of difference appealed across class and ethnic lines because it evoked the problem of injustice, and yet it displayed a blindness to culture and ethnicity that deflected delegitimizing accusations of antirepublican ghettoization that had been directed at activists in the area by the local and national media.[14]

From "Under the Pavement, the Beach" to "Behind the Wall, a Garden"

The mobilization for the park materialized several broad ideas combining nature, the urban future, and environmental justice. At an immediate level, the demand for a park sought to prevent the construction of the proposed diesel-truck depot or garbage-processing facility without putting the residents in the position of simply being "against" the projects. In contrast to NIMBYism, the demand for a park amounted to a resident's vision for the neighborhood with which authorities would be forced to directly engage— and deny—if the truck depot or garbage facility was ultimately built.

This vision was based on environmental justice arguments that not only opposed the depot and garbage-processing projects but stipulated that the residents should have the same level of access to green space as other Parisians. Moreover, the environment and nature provided a symbolic idiom with which to speak about the complicated social processes that reproduce social inequalities in northeast Paris. In a manner similar to (and consciously borrowed from) community garden movements, the mobilization for a "public garden" (to employ the literal translation from the French, *jardin public*) was oriented toward a civic ecology.[15] The public garden was meant to cultivate far more than trees, shrubs, and lawns. It provides both a metaphor and a catalyst for a broader social and political intervention by way of greening the built environment.

The Éole mobilization was informed by the global urban gardening movement. An especially formative experience for the leadership had been participation in the Forum National de Jardinage et de la Citoyenneté (national forum of community gardening and citizenship) held in Lille in 1997. This international conference brought together "citizen gardeners" from throughout France, as well as Belgium and New York, in a global forum on the state of community gardening. Presentations by the Green Guerrillas, a New York City group that used gardening as a way to recover abandoned lots, were especially influential for Tomi, who had traveled to New York in the late 1990s to observe community gardening there. For conference participants, the creation of gardens was not simply about adding more greenery in neighborhoods or "brownfields," but a broader political intervention in struggles over urban land that were becoming more pronounced in postindustrial, gentrifying cities. Despite the Éole mobilization's local approach, the emergence of the group must be understood in the context of this global trend, itself a product of deindustrialization and burgeoning urban environmentalism in North America and Europe.

But, unlike the "community gardening" movements, the Éole activists had as their aim a policy change: it was the city and elected officials who should act to create a "public garden"—there was no interest in creating a temporary community space that would likely disappear when a "legitimate" use for the Cour du Maroc was found by more powerful interests. By 1998, when the construction on the Éole commuter line was completed, there was a gap in expectations between elected officials, who had apparently forgotten the plans for a six-hectare "Jardins d'Éole," and the residents who lived near the Cour du Maroc, who had been greatly impressed by the visit of elected officials and the tree planting. On a walk through the neighborhood in 2008, Marc, one of the group's founding members, told me: "Most people you met on the street thought after the electoral campaign event that there was going to be a park built here, because of what the politicians did." Indeed, the name the "Jardins d'Éole" was invoked by the activists as a *reminder* of this apparently broken promise.

The Éole activists "fashioned" their mobilization, and in particular the visual composition and "feel" of events, in a highly strategic and specific manner. The aesthetic might best be described as part of the cultural afterlife of May '68. It emerged in relation to a middle-class "generation" of the French Left that was also well represented in the Socialist Party that came to power in Paris in the early 2000s.[16] This style is less visual than social and atmospheric; it infused the affect, atmosphere, and social milieu that the association created in its protests and gatherings. It is most visible (and politically important) in a type of protest the Éole activists utilized starting in the late 1990s, which they called *manif-festives*. This term, a contraction between *manifestation* (demonstration or protest) and *festive*, described a kind of protest that resembled a whimsical, carnivalesque, and polemic take on a block party. Many aspects of the events were evocative of an anti-modern, rural nostalgia for village festivals, Romani imagery, and circus and sideshow performers that have been associated with France's middle-class counterculture since the late 1960s. Protests often combined performances of puppetry, circus acrobats, and a typically Romani- or Balkan-influenced music ensemble making heavy use of a rustic, "exotic" sound grounded in accordions and horns. In many respects, the *manif-festive* substituted the anticonformity message conveyed by the zany circus performer aesthetic from the level of the individual with that of the urban space where the protest was centered: it was the neighborhood that was a pariah—quirky, somewhat exotic, and a wellspring of creativity. This atmosphere was enhanced in the early 2000s when a traveling circus troupe known as Cirque Électrique occupied the Cour du Maroc with the activists' support for several years.

This strategy of protest is notable in that it sought to make use of northeast Paris itself. Instead of meeting with politicians in their established sphere of arrondissement councils and committee meetings, the activists aimed to stage confrontations with politicians on their own turf, where they could arrange a spectacle and control the terms of the conversation through the *manif-festives*. The events combined the visual impact of a protest, including masses of chanting residents holding signs and placards, with the atmosphere of a party, as food was served potluck, games were played, and musicians performed. Whereas most demonstrations might march through neighborhoods and culminate at a politically symbolic site such an arrondissement's *mairie* (town hall), the *manif-festives* stayed put in one place in the neighborhood, either at the Passage Goix (a narrow lane lined with the neighborhood's most dilapidated apartment buildings and squats) or, later, at the Cour du Maroc itself. The mood was not angry but earnest, at times even fun-loving and welcoming; it eschewed a political aesthetic of anger in favor of one of celebration and friendliness, bonding and solidarity. The lingering presence of the *manif-festives* soon became a fixture in the neighborhood and continued well after the construction of the park in 2007.

The activists also embraced a Situationist-style penchant for transforming the neighborhood's spaces into surreal settings. The crumbling alleyways and weed-strewn lots that were the sites of the *manif-festives* were often decorated with potted plants, small trees, and even pictures of parks and greenery—one might say that these northeast Paris activists replaced the May '68 motto "Under the pavement, the beach" with "Behind the wall, a garden." Such imagery and sounds resonated as a "signifying practice" evoking a middle-class aesthetic, political, social, and even moral sensibility instantly recognizable among France's *soixante-huitards*, who remain prominent in Paris's Socialist and Green Party establishment.[17] Éole mobilization politics came to be marked by a carnivalesque style of playful absurdism combined with middle-class conviviality that could be contrasted with the anger-infused "street politics" of mobilizations such as the *sans-papiers* (undocumented immigrants movement) and Droit au Logement or DAL (the right-to-housing movement). This style marked the Association Jardins d'Éole as part of a mythical legacy of May '68 shared by the Socialist Party, but it situates the group amid an increasingly active set of *soixante-huitards* in the neighborhood politics and gentrification of Paris's outlying working-class neighborhoods.[18] In an era in which the global city is at once a gentrifying city, class-inflected style is therefore a crucial element in marking urban movements' legitimacy in the eyes of the powerful.

At times, *manif-festives* took on the character of pranks. Finding themselves locked out of negotiations between Vaillant and the SNCF over the future of the site, the group held a traditional demonstration in front of the eighteenth arrondissement town hall, waving placards that called for a "halt to authoritarian urbanism." When locked out of another meeting at Tafanel's headquarters, the group gathered at the company's entrance with signs, and in the words of one activist, "politely offered coffee" to the participants as they arrived for the meeting.

Such gentility (often rendered absurd and poignant by the dehumanizing postindustrial landscape where the events are held) is a signature trait of the group's style. For example, the activists once mailed hundreds of postcards with photographs of the abandoned "Cour du Maroc" to the arrondissement (an ironic message in one of the world's tourist capitals) and covered apartments buildings near the site with garish banners. When the group was allowed into meetings, Tomi noted that "it wasn't only two or three people that came to ask questions at arrondissement council meetings, but ten, eighty, even two thousand—then they are obligated to listen." By using sheer numbers, the activists sought to, in the words of Paul, "force the politicians to work."

Manif-festives had a practical function. The Éole mobilization used the events to inform residents about new developments in the struggle and the presence of industrial pollution emitted by the SNCF and Tafanel's vehicles, and to draw more core members from the wider population of northeast Paris. But these practical successes also contained potent symbolic elements. One journalist marveled at how "the Cour du Maroc was transformed in the space of minutes into a veritable garden."[19] Two leading members of the association described how the multiple goals of the *manif-festives* were closely tied to residents reimagining the social and built environment of the neighborhood itself. Paul, Rachel, and Tomi once described *manif-festives* in the following terms:

> PAUL: We did it to give desire when people passed by, because in the site there was a huge wall and no one could see there [into the Cour du Maroc]. So, to attract people to the event we put up trees and plants and stuff like that, so that people could discover the grandeur of the site, so that people would have the desire to have a park there, to enrich their lives.

> RACHEL: We had to get the people to imagine a park there. For one of the *manif-festives,* for example, we searched in stores for images of parks so we

could tell people "you could have that," to tell people in this impoverished, deteriorated neighborhood, in the social housing, to "imagine having this" and show that we could take the initiative, get things moving, to get this park. So it's true that a goal of the *manif-festive* was to introduce the people of the neighborhood to the land and to inform them. And more, there were concerts, games, some food—

TOMI: —and to make the politicians come, so they could see the number of people present.

Not only did *manif-festives* appeal to "needs" such as housing or play areas for children, but, at a visceral level, the group sought to create a "desire" for a green space as well. In most of the demonstrations, the group would invite people into the Cour du Maroc itself, which was decorated with spontaneous vegetation and often featured music, games, and a forum for debates. In this way, by symbolically breaking down the wall along the Rue d'Aubervilliers— which at least one journalist could not resist dubbing a "Berlin Wall"—the group sought to show the possibility of a changed future by exposing the vast openness of the Cour du Maroc itself to the inhabitants.[20] This pedagogical form of protest served to demonstrate the vastness of the *terrain vague* and allow other neighborhood residents to imagine what a green space might look like—often by showing images of parks and gardens. The idea was to create—"manifest"—if only for a short time, the sociality and community that the movement sought to realize in the creation of the Jardins d'Éole. The *manif-festives* thus produced a space of desires and dreams while also making political demands.

The numbers of residents on the streets as well as the mobilization's success in publicizing the events began to feed the spectacle, drawing in journalists from local newspapers, and quickly thereafter, politicians. While local Socialist Party figures such as Daniel Vaillant and Roger Madec were eager to be seen in streets that have long been a left base in French politics, representatives from city hall (presided over by Jean Tiberi at the time) also began to make appearances. A decade later, Tomi remained amused at how eager even opposing elected officials were to mingle with the crowd. For him and other activists, however, the crowds were not simply there to "welcome" politicians or impress them with numbers, but to influence them. Tomi recalled the politicians' presence at the *manif-festives* with a chuckle:

> At each party there would be between ten and twenty politicians, from across the board, left, right, from the arrondissement and the city of Paris. I used to tell mothers to tell their children to go say, "Oh, Mr. Mayor, we must have a park here," and I would tell the kids to go pull on the politicians' hands. That was funny, all of that, but you absolutely had to motivate the politicians. When the elected officials came into the Cour du Maroc, with the grilled meats and about two or three hundred residents—everybody was there—and they saw the people wanted this place, and then the people were asking them questions about whether this place would become a park or not—[he pauses for a moment, seemingly lost in reminiscence]? At those parties I remember looking over my shoulder and noticing, Oh, there is a politician! And another one, and another, and another . . .

The *manif-festives* served as a spectacle for the seduction of elected officials who arrived seeking votes from residents who spanned various ages and ethnicities. Aided by the wafting smell of Maghrebi-style lamb sausage being grilled over an open flame, the *manif-festive* offered a mouthwatering sight for politicians: the "neighborhood" in all its generational, class, and ethnic diversity. Many aspects of the events seemed to play to the desires of politicians in an almost a satirical manner: there was ample space for photo opportunities with children and opportunities to sit and eat alongside residents. Not merely a gathering of residents, the events made for a spectacle of neighborhood conviviality and diversity that sought to displace a predominant image of the area as run-down, torn by interethnic strife and youth delinquency. Activists were, in some respects, "serving up" the neighborhood to politicians, but in doing so, they were also constituting its power.

As a form of grassroots political theater, the *manif-festives* offered both a cause and a presentation that were more than palatable for Paris's Socialist Party establishment. In contrast to more radical and nationally prominent movements in northeast Paris such as the *sans-papiers* and Droit au Logement, the Éole activists eschewed a common tradition of radical street politics rooted in barricades and open confrontation. In contrast, they focused on face-to-face politics, exposing the politicians to the people (and thus stirring their desire for power—or at least their obligations to their constituents). Park politics cultivated a milieu of middle-class civility and conviviality, often heavily inflected by an aesthetic of merrymaking and the carnivalesque. Ironically, the May '68 sensibility signaled legitimacy and participation in— as opposed to radical alternatives to—the emergent and rapidly expanding power base for the Socialist Party in Paris.[21]

In these events, as well as the broader discourse associated with the Éole mobilization, nature was a theme of overriding importance. Nature, often conservatively gendered in a female fashion, became closely linked with raising children, the life cycle, and social reproduction. Parents' associations in the area's schools were closely tied to the mobilization from the start. Parents—frequently mothers—were important not only in planning activities at the *manif-festives* for children but in constructing an improvised sandbox and playground (little more than a large pit of dirt) in the Cour du Maroc itself. Their presence was indicative of the fact that northeast Paris's urban inequalities seemed to threaten social reproduction itself. Calls for a park were therefore commonly articulated by residents as focusing on a "play space for children" and an "infants garden," "a place for the mothers

Parents with children at a *manif-festive* for the Jardins d'Éole. Photograph by Daniel Keller.

to meet," and "a traditional park offering shade and a place for mothers and their children." Parents with children became some of the earliest appropriators of the Cour du Maroc, claiming a corner in the space for themselves, while teenagers practiced break dancing and deejaying in the abandoned buildings nearby. This particular version of urban nature identified the space with ideas of the future generation's needs while also reinforcing a highly domestic notion of women's gender roles.

A particularly rich source of the ways northeast residents constructed their desire for a park in the Cour du Maroc can be seen in a set of petitions the Éole activists collected during its campaign. Designed as testimony to pass on to politicians and local officials, these statements by residents about the need for green space are flawed in that they contain no information regarding a petitioners' gender, ethnicity, or class background. It is only known that the "survey respondents" were approximately 20 percent under twenty years of age, 60 percent between twenty and sixty, with the remainder being older residents. The majority (70 percent) were not affiliated with the mobilization itself, and the main arrondissements where respondents lived were the nineteenth (54 percent) and the eighteenth (42 percent). The activists obtained written "imaginings" of a park from 141 residents (the vast majority were collected at the *manif-festives*). Although one cannot treat the responses as statistically representative, the "testimony" offers an informative collection of views on the politics of green space, nature, and the environment in the city, and, more important, an example of how activists represented the neighborhood on these issues.

In many cases, residents articulated nature specifically as a need of children. Thus one resident longed for a "real green space where one can see nature at work and show young Parisians of the neighborhood the cycle of the seasons, and how plants grow (other than the weeds that come up through the sidewalks)"; nature was thus linked to a pedagogy of life itself. Another called for "a space where children and people of the neighborhood discover—or rediscover—the cycles of nature." Yet another saw the park as not only a "garden for children" but a "space for children to garden," with a request for "goats and sheep for children to see" (another resident envisioned a park with cows and chickens). In multiple instances, it appeared that residents linked children's exposure to nature and symbols of rural life as an escape, relief, or redemption from northeast Paris as a place of physical, environmental, and even moral degradation and deterioration. The emphasis on the redemptive power of green space for young children was especially meaningful given the degree of anxiety over adolescent delinquency that was articulated in local settings (schools and neighborhood meetings) and the national media alike.

An expression used by the activists—*espace de vie* (living space) seemed to capture many concerns that residents voiced about the importance of life and vibrancy. In the postindustrial landscape of northeast Paris, where capital disinvestment had resulted in the visible deterioration of the built environment, vitality appeared to be at the forefront of individual consciousness when envisioning rebuilt urban space. Thus one resident spoke at length of a "place of life," "lots of lush greenery and water," "a wooded valley," and a "garden that could transmit life across the generations, a park of human values." Nature was seen as having a healing effect on industrial activity and the pollution that accompanied it. One resident stated that the "minimum to obtain is for nonpolluting trucks and engines—no noise, no diesel—it's hellish." Another called for "trees to recuperate a maximum amount of oxygen and clean the pollution." The park was seen as an "oasis" of life as well as being restorative of it.

Frequently, these images of life, whether related to healing or lush vibrancy, intermingled the realms of the social, biological, urban, and cultural. The mobilization itself made a slogan out of the call for a "great park to heal the wounds of a suffering neighborhood." The following quotes show how some residents drew parallels between horticulture, social diversity, and political vitality for the neighborhood:

> A place of awareness for culture as well as botany. Just as well, it could be a space to play for little ones, but equally for the teenagers who could move their basketball courts out from under the scandalous spaces under the metro and have them in the park. I'm thinking also of a place for health, and imagining a meeting place (for debates, different events, a sociocultural place).

> Heavily wooded and flowered. It really should be a meeting place for residents of the nearby neighborhoods for cultural activities and sports.

A place where the neighborhood might have the possibility of discovering the beauty of the changing seasons. A place of calm and meditation for some. But in another way, a feast of oxygen, and above all a place of life for demonstrations to improve the neighborhood and its residents.

Green! Green! Green! Lots of trees to heal the pollution in the neighborhood. A play space for children (of which the eighteenth arrondissement currently suffers a serious deficit). A space for encounters between different types of people: a space of communication.

A real working-class park (don't make it like the buttes) [a reference to the highly stylized, Haussmann-era Parc des Buttes-Chaumount in the nineteenth arrondissement].

A large portion should be occupied by GARDENS for the NEIGHBORHOOD ASSOCIATIONS. That's to say, semipublic—open to residents of the neighborhood, the schools, disabled people, unbalanced people (addicts, etc.) to give a taste of the earth, and of plants. All of this could be done thanks to a personal investment that the associations could offer.

Much of this aspirational discourse intermingled and juxtaposed images of a vibrant floral setting with a social, political, and urban "flowering." Images of lush, vibrant gardens parallel cultural diversity and *mixité social,* and the intermingling of plants and species is envisioned in the same breath as "encounters between different types of people." Such a space of "communication" could enable political consciousness and activity: it would be a "working-class park," a space for "debates," and, according to a few residents, a place largely managed and controlled by neighborhood associations. Both residents and the neighborhood itself could benefit from exposure to the natural cycles of life ("the changing seasons" or "a taste of the Earth") and nature as a restorative power for city and children alike. The park would be an *espace de vie* in a natural, cultural, social, urban, and political sense. Most important, the imagery of nature and green space provided a shared idiom with which residents could grapple with political and social struggles facing the neighborhood. As a "public garden," it would be a site of cultivation for a renewed northeast Paris in a social, ecological, and democratic sense.

Toxics, Trains, and Elections

These visions of urban nature gained political currency in the midst of multiple revelations of ecological injustice that began to appear in the late 1990s. First, the discovery of toxic waste–filled barrels on the site in 1998 served to enliven the debate of the Cour du Maroc's future, if not change its terms. Tests revealed that 2.5 metric tons of sodium cyanide were found illegally stored in the site, though the toxic chemicals were also discovered to be safely contained within barrels.[22] The discovery drew Europe Écologie Les Verts—the Green Party—into the debate. Its support, together with the considerable press attention drawn to the issue by the toxic waste, increased pressure on a now deeply embarrassed SNCF, even though the railroad was absolved from being primarily responsible for the waste (two other companies that were tenants of the SNCF were later fined). Similarly, the short-lived but very public deliberation by Mayor Tiberi to locate a municipal garbage-processing facility on the site only strengthened the perception of the neighborhood as a victim of more powerful interests. Both incidents served to galvanize wider support for the Éole activists.

Given the neighborhood's historical and geographic position relative to the railways, there was no shortage of ill feeling or willing participants in a campaign against the SNCF, as well as the Tafanel corporation. The Éole activists found an enthusiastic partner with Fabrice, the La Chapelle–based activist who had long fought with the SNCF over air pollution (see chapter 1). A particular focus was placed on the noxious effects of diesel fumes spewed by the delivery trucks (especially those of Tafanel) and, most of all, SNCF yard engines. Diesel-powered locomotives are run through the neighborhood day and night, and have been used for scheduled and nonscheduled (yard-engine) service alike. In addition to a virulent letter-writing campaign to elected officials and the SNCF, the associations were able to conduct press interviews leading to a full-page article in *France Soir* titled "A Poisoned Neighborhood."[23] Not only did the article draw connections between the toxic waste, the diesel fumes, and the number of children living in the area, but it branded the railroad, ironically enough, as the ecological antagonist.

Thus it is perhaps not surprising that by 2000, a publicly cowed SNCF was now offering the association a garden of 30,000 square meters, with an area of 12,000 square meters set aside for Tafanel. Not only was the new offer ten times the amount of green space first proposed in 1998 but it included a total withdrawal of the SNCF's own facilities from the site.

This did not mean that the Éole mobilization was without opponents outside of the SNCF or Tafanel. The Communist Party (PCF) took up the cause of Tafanel on grounds of reviving industrial employment in the eighteenth and nineteenth arrondissements and in support of rail-based freight delivery. Others, including some residents with whom I spoke, cited the need for housing more than parkland. Éole mobilization activists had treated this debate delicately, acknowledging, as one activist told me, that "housing is a principal urban demand," but frequently citing the already high population densities of northeast Paris and its lack of green space. Paul stated that "in that case, it wasn't good versus evil," and acknowledged that there were arguments to be made for housing and employment in the form of jobs with Tafanel and the SNCF. Rather than counter such arguments directly, the association preferred to point out that when it conducted the survey of 141 residents, a majority wanted the park. Whether or not the survey truly represented the views of the neighborhood, no other associations emerged in opposition to the goal of building a park, and at this critical period, housing-rights groups such as DAL (Droit au Logement—discussed further in chapter 6) did not join the debate or suggest that housing should be built on the land instead.

It was a matter of no small importance that all of this contestation (including the widely publicized cyanide barrels scandal) occurred during the buildup to Paris's 2001 mayoral race, in which an energized left-wing coalition (PS–PCF–Green) saw an opportunity to seize the mayor's office for the first time in modern Parisian history. By polling day, Jean Tiberi, the right-wing incumbent, had been weakened by several scandals involving vote rigging and the illegal possession of a firearms cache in his apartment. His party (the Gaullist RPR—Rassemblement pour la République) split its ranks because of the scandals, and ran a second mayoral candidate in the final hour. Bertrand Delanoë (PS), a former city councilor and one of France's few openly gay politicians, who also happened to be from the affluent but left-leaning Montmartre neighborhood in the eighteenth arrondissement, won the election handily against the split opposition. Delanoë's electoral campaign had publicly supported the Éole activists in their opposition to Tiberi, and his new administration was quick to tout a park at the Cour du Maroc. This was a populist gesture in a city long known for its leaders' pharaonic penchant for large projects in central locations (away from the city's outlying *quartiers populaires*). Moreover, the election of a Socialist Party mayor now meant that there was a direct political alignment by party between the arrondissements of northeast Paris and city hall. The impact on the negotiations with the SNCF was swift: according to Paul, after the election of Delanoë, the terms of the debate surrounding the park went from "'yes or no' to 'what size?'" To make matters worse for the SNCF, the eighteenth arrondissement mayor, Daniel Vaillant, abruptly became an outspoken supporter of the park.

The Éole activists were now in an enviable position: not only did the eighteenth and nineteenth arrondissements have a close ally in city hall, but beginning in 2001 Vaillant won a presidential appointment as interior minister: he now sat at the apex of France's domestic policy apparatus, behind only the prime minister and president. The importance of this alignment of political stars should not be underestimated. The year 2001 was indeed a fortuitous one for politics in the eighteenth arrondissement. These politicians formed the backbone of the Socialist Party resurgence in Paris that would, over the next decade, strengthen the national campaign to unseat Nicolas Sarkozy in 2012 (though President Hollande emerged from a different faction within the PS). The resultant change in political currents was quick, and by December 2001 Paris had all but approved a 4.2-hectare garden, part of which would now be built on top of a 4-000-square-meter Tafanel facility.

Over the next two years, the railroad and its tenant Tafanel were forced to renegotiate their claim to the Cour du Maroc in ever-decreasing sections. Finally, they were driven off the site altogether, having been pressured to sell the property to the city. By the end of 2003, the SNCF had canceled the plan to allow Tafanel access to the site, though by then it was too late to remove an artificial hill from the design intended to accommodate an underground facility for the corporation. This legacy of Tafanel's influence led to

Politicians at a *manif-festive* after the city chose to side with the residents and pursue the creation of a park at the site. Roger Madec, mayor of the nineteenth arrondissement, is on the far left; Paris mayor Bertrand Delanoë is in the center; architect Michel Corajoud is on the far right. Photograph by Daniel Keller.

unresolved design problems and conflicts over modes of park usage (see chapter 6). Nonetheless, the Cour du Maroc would now be set aside purely for the Jardins d'Éole. If the campaign for the park had been declared a victory over the SNCF in 2001, it now represented a trouncing of the Tafanel plans as well. Residents were able to claim a victory against the "powers that be," and ironically, so could the Socialist Party and the incoming mayor of Paris.

Conclusion

Thanks to a combination of political timing and shrewd coalition building, the Éole activists and their allies managed to win a sizable prize— the planned construction costs for the eleven-acre park were estimated at

Production of nature: the Jardins d'Éole construction site, 2006. Photograph by
Daniel Keller.

$26 million—in the face of powerful opposition, in roughly six years' time
(1998–2004). The victory was all the more remarkable in that it occurred in
an area whose residents have been historically marginalized—politically,
socially, and economically. For residents, the building of the park was linked
to the end of an "authoritarian urbanism" and viewed as a coup for local,
grassroots democracy. Activists envisioned the proposed green space as
linking ecological concerns with housing, health, safety, quality of life, and
a strengthened political consciousness of the "neighborhood" as a force in
favor of democracy.

The contentious politics swirling around the building of the Jardins
d'Éole is part of a spatial strategy of grassroots politics that transcends the
issue of the park itself. Spatial interventions such as the Éole mobilization
are ways that residents attempt to manipulate the constantly shifting terrain of the city for their own ends. The demand for the park had its roots
in an attempt to recast *what the city is for* at a basic level (sustaining life as
opposed to extracting value) and to radically reimagine *who the city is built*

for, especially at the level of gender and class. In this regard, it is important to remember that the Éole mobilization's focus on the park was a highly successful strategy to prevent what policy makers and corporate leaders had otherwise planned for the site: a diesel trucking depot or a garbage-processing facility.

The "production of nature"—to reappropriate a phrase coined by Neil Smith—is a significant part of this strategy.[24] As a result, the concepts of life, the neighborhood, and the environment were often used interchangeably in a tripartite conflation of the urban, horticultural, and biological. It represented an attempt to heal what was viewed as a wounded city.[25] Indeed, it is not enough to say that the park was a stand-in for other social issues: the nature-based discourse surrounding the park shaped the ways in which activists constructed social problems as varied as poor housing conditions, industrial pollution, and the lack of facilities and spaces for child care. It would not be inaccurate to describe the demand for the park as a form of political ecology analysis undertaken by the activists themselves.

The style in which this analysis was conveyed was important, and aesthetics proved to be a significant aspect of the strategy as it played out in Paris as a global, gentrifying city. The "fashion" of the outer arrondissements—in the world of middle-class neighborhood politics—is itself an afterlife of the Paris of May '68: an *écologiste* version that has evolved from "back-to-the-land" antiurbanism to the green urbanism of the Jardins d'Éole. It is a style that embraces playful exoticism in the form of music and pageantry, and prefers pointed satire or surrealist irony to the barricade-and-march version of '68 politics that might be associated with groups such as the *sans-papiers,* Droit au Logement, or the alter-globalization movement in France, the Altermondialistes. It is also eminently palatable to Paris's Socialist leaders, who since 2001 find themselves in the role of deciding what type of city a Socialist-led Paris should be. Style is an important part of grassroots politics as a war of position in which activists situate a movement within a recognized symbolic terrain—and idiom—of politics.[26]

Beginning with the election of Socialist Bertrand Delanoë as mayor in 2001, May '68 came to the forefront as an important political idiom that signaled a temporal shift for a new era in the city. By the mid-2000s, Paris had adopted some of the most outwardly important referents of the May '68 protests in a wide range of urban policies that more often than not served to reconstruct Paris as a brand. Most notably, the Delanoë administration recast the famous slogan "Sous les pavés, la plage" (Under the pavement, the beach) as part of a quality-of-life/tourism strategy called "Paris-Plages" (Paris Beaches). The centerpiece of the city program is the transformation of the Pompidou Expressway (the urban project that crystallized the post-'68 *écologiste* movement in Paris) into a beach by covering it with truckloads of sand, beach chairs, and umbrellas, and adding live music and DJs to round out the scene. Other programs emphasizing a populist retaking of the streets include Fête de la Musique, a summer solstice festival in which musicians (amateur and professional) are invited to perform outdoors and around the city all night. Starting with Delanoë, a new afterlife of that famous insurrection emerged: May '68 as logic of accumulation, providing Paris with a distinct "niche" and identity among other global cities. The Jardins d'Éole project aligns with that vision.[27]

The beach "above" the streets: one of Bertrand Delanoë's signature spectacles, Paris-Plages (Paris Beaches), is held during the Jardins d'Éole's inaugural summer, 2007. Here, a beach chair of surreal proportions rounds out the scene.

The victory of the Éole activists raises no shortage of questions, chief among them being what kind of park—if any—could address such a variety of concerns, including how such a park would be designed. But as the following chapters show, the mere fact that a neighborhood movement was playing a central role in reshaping and "greening" the urban landscape points to the inescapable reality that the mobilization was now implicated in the kind of urban and social transformation often associated with urban planners and developers and was an important intervention into national politics: Paris's green spaces are, after all, national monuments of a sort. The completion of the park would represent a victory on the part of the activists but also a beginning surrounded by uncertainty: what this new transformation would entail—and who controlled it—would remain contested.

3 Cultivating the Republic?

Parks, Gardens, and Youth

> Little by little, as I become more interested in the context, gradually I came to understand that the question was not about completely transforming the space but to intensify what was already there. Not forcefully, but to delicately intensify . . .
>
> —Senior architect, Jardins d'Éole design team

Sabine and I stood in the courtyard of an HLM high-rise on Rue de Tanger surrounded by dozens of children. The kids, variously yelling, running, and crying, were nearly bounding off the walls of the concrete plaza, where a few old hardwood trees provided shade and raised garden beds containing tomatoes and green beans rounded out the scene. This space was the work of Vivre Ensemble, an association that Sabine had founded in the early 2000s and run almost single-handedly (sometimes with the help of an intern) since then. I had originally heard about Vivre Ensemble because it created community gardens expressly for the families who lived in the high-rise HLMs, but what I found more closely resembled recess time at an elementary school. Vivre Ensemble held a variety of weekend and summer "playtimes" for nearly a hundred children who lived in the high-rise towers adjoining the Rue du Maroc, Rue de Tanger, and Rue Riquet, which feature some of Paris's highest residential densities (roughly a thousand people per square kilometer) and among its highest proportions of children and young people (one in four residents are under twenty).[1]

Vivre Ensemble appeared to resemble a day-care program, and Sabine once described her reason for founding the association in straightforward terms: "We created these gardens for the kids, not adults, but of course parents end up coming out too." She referred to her experience over the past two decades in which she'd lived in the buildings: "We didn't have anything in this neighborhood then, certainly not like the Jardins d'Éole, so the kids just played in the street all of the time."

At other moments, however, it became clear that playing "in the street" versus playing in "the gardens" held a deeper social and even political meaning. Vivre Ensemble, the name of the association, was, after all, a reference to the ethnically diverse makeup of the buildings, which contained a plethora of immigrant-origin families from West Africa and the Maghreb as well as residents from East Asia, South Asia, and a significant Jewish community; the children present at many events appeared to fairly represent this diverse population. The gardens at Vivre Ensemble, said Sabine, were created to avoid a situation in which "you don't know the cultures of others, why people conduct themselves differently." Instruction for children in basic urban gardening therefore operated as a kind of pedagogy in culture and citizenship. It was intended to counter what Sabine described as "mal-intégration." To this she added: "We in France have a way of living that's definitely not the way people live all over the world."

When she made this comment, her intern, a young college student of French origin who assisted with the technical aspects of urban gardening, seized on my question to instruct me as a foreigner (and specifically as an American) about what "integration" meant in France, in a near-textbook articulation of assimilationism: "In France, people must absolutely adopt a French way of life, or a European way of life, in any case. Of course, when you look at the United States, it's somewhat the opposite; people keep their culture, in their neighborhood. In this association, we try hard to avoid the ghetto."

In discussing why community gardening for children—or what might be called gardening the community—was important in a multiethnic neighborhood, Sabine and the intern had just expressed two slight variations of an assimilationist republicanism. While Sabine discussed issues of mutual incomprehensibility and made a point of associating "peculiarity" with France (as opposed to the culture of the immigrant), the intern voiced a more nationalist iteration of republicanism that associates cultural differences with social fragmentation, and deploys the urban (i.e., racially divided) United States as a case in point (thus the invocation of the term "ghetto" in its contemporary English usage).[2] Last, but not least, this articulation of belonging posits a fixed notion of a French—or European—way of living as normative. Vivre Ensemble was not simply conceived to care for children in a neighborhood lacking appropriate public facilities. Rather, the garden— an environment that emphasizes nature, nurturing, and attention to the life cycle in a carefully ordered, bounded setting—was invoked in explicit contrast to the unregulated "street." In this regard, Vivre Ensemble's vision of community gardening in northeast Paris merges with the cultivation of political belonging in children.

Republicanism is sometimes defined as a form of citizenship, an ideology of governance, or a political tradition.[3] Anthropologists studying contemporary France focus on the importance of republican citizenship as a basis for belonging and exclusion in the nation: the preservation of republican values is often cited as the justification for a number of assimilationist policies.[4] For example, the banning of the head scarf in schools and of the burka in public space as a whole is cited because of a need to safeguard laïcité (state-guaranteed secularism meant to preserve the separation of religious institutions from the state, and hence equal treatment for all).

In this chapter, I use youth activism and conceptions of human–nature relationships centered on gardening as an opening into new understandings of how republicanism might be "lived" or practiced in varying ways by individuals on the ground. Mustafa Dikeç has used the term "actually existing republicanism" to describe the gap between the ways that republicanism is discussed at an ideal level and the implications of republican policies for politics in everyday life. For him, "actually existing republicanism" differs from idealized versions because—in practice—urban policy does indeed result in discrimination against different ethnic groups. While this is undeniably the case, I also suggest that the recognition of (and hence the reproduction of) difference in practice is not limited to either discriminatory practices or public agencies. Thus, I invoke Dikeç's notion of "actually existing republicanism" to refer to civic engagement around urban and environmental themes as one of many such places where residents recognize, promote, and politicize differences in a manner that opposes a hegemonic assimilationist version of republicanism.[5] Indeed, during the Sarkozy era, even the president of the Republic himself was prone to breaching the neutrality of the public sphere in speeches by invoking what he termed France's Christian heritage.[6]

Youth activism as well as gardens (of both the public and community variety) offer bountiful analytic ground for rethinking everyday political belonging in France. City parks and community gardens are landscapes that help redefine the boundaries between nature and culture, difference and sameness. At the same time, these settings are often understood as sites of explicit public socialization—especially in multiethnic districts—that emphasize a mix of pedagogy with articulating the "nature" of differences.[7] Both youth activism and gardens focus on naturalizing various forms of transformation and becoming as part of the life cycle, including citizenship and political belonging. Practices such as gardening and landscaping (and even nurturing children) invoke the agency of nature alongside citizenship; as a result, the qualities of malleability, development, and becoming are highly important. Discussions of nature highlight the degree to which republicanism is a multifarious, indeterminate concept.

However, possibilities for plural interpretations of the Republic are erased when republicanism is glossed as a static, Islamophobic ideology underlying increasingly powerful nationalist, xenophobic voices in French public discourses on difference and integration. While nationalist tendencies in supposedly republican discourse are both real and a politically urgent target of analysis, there is an unfortunate tendency to homogenize republicanism, and only the exclusionary aspects of it become the target of analysis. This is ironic, because doing so can marginalize other types of republican political belonging that only become visible when one focuses on practice, as opposed to the media depictions, policy documents, and speeches of politicians. Republicanism is, after all, a theory of "natural law" based on a priori assumptions about the innate qualities of humans, in which rights and political privileges are afforded to all on the basis of shared equality and unity. This fundamental aspect of the philosophy becomes visible when I examine varying republicanisms in place and as practices that are at once spatial, urban, and linked by most people to the "nature" of human and nonhuman forms of life alike.

Spaces of Anxiety

Anthropologists and other cultural critics mostly discuss republicanism in the context of high-profile debates over the status of Islam and Muslims in French society. The specific issues have evolved since the debates first generated public interest in the 1980s, moving from the wearing of head scarves in schools, to the veiling of women's faces in public, to a 2012 moral panic centered on the ubiquity of halal meat in French supermarkets and restaurants. Indeed, the January 2015 attacks on the newspaper *Charlie Hebdo* were widely cast by media and politicians alike as proof that the republican values of freedom of expression and *laïcité* were under a violent threat in France. In each of these controversies, a great deal of anxiety has been aired by media outlets and politicians (from the Right and the Left) about the encroaching threat that religious values (almost exclusively Islam) hold for France's nominally secular public institutions, civic values, and public culture more broadly. The political intensity of France's moral panic over Islam is best exemplified by the 2010 burka ban. One need only reflect on the differences between France's total national population (65 million) and the total number of women estimated to wear the full burka (estimated at two thousand) to be impressed by the political drive to preserve a secular, undifferentiated public space.[8] The 2010 ban passed by a margin of 335 to 1 in the French Senate. While patent Islamophobia is not hard to uncover when searching for justifications for the ban, the most common reasons cited by mainstream policy makers and the media are the need to preserve and the *laïque* nature of public space itself.

However, republican anxieties are not *only* expressed over the presence of Islam and Muslims in French society; a large part of France's regime of urban planning and design—that is, the way cities are conceived, envisioned, and built—has been greatly shaped by concerns over the preservation of a citizenry that is secular and undifferentiated by ethnicity, religion, or race. As some excellent historical and ethnographic scholarship has shown, French urban policy since World War II has long been oriented toward creating the nation by way of the modernist city.[9]

Most of this scholarship has focused on the importance of housing, and for good reason. Housing policy in postwar France began as a triage process aimed at hurriedly sheltering the victims of an acute housing shortage, resulting in, among other problems, criticisms of the public-housing bureaucracy as autocratic and the low quality of the buildings themselves.[10] By the mid-1960s, however, social housing became a home-front intervention in the process of decolonization. For French citizens, guest workers, refugees, and other migrants from the colonies during the Algerian war, social housing offered a modern alternative to both *bidonvilles* and deteriorating apartments in towns and cities themselves (40 percent of all of France's residences lacked running water as late as 1954).[11] Social housing was employed as an architectural strategy of containment and assimilation to prevent the emergence of immigrant enclaves within the city.[12]

After the cracks in the facade of this modernist dream appeared in the 1970s and 1980s, French urban policy began to chart a different course, emphasizing special policy zones over the creation of new towns. Zone-based policy had long been an important feature of the development of modernist housing, but by the 1980s the policy began to use this spatial logic as a method of social intervention, and not only of urban development. The specific nomenclature for policy zones, and the initiatives themselves, vary widely depending on the program, from ZACs (Zones d'Aménagement Concerté—zones of intensive development), to ZRUs (Zones de Redynamisation Urbaine—zones of urban redynamization), to ZUSs (Zones Urbaines Sensibles—sensitive urban zones), and, most recently, under the Hollande administration, ZSPs (Zones de Sécurité Prioritaire—priority security zones). In each case, a social issue (ranging from poverty, to underdevelopment, to delinquency) is identified by policy makers, and the problem is spatialized as an urban issue. For this reason, Dikeç has argued that France's urban-policy approach has provided a legitimate republican way of constructing and reproducing difference within society by way of space, as opposed to ethnicity or cultural difference.[13] While such "zones" are popularly imagined as *banlieue* areas, most large French cities—especially Paris, Lyon, and Marseille—have been the targets of zone-based urban policy since its inception.

Indeed, when one takes a historical view, northeast Paris appears to be an unceasingly problematic space for planners and policy makers. The area has long been targeted with continual (and often heavy-handed) doses of urban policy that appear to come and go every few years. These include the

ZACs, ZUSs, and ZSPs, as well as CUCS (Contrat Urbain de Cohésion Sociale—a zone-based strategy emphasizing social cohesion in neighborhoods); OPAH (Opération Programmée d'Amélioration de l'Habitat—urban-rehabilitation program that focus on the built environment); a POS (Plan d'Occupation des Sols—targeted land-use plan); a GPRU (Grand Projet de Renouvellement Urbain—large urban-renewal plan); and, at the city level, three "quartiers de la politique de la ville" (municipal urban-policy neighborhoods). From the base of Montmartre to the Canal de l'Ourcq, it is hard to find any stretch of land north of the pre-Haussmann city limit (now metro line 2) that is not encompassed by one or more of these special policy zones.

On the ground, however, such policies often unfold in ways that are quite different from the assimilationist spatial strategies they are frequently intended to be. Policy makers in northeast Paris have often employed "fine-tuned" forms of urban policy that are less assimilationist and even gesture toward a preservation of difference and distinctiveness in the neighborhoods. In contrast to the assimilationist urban policy of the postwar era, which sought to fracture ethnic enclaves, one eighteenth arrondissement official stated that one of the goals of local urban policy was to "keep the people in their place" and acknowledged that "there have always been opulent neighborhoods and working-class neighborhoods [quartiers populaires]; the objective of mixité sociale is not to erase that reality, but to mitigate it."[14] In this case, a housing policy that invoked mixité sociale as the deliberate "social mixing" of classes and populations would be the goal, but because the eighteenth arrondissement had long been understood as a working-class, immigrant enclave, as opposed to a new town, this implies—as another official put it—the "need to conserve the neighborhoods' proletarian character [aspect populaire]." Mixité sociale represents a highly republican way to speak about difference by valorizing a controlled version of diversity without actually giving lip service to any specific group. This shift from a strategy of conquest to one of "conservation" represents an inversion of the integrationist approach of intentional social mixing that characterizes the suburban new towns. In some cases, policy in neighborhoods such as La Chapelle and the Goutte d'Or would be aimed at preserving distinctiveness rather than dissolving it.

Even with the ambiguities around the spatial language of neighborhoods, some considered this discourse emphasizing the conservation of difference as very threatening. Romain, a longtime left-leaning activist and participant in a *conseil de quartier* (neighborhood council) in the eighteenth arrondissement, surprised me with his views on this matter when I first met him. His anxieties about the neighborhood revealed several assumptions about the nature of difference that commonly undergird arguments in favor of active assimilationist policy. When I asked him about the dominant political ideology of leaders in the neighborhood, his face showed a bitter expression, and he quipped:

> It's an opportunistic Left that has a ghetto ideology in its head, one of letting go *[laisser-aller]*, and one of self-management *[autogestion]*. It's above all the postcolonized, the Maghrebis, the Africans, some Asians, but mainly the Maghrebis and Africans. Here, it's the Algerians essentially, at least over at Barbès it's the Algerians, and now more Africans.

Romain was particularly bothered by public spaces such as Barbès, a congested stretch of sidewalk in the Goutte d'Or where street vendors selling everything from African crafts to cigarettes intermingle with the often multiethnic crowd leaving the Gare du Nord. Such places were, in his words, "manifested, created, and mis-en-scène" by this "ghetto ideology" associated with policies of "letting go" and "self-management." Despite the tremendous amount of statism present in the neighborhood (renewal is based largely on state funds and national-level urban policy), Romain viewed *mixité sociale* as a sign of state withdrawal from its duty to curb expressions of cultural difference in public space. By the mid-2000s, the mere presence of "ethnic" vendors and grocers and halal butchers had provoked public discussion of the threat of so-called ghettoization, and in 2011, when overflow crowds from a Goutte d'Or mosque began praying in the streets, a public controversy erupted.[15] Such public displays of difference capture what Romain was expressing in his discussion of the "ghetto": difference as a kind of uncontrolled growth resulting from a lack of policy intervention at the level of assimilation. In this regard, northeast Paris represents a spectacle of unchecked cultural heterogeneity that is a public affront to assimilationist republicanism; it is a

Storefronts in northeast Paris. Many media depictions of Paris's northeastern neighborhoods conflate images of graffiti-covered walls and crumbling buildings with a visible immigrant presence as part of the call for urban renewal as a spatial form of cultural assimilation.

space where "differences" have been "allowed" to develop in a wild and un-controlled fashion.

Public Gardens and the Nature(s) of Republicanism

> Public gardens. The expression pleases as much as other similar-sounding terms: public school, public monument, public transport, public place. It signifies a principle in which no one is excluded, and we have the right to hope that it embodies the popular will.
>
> —Pierre Sansot, *Jardins publics*

Romain's conception of northeast Paris's public spaces as "ghettos" that threatened the republican social fabric was anything but unique to him. In the wake of the *Charlie Hebdo* attack, media outlets were abuzz about the "Buttes-Chaumont cell." This name, which refers to the northeast Paris park where the perpetrators of the attack jogged and played soccer, directly con-nects anxieties over public spaces in multiethnic neighborhoods (and urban parks in particular) with fears of terrorism. Parks, public spaces, and green spaces of all kinds (especially those that emphasize "urban nature") have not been the focus of national-level policies such as the *cité*.[16] However, these spaces play an important but less appreciated role in France's politics of belonging. In contrast to housing, which can be understood in a very direct way as a locus of power where urban planners attempt to sculpt the social world of inhabitants at a domestic level, parks and public spaces are open, ostensibly free (but no less mediated) sites of encounters between strangers, self, and other. By definition, these areas constitute publics and other forms of solidarity, whether those who use them are ostensibly there as atomized individuals or "occupying" space in a conscious effort to claim territory or make demands as a self-defined collective. For this fundamental reason, parks can function as an unpredictable commons of a city and as such are a threat to any political order that invokes an idealized vision of the "public" as a claim to legitimacy. As a result, parks, public squares, and open spaces in general are a source of continual anxiety for those seeking to safeguard normative definitions of the public. Therefore, parks and public spaces are often subject to continual efforts to "fix" what can prove to be unruly if vibrant urban commons.

In addition, parks and public gardens have the added complexity of being sites where the social is inevitably drawn into dialogue with nature. As I have argued elsewhere, a "successful" Parisian public garden is frequently understood by the Paris Parks and Environment Department (DEVE—Direction des Espaces Verts et de l'Environnement) as a zone that spatializes and naturalizes republican values. And while having never received the same level of attention from historians of assimilation and cultural politics as social housing, Paris's park system has a far longer history in civilizing, cultivating, and reproducing an ideal (re)public, one that stretches back to the birth of the secular public itself in the wake of the French Revolution. Indeed, from the time of the Revolution, when the royal Tuileries Garden (which is sited at the base of Paris's traditional westward facing axis of power) was temporarily renamed the Jardin National, public gardens have played a central role in spatializing—and naturalizing—republican forms of citizenship and the nation itself.[17]

This point is best illustrated by briefly examining the defining features of a "classic" public garden—for example, the Parc Monceau—situated in the affluent eighth arrondissement. The first thing one notices when visiting it are its monumental gates, which are more than eight meters in height, painted black with gold embellishments, created by Gabriel Davioud for a renovation planned by Haussmann. This emphasis on boundary making is no accident: the park is designed to reinforce a series of dichotomies, chiefly that between garden/city and nature/civilization. Moreover, gating serves an important disciplinary function linked to these distinctions: parks are not public spaces like the surrounding streets. Conduct, behavior, and even movement are subject to regulations that sharply distinguish the public garden from other public spaces. This feature brands parks as public socializing agents much like schools.[18] In the Parc Monceau, like most Parisian public gardens, an extensive list of rules and behavioral standards meant to be uniformly enforced in all public gardens in the capital are clearly posted by the main entrance for all to see (the *réglementation générale*).[19] The document, divided into five chapters with eleven articles, reads like a "constitution" of sorts, in which a person, upon passing the gates, enters into a citizenship-like contract with the DEVE by becoming a park "user." As secular, anonymous, and undifferentiated subjects, "users" are guaranteed access to the territory on equal terms as long as they accept the rules of the parks as formally defined by the DEVE.[20] Examples of these regulations include the careful delineation of opening hours (marked by a ritualistic practice whereby uniformed DEVE staff open gates each morning and often close them with a blowing of the whistle—see chapter 6), observing "standards and dress and behavior in keeping with public decency," and limiting sports and ball games to carefully proscribed areas.[21] In general, this careful enforcement of social and architectural boundaries emphasizes the importance of civility, mutual respect, and peaceful cohabitation by a state agency blind to all social distinction. These practices also reinforce the mission of public gardens as being simultaneously pedagogical, political, cultural, and social.

The Parc Monceau is celebrated by the DEVE as one of the most beautiful gardens in the capital.[22] On weekends and warm summer days, it boasts the crowds to prove it, though at eight hectares in total area, it is designed with an adequate number of large open spaces and wide paths to rarely give one a sense of feeling claustrophobic. The park attracts both international tourists and "locals," and one can often find groups of friends having picnics,

A *réglementation générale* (here termed *règlement*) posted at the entrance of a public garden (in this case the Jardins d'Éole). Here, evidence of the public's contested nature is literally inscribed on the document itself.

individuals reading or dozing on the lawn, and families with small children. Parents with strollers are especially common. Other than the paths, which are used by joggers, however, it is a remarkably conservative design thanks to its lack of facilities for sports or other rigorous activities. Despite the park's great size and large crowds, it has just two playgrounds for children and one small area for roller-skating. Therefore, it retains a traditional notion of usage designed into many classic landscape gardens: it is intended as a museum-like space for a public that behaves in a docile manner, is given to reserved and private forms of sociality, and that valorizes solitary strolling, contemplation, and seeing over more physical forms of activity.

The Parc Monceau demonstrates the power of landscape architecture to naturalize *patrimoine* or heritage and nation. *Flânerie* is elevated to a form of

Enjoying culture as nature at the Parc Monceau.

Encountering the other at the Parc Monceau. This 2012 "Jardins du Monde" (Gardens of the World) display depicts an "African garden," among several other examples, including Japan and France.

communion with heritage, as one takes in views of the Arc de Triomphe framed by tree-lined alleys, statues of cultural figures such as Maupassant, and paths that have barely changed since the time when Proust, Monet, and Bizet favored them. At the same time, the park reaffirms nation and civilization by prominently deploying the mirror image of the other for the viewer. The landscape architect Louis Carrogis Carmontelle—who was also a painter, dramatist, and set designer—placed a series of follies evoking exoticism and foreignness throughout the park, some of which, such as an Egyptian pyramid, are still present. The DEVE has maintained this tradition. A "Jardin du monde" (global garden) on display in 2012 featured a set of culturally themed gardens in the Parc Monceau, including a Zen garden (Japanese), a tropical garden (Aztec), an arid climate garden (African), and one that was described as "classic and sustainable" (French). To visit the Parc Monceau, walk its paths, and indulge in its intricacies is to experience the nature of republican political belonging and know the self by encountering the other in a carefully cultivated and controlled environment at the level of aesthetics, social life, and nature.

The antithesis of the Parc Monceau might be the Square Léon, which is a very different type of green space and is exactly the sort of place Romain would have described as a "ghetto." Located in the largely West African and Maghrebi Goutte d'Or neighborhood, the Square Léon sits on the most elevated point in the area, at a site once used for gypsum processing from the nearby quarries. It is just a fraction of the size of the Parc Monceau but serves a district that is, in some places, four times as densely populated.[23] Because the Square Léon is a public garden like the Parc Monceau, one also finds an identical set of rules there. However, the first thing one notices when crossing through its decidedly less magnificent threshold is the crowded sensation of being within, as opposed to being outside. It is not a space of expansive views and wide-open lawns (there is only one), but rather one in which movement feels carefully managed and channeled. Rather than a meandering path with views into open space, one follows mostly straight paths into small gravel plazas carefully bordered by shrubs, plantings, and fences. In contrast to the Parc Monceau, it is a place designed *against* the idea of surprise; here spontaneity is a threat, not a source of wonderment or playful discovery. Those who visit the park are almost exclusively residents of the surrounding neighborhood, and the uses of the space itself seem clearly delineated, if not segregated. To the park's south end, the path is widened to accommodate several chess tables, which are the near-exclusive domain of West African and Maghrebi men, particularly elderly men. The park's northern end features its sole lawn. Here one often finds families—mothers, fathers, and children of Maghrebi and West African origin. A favorite place for adults to linger and greet neighbors passing through the park is the edges of the central path, which is essentially an extension of a north–south axis street that transects the Goutte d'Or. Nearby, there are athletic areas where large crowds of teenagers meet; groups of friends gather on the surrounding paths and break the monotony of summer days with loud outbursts of jokes and teasing that seem meant to capture the attention of bystanders. This is not a space of social restraint. The Square Léon has the same number of playgrounds as the Parc Monceau (despite being a fraction of its size) and a far greater proportion of its users are children and youths. It also boasts a basketball court and an artificial-turf soccer field; these athletic facilities are nearly always crowded and very popular with neighborhood

The main lawn of the Square Léon. This is the primary open space in the park (and in the Goutte d'Or neighborhood as a whole).

The design of the Square Léon often gives one the sensation of being "within"; movements often feel channeled and controlled.

youths. The Square Léon is a place of circulation, movement, and exercise. It gives the impression of being designed less for contemplation than for the controlled release of pressure.

The DEVE has long considered the Square Léon a public garden marked by social dysfunction. It is the focus of continued anxiety, and scrutiny by the agency has been the subject of a great deal of research. The principal sources of concern are "conflicts of usage," or tensions that arise because a single group of users manages or redefines the space in a way that interferes with the rights of others to use it. In a logic that parallels arguments in favor of the burka ban and *laïcité,* these acts of appropriation by one group threaten to usurp the state's monopoly over the power to define the purpose and the meaning of the space. In the case of the Square Léon, the conflict stemmed from illegal drug activity (primarily dealing) in the park. But rather than isolate the source of the problem to a specific group of actors, the conflict of usage was increasingly associated with all youths of Maghrebi and West African descent (who are among the most prolific users of the park). As a result, the entirety of the park itself was frequently viewed as the problem.

The DEVE's concerns with the space have been so great that officials simply felt they had to start over from scratch—not once, but twice. The Square Léon was closed and underwent two major redesigns whose logic appeared to be that by demolition and reconstruction the public garden could be "reset" as a social project.

However, many residents have somewhat different readings of the Square Léon than the DEVE. Prior to my joining the research team, the Laboratoire Vie Urbaine conducted a study of the space that demonstrated that the park was routinely filled with a great diversity of users in terms of age and gender that reflected the social composition of the surrounding neighborhood.[24] It suggested, based on interviews with residents, that those who frequented the park often had a fairly positive and strong sentimental attachment to the space, despite the DEVE's bleak assessment. In contrast to the DEVE, many residents tended to see problems as limited to specific individuals in the public garden, not the space itself. DEVE staff and administrators however, often saw a broader social breakdown at work because they could not guarantee total control of the space. Because of conflicts with drug dealers, the DEVE staff who are charged with enforcing park rules, the paradoxically named Agents d'Accueil et de Surveillance (AAS— welcoming and surveillance agents) were so terrified of the space that they sometimes abandoned their posts.[25] Gardeners, who typically do not interact with the public, were quick to retreat from the garden: according to one horticulturalist, because drug dealers preferred to hide their products among the plants, they were unable to maintain the flower beds and shrubs and so left the garden to grow wild.[26] Faced with a public (and a garden) beyond their control on both a symbolic and an operational level, the public agency's response has simply been to echo the logic of urban renewal: demolish and rebuild (a policy that deprives residents of a much-needed green space for long periods on end). While the most recent (2006) renovation has been considered far more successful, the Square Léon remains a stigmatized space. It naturalizes and seems to materialize the dystopian fantasy of a failed republican society that is warned about those who see a *laïque* nation being imperiled by immigrants.

If the Parc Monceau represents an ideal, and the Square Léon its commonly invoked antithesis, the Jardins d'Éole is yet a different project: it appears to spatialize a fundamentally divergent type of belonging that is at once highly republican and not particularly conforming to assimilationist expectations. At 4.5 hectares in area, the Jardins d'Éole is larger than the Square Léon, but half the size of the Parc Monceau, though, like the Square Léon, it serves a far more densely populated neighborhood than the eighth arrondissement.[27] The park's design places great emphasis on visibility and surveillance but it does not appear to force a particular conception of what a public garden ought to be. Like the Parc Monceau, the Jardins d'Éole is the public garden as a spectacle; but this time it is the city itself that is the center of attention. If one enters from the Rue du Département on the park's south end, one is first confronted with an expansive view of railroad tracks from the Gare de l'Est to the west, and HLM developments built at the apex of social housing's monumental period—the Cité Michelet and Orgues du Flandre—to the northeast. As with the Square Léon, there are no immediately identifiable symbols or large monuments evoking heritage or patrimony to be found. It is as if the primary element being cultivated in the garden is neither flora nor national culture but a kind of substance of the surrounding neighborhood itself.

In general, those who visit the park represent the the demographic of the surrounding neighborhood: many of its visitors are immigrants of West African and Maghrebi origin, along with a growing number of middle-class (but often relatively cash poor) students and families with small children. As with the Square Léon, the park attracts a range of ages from elderly people to small children. As a testament to its perceived safety, many residents and DEVE personnel comment on the large numbers of children whose parents let them play in the park unattended, when in fact many children are watched by parents and friends from nearby windows. On the weekends and evenings, the three playgrounds and athletic areas are nearly always full. In contrast to classic French landscape gardens such as the Parc Monceau, the Jardins d'Éole encourages people to actively create and imagine new uses: given its minimalist design and the area's history as a zone of liminality, transition, and becoming, one could say the park has been left for the residents themselves to complete.

In keeping with this spirit, the Jardin d'Éole itself "breaks" DEVE rules in some respects. One portion of park, known as the esplanade, flouts DEVE's long-established tradition of boundary making because it was designed to

The Jardins d'Éole. Note the expansive, open feel of the space and the extent to which the park's sight lines afford the visual embrace of northeast Paris's distinct built environment—while facilitating surveillance.

The Jardins d'Éole's design valorizes the site's history as a *terrain vague* or "wasteland" where nature (and the public itself) is free and unbounded by the standards of the traditional public garden, and the "users" are allowed some measure of influence in reappropriating (and hence coproducing) the space. Here, children playfully interact with the performance artist Jean-Christophe Petit during a public exhibition.

Children from the surrounding neighborhood are the most prolific visitors to the park.

be left ungated, and therefore open all night; an intricate display of multicolored lights even beckons residents to enter the area after dark. This design feature was very controversial for the DEVE and elected officials, who feared the garden would become monopolized by drug dealers in the same manner as the Square Léon; in fact, an adjacent street is a significant node in the illegal drug economy for the city as whole. Neighborhood associations responded by playing a central role in developing regular activities and even managing this section of the park. In general, the park's design and managerial logic appear to be more oriented toward playing with limits and boundaries than reinforcing them.

Ironically, however, as chapter 6 describes in more detail, a pattern of drug trafficking and usage did eventually take hold in the Jardins d'Éole. This occurred in one of the more "traditional" parts of the garden, an interior set of alleys surrounded by hedges and bamboo plants. As had been the case in the Square Léon, DEVE gardeners told me they could no longer trim back the hedges, but in this case the AAS personnel felt they could "share" the space with the drug dealers and still do their jobs. Residents, for their part, simply avoided lingering in that particular area, and many—perhaps most—people were unaware of the drug activity altogether.

Moreover, in the case of the Jardins d'Éole, the DEVE's reaction was quite different from the Square Léon: the park was closed for a period of two weeks and the hedges, bamboo plants, and some taller grasses that had been intentionally planned by the architects to grow in "natural" fashion were mowed (as was the case at the Square Léon, social problems in the park prompted careful attention to the grooming of the flora in the space). After these changes, the park was reopened and continued functioning as before with little fanfare. In this regard, the design embraces the ideals of *autogérer* so disliked by Romain: rather than entrusting the governance of the space to the state, citizens' associations play a leading role in defining how the space should be used, and by which public.

In some cases, these alternative visions of republicanism, in which the creative reappropriation of space is tied to new forms of belonging, were displayed by some of the park's most devoted "users," making them, in essence, coproducers of the space.[28] My friend Meryem provides one such example. I met Meryem because she was an acquaintance of several activists involved in the campaign to build the Jardins d'Éole. A native of Turkey who had lived in France for two decades, Meryem lived by herself in one of the large HLM buildings on the Rue d'Aubervilliers. For several months each year, she worked as a housekeeper and cook near the wealthy resort town of Deauville; otherwise, she survives from public assistance and some occasional help from her adult children, who live elsewhere in France.

Meryem was a participant in Paris's Main Verte (Green Thumb) program, which, for an annual fee of ten euros, entitled her to a two-square-meter community garden plot at the Jardins d'Éole. One day, as she and Nadia, a fellow gardener of Tunisian origin and roughly the same age, were describing the importance of the garden, I found that their remarks blurred the boundaries between the cultivation of herbs and vegetables and more political forms of belonging.

"Every evening" she said, "I meet my Maghrebi friend [Meryem smiles to Nadia], and I learn her culture, and she learns Turkish things from me. You learn the *savoir-vivre* and all that, so we learn together. I think life is better that way."

When I added that the garden must be a nice place to meet people, she said, yes, "And you might have mint, rosemary, and other herbs, so we exchange plants. And we exchange seeds."

However, for Meryem, the community garden has a more profound and expansive function. I found it noteworthy that she equated her enjoyment of encounters with others and making new friends with something more than mere sociality—exchange, dialogue, and creation. Moreover, *savoir-vivre* (often translated as etiquette or manners) implies learning to "abide" cross-culturally. Thus, the garden is not only a space of exchange for mint, rosemary, and cultural know-how, but a place for the development of sociality predicated on the encounter with difference. Indeed, as an "exchange of seeds" implies, the garden is a site for the creation of new forms, social and organic.

When I asked Meryem if there was anyone from the Main Verte program (i.e., the city) who provided counsel with the practical matters of what to do or how to cultivate different plants, she said: "Well, yes, but me, I know too, since, in Turkey, where I grew up, my parents were farmers. *It's me* who helps everyone [she laughs]."

Meryem marks the garden as her territory, where her experience from her homeland serves to define her creativity and her influence on the space. Thus, in the urban garden, agriculture becomes a space where one's self-defined distinctiveness is intimately tied to one's capability to transform the environment and make it one's own.

In fact, according to Meryem, the presence of "foreigners" is especially important in the social life of community gardens. She referred to some of the other urban gardens in the neighborhood, as many of the other sites such as Écobox (discussed in chapter 1) are scattered throughout vacant lots and the courtyards of HLM buildings. Oddly, she noted that she preferred many of those other gardens to those at the Jardins d'Éole:

"It's the same [in the other community gardens], but different. Before, I was over there [she points at a large HLM building down the street], on the other side. I actually found it better, more agreeable."

"Oh, yeah?"

"Those people there are nicer."

"Oh, really. Why?"

The community garden at the Jardins d'Éole is part of the Paris's Main Verte (Green Thumb) program.

"Here [at the Jardins d'Éole] there are lots of French people. I don't get along with them." [Nadia and I laugh somewhat uncomfortably.]

She continued, with a slightly defensive tone: "Those people [she points toward the HLM building to refer to immigrant-origin residents in the other garden] are more gentle [plus doux] and more understanding [compréhensifs]." Everyone was silent for a moment.

Meryem then clarified her position: "There are lots of foreigners here, and we have to learn to live together, and the garden is a place where you meet someone for the first time [faire la connaissance], and you help others, you learn the culture of others—the richness of other people's cultures."

Meryem's comments offer a window onto the everyday experience of diversity in northeast Paris as mediated through urban gardening. Her words convey the routine importance of community gardens for a diverse group of immigrant-origin residents in northeast Paris to meet, become acquainted, and provide support for one another in recognition of their often tenuous social and economic positions—it is a place of understanding at the level of both comprehension and compassion. Although her emphasis on "learning," "cultures," and "encounter" shows the impact of the popular discourse of *mixité sociale* on her own thinking, Meryem's articulation of gardens and difference has a slight but important twist. Most interestingly, the diverse group of gardeners' *self-identification as foreigners* becomes the common basis for a form of solidarity. Although this sounds close to the assimilationist message of the Vivre Ensemble association discussed at the start of this chapter, there is an important difference: Meryem associated French residents with a more reserved form of sociality, and therefore they do not participate in the exchange and "cross-fertilization" the way the other immigrant-origin residents do. The new city-run community garden at the Jardins d'Éole, interestingly enough, is associated with French residents, whereas the older community gardens used primarily by HLM residents are not—which would suggest that the new Jardins d'Éole is at times viewed as a space associated with "France" when compared to the HLM buildings nearby.

If Meryem's views may be rooted in a stereotype of French residents, she nonetheless highlighted an important relationship between urban gardening and the cultivation of forms of belonging that are distinct to immigrant-origin residents. In this regard, her use of the concept *savoir-vivre* (manners) is significant. It implies the adoption of a sociality that is different from the French *savoir-vivre* and yet belongs to no one particular group. In this regard, the garden (like the neighborhood itself) becomes a crucible of sorts for a hybridization that resonates with basic republican tenets such as "civility" and equal participation, embodied by balanced reciprocity in exchanging seeds and gardening know-how. At the same time, however, it is a sociability that is transformative in its rejection of static, monocultural notions of Frenchness that underlie both assimilationist and even some integrationist articulations of republicanism. Ultimately, the garden gives rise to ways of abiding, exchange, and creativity that transcend multiple cultures, and yet it belongs to no particular one, including the dominant French culture, however it may be imagined. Could such ideas contain within them the seeds of a radical republicanism?

This notion of the Jardins d'Éole as a space for alternative forms of belonging is reinforced when one juxtaposes Meryem's understanding of the space with the vision of one of the senior architects on the park's design team.

When I asked Guy, a landscape architect who has worked on urban parks throughout France for several decades, what the meaning of a "public garden" was, he said: "A garden is a space of pleasure, civility, rapport between communities, and a place of integration." In this understanding, the garden blurs the boundaries between nature and culture because its a priori function is social and interpersonal, despite its status as a cultivated "natural" landscape in the city. The architect, like Meryem, favored the language of "rapport" and multiple "communities"—the language of pluralism—over the language of assimilation.

This emphasis on generating rapport and connections across boundaries transcended a concern with culture, extending even into the realm of non-human species. This approach was based on a choice of plant species that had, according to him, the "function of nourishing birds." Birds were valued through an "ecological approach" that emphasized the "rapport between people and the birds" and the need to have a "diversity of birds" in the park. While this approach undoubtedly built on the Éole mobilization's emphasis on the park as a "space of life," the focus on what the architect called the "animal presence" helped to create an atmosphere of liveliness and vitality in what had long been considered a moribund postindustrial brownfield.

The cultivation of "rapport between people and birds" was built into the park through the design of the park's western wall. Designed by the artist Carmen Perrin, it has the appearance of a porous screen and is made up of numerous miniature cells that were envisioned as potential nesting sites for birds. This combination of an avian-focused built environment and a floral setting has both ecological and social importance (and in fact blurs the two). Birds aid seed dispersal, and their presence also evokes an ideal of a garden as a place of harmony where humans live in peace with animals. Even more important, the integration of birds with human uses helps to naturalize the idea of the garden as a space where connections are made in spite of differences, be they cultural, social, geographic, or species-based.

A strong valuation of biodiversity associated with this image of avian–human ecology is central to understanding the Jardins d'Éole as a site for the creation of new forms of social belonging. Urban biodiversity (see chapter 4) is a discourse of power, embraced the world over by sustainability-minded policy makers, urban planners, and architects. It is also a significant step in the direction of ecological urbanism, which places special emphasis on the role played by landscape architects in blurring the nature/city dichotomy, and their role in orchestrating the flows and circulation of both human and nonhuman life-forms in the city.[29] Urban planning therefore becomes synonymous with the production of nature, and hence the naturalization of social and political relationships in an urban context. Paris's official Biodiversity Plan, first released in 2011, provides an excellent glimpse of how this approach is put into action. The plan focuses on the importance of railroad infrastructure (active and disused) as an important pathway for circulation of wildlife (and hence the production of biodiversity) throughout the urban region. The Jardins d'Éole is specifically mentioned—given its proximity to railroad infrastructure—as an important node in this living, but nonhuman, part of the city's metabolic system.[30] The site's previous function as a way station is therefore revived, but this time with a focus on migrant bird species. This image's suitability as a metaphor for the immigrant-origin population of the neighborhood should not be ignored, and neither should the discursive power of biodiversity for "naturalizing" that idea of Jardins d'Éole and the ideals of cultural diversity associated with it.

Meryem and Guy, whose firm has close connections with elected city officials, occupy vastly different social positions. There are important differences in their perspectives, especially Meryem's notion that the Jardins d'Éole is relatively less friendly for cross-cultural exchange. However, the visions of both reinforce the idea that as a *social space,* the Jardins d'Éole is an important departure from a tradition of French public gardens. It is not that the Jardins d'Éole fails to spatialize republicanism. Indeed, many of the expressions and terms used by Meryem and Guy (such as *vivre ensemble* and *rapport*) could well have come from the dominant republican discourse of belonging that can be found in media outlets and government initiatives. Rather, the Jardins d'Éole is a site where alternative notions of republicanism are both spatialized and naturalized in ways that differ from the classic assimilationist vision of the public garden.

The emergence of these forms of belonging, or, more precisely, the intensification of existing tendencies (to draw from the architect's quote at the beginning of this chapter), did not go unnoticed by those who view themselves as the guardians of assimilationist republicanism. In 2010, the Paris city council performed a symbolic gesture: it placed (but did not plant) a "tree of *laïcité*" in the Jardins d'Éole. The tree of *laïcité* was championed by a subgroup of the Socialist Party called the Republican Socialists, and it had two stated goals: to aid in the education of neighborhood schoolchildren and to "demonstrate the commitment of the capital to the principle of *laïcité* at a moment when it was being questioned, especially by the head of state."[31] It seemed placed as a reminder that even here, in one of the most multi-ethnic parts of Paris, a *laïque* vision of France is alive and well. When I saw the tree in the summer of 2012, however, I was left with precisely the opposite impression about such attempts to use the Jardins d'Éole as a place to re-inforce the commitment to state-enforced secularism. The tree of *laïcité*, in reality not much more than a sapling, remained in a wooden box tucked away in one of the park's less trafficked corners, surrounded by a grove of bamboo plants. A resounding symbolic statement commissioned by power-ful elected officials, it nonetheless seemed marginal to the everyday life of the park, including the lived reality of republicanism that one finds articu-lated and reproduced there.

An Alternative Republicanism Comes of Age in Northeast Paris

These alternative visions of republicanism are not limited to the often sym-bolic realm of public gardens. The more traditional public sphere of grass-roots politics—that of associations and local electoral races—is an even more important site where "insurgent" forms of republican citizenship simi-lar to the ideas expressed by Meryem and Nadia percolate up to the realm of governance.[32]

The unfolding political career of Mamadou provides a case in point. Nearly two years after our first meeting, I met him in his professional setting of the nineteenth arrondissement's ornate *mairie* (town hall), adorned with the iconography of the Republic and more lavishly decorated than most American city halls. Here, in his official capacity as an aide for youth affairs to Roger Madec, then the Socialist Party mayor of the arrondissement, he carried himself very differently than in our first meeting on the streets near the Jardins d'Éole. From behind his desk, he dwelled not on music but on his other passion, which could be described as the political cultivation of youth from the nearby neighborhoods where he grew up. As he often did, he turned to his own adolescent memories of him and his friends when describing his own turn toward civic participation and public life, saying:

> We decided to create an association, primarily to give a new image to youth, not the image of delinquent youth, not the image of youths as violent, not the image of youths as drug dealers. It was an image of youth who would reappropriate the neighborhood and add dynamism to it. That's why we did it—to get away from the violence at the time, which was physical as well as moral. It was a troubled time and we had a choice. Either you would be a delinquent or an artist, except we wanted a different choice, not just creating a movement of youths in a *bande* [gang], we wanted to create a movement of youths, like a *bande* but that emerges like an association.[33]

Mamadou's adolescent transformation, which occurred against a background of youth subculture related to hip-hop and *bandes,* led to his political awakening. The vocabulary of place making and territoriality inherited from hip-hop and working-class youth subculture merged with the framework of republican citizenship engendered by the tradition of associations. The term "association" is frequently used to refer to "grassroots" organizations or "neighborhood"-based associations. The term itself serves as an invocation of the "right to associate," which was established in the French civil code in 1848, repealed, and then reformalized in 1901 (thus many associations describe themselves as "associations according to the law of 1901"). Associations represent an alternative form of political activity to the violent confrontation that pitted him and his peers against skinheads who arrived in the arrondissement to protest the Adda'wa mosque (discussed in chapter 1).

Other than voting, associations become a key method by which political participation and the full rights of citizenship are performed under the auspices of republican civic traditions. Indeed, by the 1990s, many analysts argued that associations had supplanted participation in social movements, voting, and unions, in what some observers termed a "new associativity" or a boom in "micromovements" and "localism."[34] Associations provide one facet of the evolving tradition of republicanism and provide one way in which republicanism can be viewed as a set of citizenship practices, and not merely the discourse of elites and policy makers, as it is frequently imagined.[35]

However, as Mamadou's politics in northeast Paris shows, the slippage between local and national politics was profound in these neighborhoods. This is not a case of residents retreating from the national to the local sphere of politics by way of associations, for such an analysis would reify each scale. Rather, activism such as Mamadou's is a way of remaking scale by harnessing the local to reimagine the national, and at times even the global.

The association founded by Mamadou and his friends was called Braves Garçons d'Afrique (BGA—Brave Boys of Africa) and was ideologically an outgrowth of the hip-hop influenced subculture of *bandes*. BGA meetings and activities featured lectures on a variety of historical leaders from anti-colonial figures such as Toussaint-Louverture to civil-rights icons such as Martin Luther King Jr. The association's culminating achievement was called the Festival Afro: a ten-day conference drawing more than a thousand attendees and featuring scholars and activists from around the world lecturing on a wide variety of themes, including sports, solidarity, health, citizenship, gender, and memory.[36] Above all, importance was placed on the historical significance of slavery, empire, and the broader African-Atlantic diaspora for France's *jeunes issus de l'immigration*, regardless of whether one's origins lay in West Africa, the Maghreb, or the Antilles.

The BGA's project drew the attention of the national media to the convention as well as to northeast Paris. Journalists writing for outlets such as *L'Express* described the Festival Afro by placing it in the context of an "urban no-man's-land marked by unemployment, troubled schools, delinquency, racism, and the rise of communitarianism."[37] *Le Point* drew in readers with a tagline highlighting "the rise of communitarianism on the part of Muslims and blacks," and introduced the BGA (and northeast Paris) with the following rhetorical device:

"Do you define yourself as French-Caribbean? French-Maghrebi? Full-blooded French? Circle the corresponding box." This type of administrative questionnaire, as surreal as it may seem to our republican ears, could well become normal in a few years' time.[38]

The article raised the image of a "communitarian vulgate" and stopped just short of accusing the BGA of outright racism when describing the Festival

Afro. The specific way the BGA invoked a shared consciousness linked to slavery provoked ire in a political context marked by deep hostility to "Anglo-Saxon" models of "multiculturalism" and American notions of racial "consciousness" in particular. Such reports treated the BGA as little more than misguided youths under the sway of globally hegemonic, but nationally corrosive, ideas of race and black nationalism imported from America. It is worth noting that none of these often patronizing—if not racist—reports, which followed a predictable journalistic template for the construction of sectarian minorities, even entertained the notion that Mamadou and his peers might have been in the process of actively creating ideas of their own.

It was not lost on *Le Point* that the supposedly antirepublican BGA enjoyed the full support of the Socialist Party in the nineteenth arrondissement. The arrondissement's mayor, Roger Madec, was allied with the antiracist Left, a position that is far from taken for granted for PS politicians. At a national level, the PS is frequently restrained on questions of immigrant rights, and it is arguably as forcefully opposed to ideologies that seem to embrace "multiculturalism" as the center-right party Union for a Popular Movement (UMP) of then President Nicolas Sarkozy. In northern Paris, however, the PS has proven remarkably quick to embrace movements from the anti-racist Left (chiefly SOS Racisme and the Mouvement contre le Racisme et pour l'Amitié entre les Peuples or MRAP) and even more controversial issues. For example, Madec has advocated publicly for the Adda'wa mosque and supported its rebuilding after the 1998 pipe-bomb attack, and continued his support even after captured "insurgents" from Iraq were reported to have met in the congregation.[39] Madec's embrace of Mamadou in his role as an official in charge of youth affairs is a recognition of the sensitive predicament facing young people in the area, and it conveyed legitimacy to the kind of associative politics practiced by the BGA.[40] Such gestures have provoked a great deal of ire and finger-pointing not only by the Far Right, but by assimilationist-minded republicans on the Left such as Romain, who accused the Left in northeast Paris of espousing a "ghetto ideology."

Soon after the start of his new role in the nineteenth arrondissement, Mamadou faced the first big test of the inclusive form of republicanism that was emerging there. In June 2008, a seventeen-year-old Jewish youth was severely beaten by two Muslim youths of West African and Maghrebi descent in an attack that was widely understood to be anti-Semitic. The attack occurred in the heart of the nineteenth arrondissement and received international media coverage. In an evocation of the 2005 riots that shook Paris's *banlieues,* the *New York Times* published an article along with a picture of a burned-out car (despite the strong association between car burnings and the 2005 civil unrest, finding a burned car is a rare event in this neighborhood) and described it is a place of "young Muslims and blacks in low jeans, sunglasses and hoodies, often with a kaffiyeh knotted carefully around the neck, and sometimes, now, with guns."[41] Again, the incident was incorporated into a popular geography of difference stressing northeast Paris's externality to the nation, a discursive move that is not only an act of "othering" but politically delegitimizing to the efforts of activists and officials in the area.

Under the direction of Madec and Mamadou, the nineteenth arrondissement pursued a solution that in many ways resembled the Festival Afro: a committee called Vivre Ensemble (not to be confused with the gardening association of the same name) was organized in which different cultural associations met in a regular series of forums. One of the principal goals of this publicly led Vivre Ensemble was to create a gathering space for youths. As Mamadou described its goal to me, I was struck by his use of the term "community," which could prove controversial given the emphasis in assimilationist discourse on the dangers of communitarianism:

> There are several extremely important communities in this arrondissement. There is an extremely important Jewish community, a black community that is very important, and a strong Muslim community as well. It's true that the different communities have lately had difficulties living together. But one must ask, Who are the actors in making this work? It's the associations. To answer your question about diversity, and who preserves it, it's really the associations, the neighborhood associations, the public spaces, and all the places where the residents, the inhabitants, the youths, the children meet to do activities and events.

Mamadou's descriptions of the stakes behind Vivre Ensemble are revealing for several reasons. First and foremost, despite being led by the state itself, Vivre Ensemble is easily less assimilationist than the Vivre Ensemble community garden that was described at the start of this chapter. Indeed, for Mamadou's program, "communities" are "important" for themselves, and in fact his definition of each as "black," "Jewish," or "Muslim" is a form of official reification, and therefore political legitimation. This acknowledgment—and indeed, valuation—of particular communities by a member of the government is rare in France, and the establishment of a project by local government to further this goal is also rare, and even taboo in the eyes of some. The idea seems contrary to the notion of the state's role in "dissolving" difference that permeates assimilationist republican discourse such as that of the Haut Conseil à l'Intégration.[42] And this is pursued through the highly conventional vehicle of "neighborhood" associations and public spaces. The goal of such initiatives is to preserve a diverse, even differentiated, republican citizenry. The arrondissement's role is to provide a forum for this process to take place, rather than to prevent such "difference" from being reproduced.

I asked Mamadou about this curious—and potentially controversial—approach: the production of "diversity." Was he not concerned that Vivre Ensemble was "fanning the flames" by encouraging the development of "communities" in an arrondissement? Was not this, in fact, the problem to begin with? Visibly annoyed at my asking this highly assimilationist line of questions (had I learned nothing from our previous conversations?), he responded in the somewhat distant tone of a public official:

> The French Republic recognizes the one indivisible man, with no difference with regard to religions, sex, culture, or otherwise. Of course, when one looks at it this way, it's not exactly like that. One can look, for example, at the political level: men and women are not treated in the same way. One can see that also with the question of diversity, which there is supposedly more of today. So yes, there is a certain political direction, which the nineteenth arrondissement has been concerned with for a long time; where we can't continue to live with that logic, we need to wake to the reality. Yes! There are different communities present in this neighborhood here, with their own values, their own ways of living, their own routines, and yes, indeed, it happens sometimes that these values and these ways of life are not identical between communities, that the values of one community are not the same as another. So, what do you do? You show that this is the reality here. If they [critics who see Vivre Ensemble as antirepublican] continue a perpetual crusade on that, well, that does not reflect reality at all. One could find that programs like that are more like something

in the United States than France, but the reality is, well, today, this is France. Definitely, the Republic we have constructed up until today has its limits.

Mamadou's fascinating argument is not directed against republicanism; indeed, the beginning of his lecture sounded close to a civics class recitation of the classical republican ideal on the nature of the "indivisible man." Instead, he takes issue with those who would argue for national French monoculture. The "reality" is a vision of citizenship in which cultural diversity and even incommensurability are unwelcome but perhaps inevitable facts of life. The role of the republican state, as we have seen, is to foster a public and open mixing of these communities, as opposed to facilitating their disintegration through assimilation. His last line is particularly important in this regard, as he draws attention to the "limits" of the "republic we have constructed up until today," portending, it seems, a new vision moving forward. Such a view suggests that there are multiple—yet distinctly republican—approaches to difference being lived and discussed in the arrondissement.

Political approaches such as Mamadou's demonstrate the degree to which republicanism cannot be spoken about as a static "thing." Despite the claims of his adversaries, Mamadou's political approach is not antirepublican; if anything, it is too republican because it refuses to recognize any dominant culture—including hegemonic notions of "Frenchness." In this respect, the problem that conservative adversaries have with the BGA and its supporters in the Socialist Party is, perhaps, its "overuniversalism": even notions of the French nation are not sacred. Mamadou and his allies call for a humanistic republicanism that is neither French in a traditional sense nor "Anglo-Saxon" multiculturalism. History is valued not for imbuing Frenchness in the citizenry, but as a weapon against oppression. In this regard, Mamadou's project demonstrates that it is in fact in line with a tradition of republicanism, despite his focus on youth and France's postcolonial minorities.

Conclusion

Arrondissement-level politics, gardening, and even landscape design may appear to be very different domains, but each provides a way for residents as well as officials (ranging from politicians to urban planners) to talk about, think about, and engage with difference in a context that Étienne Balibar famously described as marked by "racism without races."[43] In public gardens as well as the more intimate context of the *jardin partagé* (literally, "shared garden"; note that the English "community garden" is decidedly not apropros in the republican context of France), gardeners and formally trained landscape architects actively remake ideas of national belonging and citizenship through reworking the landscape. It would be both mistaken and ethnocentric to assume that activists, urban gardeners, and other actors are merely describing and producing what North Americans often term "race" or "ethnicity" as they work through categories of belonging in these sites. Rather, a variety of gardening practices, as well as youth activism, attest to the ways that people test the boundaries of (and reinvent) the republican tradition of political belonging at a broader level. The interlinked concepts of "nature" and the city show how republicanism has a vocabulary of difference and sameness that is all its own.

These framings of citizenship and belonging reveal the way that republicanism is reworked in the realm of everyday politics. In this regard, gardening, journalistic depictions of northeast Paris, and the park designs of a landscape architect are significant for the politics of cultural belonging in France because it provides a legitimate way of discussing difference, multiculturalism, and *mixité sociale*. For this reason, the debates I describe in this chapter are a contestation not simply over the remaking of northeast Paris's built/natural environments of parks, squares, and gardens, but over the definition of republicanism and the essence of the French nation itself.

It might be tempting to explain some of these alternative forms of republicanism as isolated aberrations that are the result of electoral opportunism on the part of northeast Paris politicians. However, northeast Paris's geographic location in the nation's capital, its long history as an election stronghold for the Left, and, most of all, its role in nurturing and producing Socialist Party leaders at the highest level of government make such claims paradoxical. The pluralism championed by a wide variety of people, from Meryem and Nadia to groups such as the BGA—and even the design of the Jardins d'Éole—is in fact, central to the maintenance of the national power structure. Moreover, all of these attitudes toward a pluralistic, inclusive republicanism are not marked by a hostility to secularism; indeed, they embrace it, and arguably to an *even greater extent* than their right-wing opponents. Such practices encourage a type of politics that, far from being an assault on republicanism, implicitly reifies its core values. Indeed, nowhere is the BGA's republican streak clearer than in its use of associative discourse and forms of politics to air social grievances. It is clear from Mamadou's political trajectory and his own words that republican notions of civic involvement such as forming an association were crucial as alternatives to "delinquency" and "violence." In many respects, such a politics demonstrates the hegemony of the fundamental values of republicanism in northeast Paris, not their rejection.

This ensemble of practices—community gardening, landscape design, coordinating youth associations—highlights the degree to which the nature of republicanism appears quite malleable in the hands of residents. Even the multiplicity of views articulated at the *first* Vivre Ensemble association (the urban gardeners' association), with its efforts to keep children from becoming "delinquent" youths, suggests that assimilationist republicanism is multifaceted. In comparing the Parc Monceau with the Square Léon and the Jardins d'Éole, I have demonstrated the ways that the DEVE, a public agency that imagines itself to be a "public socializing agent," has found itself compelled to design in diversity in order for its park system to function, despite a stated aim to naturalize a homogeneous, undifferentiated public. When one looks closer at parks and gardens, the vision of Guy, the landscape architect, and even the individual gardening practices of Meryem, reveals the subtle ways in which republicanism is transformed by insurgent pluralism. Interestingly, however, the sphere of associative politics demonstrates that such changes are not necessarily viewed as a confrontation against republican values of liberty, equality, and fraternity. In contrast, the politics of Mamadou's Vivre Ensemble are *more republican* than the ideology of many self-styled republican critics because, despite acknowledging and even reproducing cultural differences, it refuses to reify any one culture as normative— including hegemonic notions of "Frenchness." Such an invocation of republicanism as a fundamental aspect of human nature is both significant and radical because it dissolves the boundaries of France as an "imagined community" that is supposedly the guardian and keeper of the humanistic ideals themselves.[44]

4 The End(s) of Urban Ecology in the Global City

> The road to sustainability runs through the world's towns and cities.
>
> —Ban Ki-moon, Secretary-General of the United Nations, "Global Town Hall" speech at Rio+20[1]

> We are all *écolos* now.
>
> —Nassima, northeast Paris resident

Five years after the Jardins d'Éole was inaugurated, during the summer of 2012 I attended a public hearing at Paris's eighteenth arrondissement's *mairie* (town hall) over so-called *conflits d'usage*.[2] By this time, residents in northeast Paris were witnessing a set of dramatic transformations of which the Jardins d'Éole was just one example. In addition to the park, the ZAC Pajol ÉcoQuartier was in the process of being completed, and throughout Paris green "transport" infrastructure was being rapidly expanded, including the widely publicized Vélib' (Paris's municipal bike-share program) and subsequently Autolib' (an electric "car-share" modeled on Vélib'). The discussion of these conflicts was precipitated by the "greening" of the city.

Such changes—and in particular Vélib' and the Jardins d'Éole—were widely publicized by officials as heralding a new sustainable epoch in the city's history. Indeed, in northeast Paris, such projects were not only discussed as a historical milestone but actually served to produce a sense of place in an area that had been a liminal space between more strongly identified areas. Northeast Paris was now the neighborhood of the Jardins d'Éole and the ZAC Pajol. In the context of the sustainable Grand Paris plan, APUR recognized this emerging importance by describing the area's neighbor-hoods as *têtes du point:* a militaristic term of conquest that is best translated as a "bridgehead."[3]

Residents react to this redefinition of place in various ways. Some activists, like those involved in the Éole mobilization, actively participate in this reimaging and remaking of the city, though not on the same terms as urban planners and policy makers. Others, like Nassima (see chapter 2), never identified themselves with environmentalism but now find themselves compelled to "assimilate" to this green identity as the city was being rebuilt around them. Nassima had uttered the words at the beginning of this chapter while staring out her window and taking stock of the new park, Vélib', and Auto-lib' stations that all had been added to her view in recent years. In contrast, there were those such as Luc, an urban gardener from Écobox (see chapter 1) who, despite having long identified themselves as environmentalists, now felt compelled to cast the label aside. Luc had taken to rejecting the term *écolo* altogether because, for him, the new vision of urban nature in northeast Paris amounted to a rejection of the social, which was the ultimate goal of environmental practice and politics.

However, the conflicts that were the subject of the hearing at the eighteenth arrondissement *mairie* provided ample evidence that northeast Paris's green turn is very much a social project, though not in a way that Luc might have preferred. In essence, the meeting amounted to a public display of conflict over which ways of inhabiting the city were compatible with the idea of a sustainable urban future. The specific point of contention was related to transport infrastructure, and in particular long-simmering tensions between pedestrians, cyclists, automobile drivers, and motor-scooter drivers. Plans to expand Vélib'-related infrastructure and change allotted parking spaces for scooters and motorcycles throughout the neighborhood had made two-wheeled vehicles (especially bikes, scooters, and motorcycles) politically charged symbols in relation to Paris's green transformation. Thus, if discussions of scooter parking and bicycle lanes seem overly technical or quotidian to some readers, the topic cuts to the heart of the profound contradictions between two central urban struggles facing Paris (and many other cities): how do we build more ecologically sound cities, and who has the right to the new sustainable city?

In my experience of attending dozens of such meetings, the attendees that day were a fairly routine group for the relatively specialized area of urban transit infrastructure. Four arrondissement-level officials were present with interests in transit and the environment, including the arrondissement mayor for a short time. There were also two transit planners from the city of Paris, a position that marked them as outsiders relative to the residents and elected officials who identified with the arrondissement, making them the equivalent of an occupying army in the eyes of many attendees. Then, the heads of the arrondissement's Conseils de Quartier (officially designated neighborhood councils) were present, along with a few activists who worked specifically on transit and biking issues, and myself. Altogether, only about twenty people were in the room. They did not represent the multiethnic demographic of the neighborhoods; there was only one person—a Conseil de Quartier representative of West African origin—from any of the area's large immigrant-origin communities. Most people were male, and well over fifty years in age (a cycling advocate and I were the youngest people in the room, and both us were in our thirties). In my experience, this type of demographic imbalance was not uncommon at meetings held by public authorities in northeast Paris.

Most of the meeting consisted of a PowerPoint presentation by city transit planners. It was met with open exasperation by many of the "locals," largely because it used highly specific terminology and appeared to have been written primarily for other transit planners. The first part, which described the expansion of the Vélib' system in the neighborhood, drew little in the way of discussion or questions. What proved irksome for many, however, was the large amount of space in the presentation that was given to describing accommodations to a constituency that drew a unique level of disdain from the audience: two-wheeled motorized vehicles, and in particular motor scooters. Many of those present seemed to grow more engaged—out of annoyance—as the transit planners described the motor-scooter "situation" in the area. First, there was a demographic portrayal of who the riders were: 87 percent are male, 57 percent are younger than thirty-five (one in four are under twenty-five), only half live in Paris, but 87 percent work in the capital. This established the scooter as an important method of mobility for young men, especially between Paris and the *banlieue,* though it should also be mentioned that the association between young men and the *banlieue* often connotes *jeunes issus de l'immigration.* Although we received no information about the income of riders, we learned that cheap, lightweight scooters made up an increasing number of vehicles in Paris, and half of these vehicles were more than three years old—and, very important—fewer than half are equipped with catalytic converters. It was then, as the planners began to describe adding scooter parking accommodations (to avoid the problem of scooters being "improperly" chained to light poles and benches) that an adjunct elected official from Europe Écologie Les Verts—the Green Party—boiled over in frustration. He interrupted the presenters, vehemently demanding an explanation for why the city should make any accommodation for scooters. Weren't their engines responsible for disproportionately high outputs of emissions? As the members of the audience, who were his electoral constituents, murmured in approval, one of the neighborhood council members asked if such accommodations would increase the dreaded problem of motor scooters driving on sidewalks. To this, the planners sheepishly acknowledged that there was indeed a "motor-scooter culture" that posed problems for civility, but providing parking places for scooters, they explained, might actually decrease the problem. Most of the attendees were unconvinced, but none chose to argue the issue further. And so the two men from the transit department, whose manners were decidedly those of technicians rather than politicians, appeared to have succeeded in their efforts to build in space for scooter riders in the city, if only barely.

The debate over scooters provides an ideal starting point for situating a global discourse of urban sustainability in a Parisian context. The resulting political issues lead me to question what I term the "end(s)" of urban ecology. My term is an intentional provocation: on one level, I foreground the idea that environmental activism in cities has reached a cusp or limit because the urban policy establishment (and urban planning) has by and large seized upon "greening the city" as a new political orthodoxy. Of course, this does not mean that the work of environmentalists at the grassroots level is done. Rather, the issue is that the incorporation of environmentalists into the urban power structure of major cities like Paris amounts to an undeniable sea change in the ways in which neighborhood or community-based environmental activists confront the urban power structure. As the quotes that open this chapter indicate, the green turn of the urban policy establishment raises important issues about the identity of environmental politics, cities, and, of course, residents as well. Ultimately, the shift toward sustainability in urban planning presents a situation that is reminiscent of the Lefebvrian idea that the production of space is not only a material process but goes hand in hand with the creation of new forms of inclusion, exclusion, and new potentialities for social transformation.

The question that follows is, therefore, For what (and for whom) are sustainable cities ultimately being built? Even if the answer is as self-evident and obvious as mitigating the impact of the cities on global environmental destruction and climate, the question remains: What environment and for whom? There is by now a veritable school of anthropology that demonstrates how categories of nature and the environment are culturally and historically contingent and can themselves result in social exclusion.[4] This chapter is an interrogation of the "ends" of ecology at the level of urban politics. By juxtaposing the ethnography of the public hearing with everyday life in Paris's streets, alongside an extended analysis of sustainable urbanism discourse, I ask: What is the social, cultural, political, and economic context for the "green turn" in urban planning? How do ecological approaches to urbanism relate to what might be called the "traditional" types of projects pursued by urban policy elites, which often involve reimaging and rebuilding the city to attract investment in competition with other cities?[5] Ultimately, who does the green turn in urbanism benefit, and who is marginalized? In order to better understand dynamics of exclusion and inclusion in the eco-city, I return for a moment, to what Tomi from the Éole mobilization once described as "scooter battles."

The tensions and anxieties displayed by residents and planners in the *mairie* were easily visible on northeast Paris streets, where the scooters' fraught relationship with ecological urbanism could become a personal and tense affair. Through the course of my fieldwork, I spent many evenings in the company of a group of young people (the vast majority of whom were young men) who passed their time on the Jardins d'Éole esplanade. While my research primarily focused on activists, a Tunisian twenty-one-year-old by the name of Ziad, his nineteen-year-old brother Munir, and their twenty-five-year-old Serbian friend Danko (his family had arrived in France as war refugees in the 1990s) had become curious—if initially territorial—about my presence around the park (see chapter 5). Over time, I developed a routine of stopping by the wall on the Jardins d'Éole esplanade where this group of friends and an extended network of neighborhood youth often sat late into the night. Most of these young men lived with their parents in apartments adjacent to or very close to the park; the place largely functioned as an extension of the home just beyond the immediate surveillance of their parents, though it was carefully watched by police, neighbors, and, starting in 2011, surveillance cameras. The place was a kind of self-contained social world or refuge for the young men, who spent their time there chainsmoking, people watching, and telling jokes at each other's expense. This made the spot a favorite rendezvous point for young people in the neighborhood, and sometimes well beyond, who owned scooters.

While this crowd of young men often elicited fear on the part of many residents—a number of whom simply assumed they were engaged in criminal activity—day-to-day life with Ziad and his friends in a public space is often one of monotony, until, that is, someone with a scooter arrived. Scooters, along with the loud noise, smell of gasoline, and the potential for instant mobility they brought, were a guaranteed source of excitement, transgression, and possibility. Inevitably, a scooter driver would zoom out of the street and into the esplanade, which was technically part of the public garden, to say hello. Sometimes, if the crowd and the driver felt particularly mischievous, he would put on a show: rev up the engine, "burn rubber," and execute spins and "donuts" in the esplanade. At night, when all youths would gather at the esplanade, some of the Éole activists themselves would frequently show up to keep a vigilant eye for precisely such "infractions." On many occasions (one example is described in more detail in chapter 6), I saw Éole activists confront young men with scooters and invoke the status of the esplanade as a "park" as the reason they should leave; often, the mere arrival of scooters was tolerated, but donuts and spins elicited an intervention. Interestingly, in every discussion that I witnessed or heard about, the otherwise brusque young men were always the ones who backed down; both sides always knew who was more likely to be favored if the confrontation escalated and the police were called. While a host of ideological undercurrents moved just beneath the surface in the confrontations between

Youths gather on the Jardins d'Éole esplanade for a hip-hop show at the park.

middle-class residents and youths, the notion of "a scooter in the park" was often the point of contention.

This everyday contestation—or, to be more precise, negotiation—suggests the ways in which new sustainable landscapes have developed their own contours of inclusion and exclusion. "Scooter battles" articulate with national-level anxieties over delinquency and youth and the "civility" of France's immigrant-origin youth. Indeed, in many respects, one could say that there is nothing new about young people of immigrant origin being the objects of surveillance and castigated over activities deemed a "nuisance" or even a "threat." However, when environmentalists are mobilized as agents in a process of exclusion, both the environmentalist project and the nature of belonging and exclusion itself are transformed. The redefinition of urban space as "a park" provided the immediate justification for the exclusion of scooters from the esplanade. The operant notion was that there is an inherent incompatibility between young people's activities and the park's status as a sanctified territory associated with nature where the public is expected to conform to carefully prescribed behaviors. In this sense, the creation of the park spatially redefined the nature of youths' infraction: now, the problem was not only what they were doing but *where* they were doing it.

In this context, the intervention of the Green Party official at the eighteenth arrondissement hearing becomes especially important. The question of polluting emissions became the entry point to a discussion that quickly led to problems of incivility and "motor-scooter culture." This term, used by the officials for the city's transit department, is highly illustrative as an example of assimilationist republicanism rooted in the worry that a "different culture can allowed to become fully developed in France."[6] "Motor-scooter culture"—the domain of young men who move between the *banlieue* and the capital—is largely defined by a lack of conformity to the rules that define "proper" forms of mobility in the city. Scooters are uniquely suited to reappropriating streets and subverting all manner of barriers to movement. Many two-wheel vehicles, and especially older models with higher levels of emissions, are cheap, and therefore make mobility between Paris and the often transit-starved *banlieue* accessible. Scooters are small and nimble, allowing drivers with the stomach for taking risks the ability to navigate between lanes on the often traffic-jammed boulevards and the Périphérique that rings the city, and quick detours onto sidewalks are far from uncommon.

However, when the question of emissions becomes the departure point for surveillance and discipline, the stakes become far more profound than questions of civility and sharing space. The affordable and often emissions-generating scooter, which is arguably the private vehicle of choice for the world's poor and socially precarious, gets recast as a global environmental menace. Ironically, scooters, which in France have a high accident rate that is strikingly gendered (94 percent of scooter fatalities are men), are discursively transformed from "in danger" to "dangerous" in a manner similar to Dikeç's observation about the *banlieue*.[7] Loud, dirty, and frequently "uncivil," scooters might be regarded as the anti-Vélib'—a menace to society *and* to the environment. In its current form, the "road to sustainability" appears to have little room for them.

Rescaling the Urban: Green as the New Global, Eco as the New Europe

Advocates for the green turn in urban policy draw a great deal of their political strength by invoking the global scale, by defining either the nature of environmental problems (global climate change) or the nature of the solution (international, often multicity cooperation on environmental policies). This global reach of urban sustainability discourse does not make it a homogenizing influence, however. As one can see with the question of "scooter battles," a global discourse of green urbanism provides a political bulwark for planners and policy makers to carry out local transformations rooted in city and even neighborhood-level dynamics. Thus, a discussion of cities' relationship to climate change and emissions can transform scooter riding from being a mere annoyance for some residents to a potential danger to planetary ecology. In this sense, discussions related to the green turn in urban policy become an important site for the production of scale—by re-imagining the global, local, or altogether new scales (such as "Europe" in the 1990s).[8] Thus, in order to understand the political significance of the green turn in urban planning and design, ecological urbanism must be appreciated for its efficacy as a scale-making project.

In this regard, sustainable urbanism has been linked to the changing intercity geography enabled by globalization from its earliest beginnings. In roughly the same period that Saskia Sassen argued that global finance capitals, and chiefly New York, London, and Tokyo, were circumventing the nation-state as units in the global economy, leaders from many decidedly lower-profile cities began to adopt the "Agenda 21" voluntary action plan developed at the 1992 United Nations Conference on Environment and Development (UNCED, better known as the Earth Summit).[9] Agenda 21 laid out a global framework for locally adaptable approaches to urban sustainability and counts nearly six thousand local governments worldwide as signatories. The widespread adoption of Agenda 21 guidelines has in turn been accompanied by the establishment of global intercity networks focused on sustainability. These include the American-based ICLEI (International Council for Local Environmental Initiatives), which includes more than a thousand cities in eighty-four countries, and the World Bank–affiliated C40, which includes forty designated "global cities" and focuses first and foremost on the reduction of greenhouse gas emissions.[10] These networks, which are primarily oriented toward policy makers and planners, serve as important sites for the diffusion of know-how and expertise in policy implementation.

Such intercity networks and the discourses associated with them allow for a reimagining of the global and the urban as intricately linked: now cities and the "urban" scale become the primary political arena to combat global

warming and other worldwide environmental concerns related to water,
energy use, and air pollution.[11] In this regard, sustainable urbanism constitutes, as both network and discourse, Lefebvrian "representations of space"
through which political leaders and urban elites reimagine the global on the
basis of interurban cooperation or competition.[12] As the existence of networks such as the C40 indicates, ecological concerns do not rival a traditional
focus on economic investment, but instead form part of a new strategy—
and perhaps even provide a moral obligation—for capital accumulation in
the form of greening the city.

This competitive scale-making aspect of urban sustainability is of special
importance in the context of European unification. The vast majority of
Agenda 21 signatories (at one point, more than five thousand of the roughly
six thousand total) are local-level governments in Europe, where Agenda 21
was enshrined as part of the then burgeoning European Union (EU) through
the 1994 Aalborg Charter.[13] The charter has been viewed for good reason as
a historical milestone in producing international guidelines for sustainable
urban planning.[14] It is also, however, an early and formative effort to define a
new urban identity—that of the "European city." Written just two years after
the Maastricht Treaty approved the adoption of the euro and the EU parlia-
mentary system, the opening paragraphs of the charter read:

> We, European cities & towns, signatories of this Charter, state that in the
> course of history, our towns have existed within and outlasted empires, nation
> states, and regimes and have survived as centres of social life, carriers of our
> economies, and guardians of culture, heritage and tradition . . .
>
> We understand that our present urban lifestyle, in particular our patterns
> of division of labour and functions, land-use, transport, industrial production,
> agriculture, consumption, and leisure activities, and hence our standard of liv-
> ing, make us essentially responsible for many environmental problems human-
> kind is facing . . .
>
> We are convinced that sustainable human life on this globe cannot be
> achieved without sustainable local communities. Local government is close to
> where environmental problems are perceived and closest to the citizens and
> shares responsibility with governments at all levels for the well-being of
> humankind and nature. Therefore, cities and towns are key players in the pro-
> cess of changing lifestyles, production, consumption and spatial patterns.[15]

Later in the document, there is a section (I.6) titled "Urban Economy towards Sustainability" that is short but of particular importance, as it introduces a key concept, "natural capital." It reads:

> We, cities & towns, understand that the limiting factor for economic development of our cities and towns has become natural capital, such as atmosphere, soil, water and forests. We must therefore invest in this capital. In order of priority this requires
>
> - investments in conserving the remaining natural capital, such as groundwater stocks, soil, habitats for rare species;
> - encouraging the growth of natural capital by reducing our level of current exploitation, such as of non-renewable energy;
> - investments to relieve pressure on natural capital stocks by expanding cultivated natural capital, such as parks for inner-city recreation to relieve pressure on natural forests; and
> - increasing the end-use efficiency of products, such as energy-efficient buildings, environmentally friendly urban transport.[16]

The Aalborg Charter defines the essence of the "European city"; indeed, the city is said to be a more durable political, economic, and cultural "guardian" than the historically more transient form of the nation-state. Cities and towns are where continuity with the past and true connections with the people are to be found; it is therefore implied that in cities and towns one finds the authentic Europe. But what other than "tradition," generally speaking, do these locales (as diverse as Liverpool and Athens) have in common? The European city is identified as one and the same with the concept of sustainable local communities. Sustainability is understood in two ways: it is a humane responsibility (penitently born out of a history of polluting industrialization and overconsumption) and it is a productive concept, linked to "natural capital."

Natural capital assigns nature the importance of capital, making nature a source of wealth its own right, as well as a source—and outcome—of investment; it is therefore part of a (circular) logic of economic accumulation and competition. Natural capital is not the same as "nature" per se; as the charter points out, it can be produced through careful investment in "cultivated natural capital," which can include parks and other aspects of the built environment. The European city's traditional historical role as "guardian of culture, heritage, and tradition" is therefore extended to the domain of natural capital, the accumulation of which is part and parcel of traditional economic capital. In this respect, the Aalborg Charter can be read as defining not only the essence of the "European city" but a competitive European urban strategy based on green capitalism.

As with Agenda 21, the Aalborg Charter mobilizes sustainability as a common thread to bridge differences of culture and nation. It is not an effort to homogenize cities into a single identity; indeed, the opening lines of the charter strike an anti-"national" tone. It has therefore been embraced by local elites in a variety of contexts. Barcelona, which has long defiantly self-identified as more of a Catalan metropolis than a Spanish city, provided an early forerunner of this "European" model. As Gary McDonogh has reported, from the 1990s onward Barcelona's leaders led a "rebranding" effort that associates ecological urbanism with a combination of luxury and slightly offbeat cultural edginess—helped in no small part by the city's hosting the 1992 Olympic Games.[17] In a local variation of a different type, Stockholm's redevelopment of the Hammarby Sjöstad neighborhood attempts to capitalize on what might be termed the "natural capital" associated with a cultivated "Nordic" image to promote not only the project itself but the eco-neighborhood as a model for profitable export far beyond the borders of Europe.[18] Such neoliberal incarnations suggest that sustainable European urbanism has made the transition from being viewed as a humanitarian responsibility to a competitive brand.

Europe's urban political leaders are, of course, far from the only elites to integrate sustainability into a place-making strategy for investment. Not to be outdone, the leadership of Abu Dhabi is in the midst of developing Masdar City, a six-square-kilometer, Norman Foster–designed, master-planned arcology in the desert with an aspiration to someday be home to forty thousand residents and a workplace for sixty thousand commuters.[19] Masdar City's mission is remarkable in that it is expected to go beyond merely adopting sustainability principles (despite its desert location) and will serve as a globally focused "test bed" and "very-fast-to-market platform" for all aspects of sustainable design (in addition to being a tariff- and tax-free Special Economic Zone).[20] Masdar City is a vivid example of sustainable design as a neoliberal strategy of accumulation that goes beyond the level of mere marketing greenwash to embrace sustainability as a form of technological fix; although in its early stages, this global "sustainability" test bed is already partnered with firms as varied as Siemens, Mitsubishi Heavy Industries, and Reykjavik Geothermal.

These aggressive approaches to cornering the market on sustainability are forcing the leaders of the world's traditional global centers to play catchup. New York City's leadership virtually ignored the green turn of the 1990s, only to see the Bloomberg administration unveil the so-called PlanNYC in 2007. Bloomberg's sudden embrace of urban sustainability in the mid-2000s was notable for having occurred shortly after the city lost an Olympic Games bid to London, which had used sustainability as a showpiece for its proposal.[21] The Bloomberg iteration of sustainable urbanism reflected his corporatist strategy of urban governance. One of the more visible elements of the plan was Bloomberg's retort to Paris's Vélib': a for-profit bike-share scheme called CitiBike, which features blue-and-white bicycles and stations decorated and labeled in such a way as to show off their obvious brand synergy with CitiBank. In Bloomberg's New York, even the charge to reverse climate change was a finance-sector-led affair.

Of course, the global discourse on urban sustainability is marked not only by regional and local variations but by distinct trends that reflect the shifts in the meaning of sustainability over time. Since the release of Donatella Meadows's influential *The Limits to Growth* in 1972, rhetoric on sustainability has been infused by a neo-Malthusian globalism.[22] By the time of Agenda 21, when the language of sustainable development had become intermingled with urban planning, the image of insatiable urban metabolism had become predominant. Thus, Agenda 21 states: "In industrialized countries the consumption patterns of cities are severely stressing the global ecosystem."[23] Since that period, sustainable urban design has primarily sought to limit the use of nonrenewable energy sources, and in particular carbon-based fuels, by focusing on public transit, cycling, and pedestrian-oriented development, implementing green building designs and more efficient infrastructure for energy, water, and sewage. In this vision, the global scale is legitimated by a combination of urban planning and environmental science to such a profound extent that the disciplines have begun to fuse in contemporary urban studies. Today, an urban-planning program can hardly be considered complete without some degree of focus on sustainability. What might be called the "sustainability" scale has now reached a degree of global hegemony in urban planning.

In the second decade of the twenty-first century, the metabolic logic of managing and governing "inputs" and "outputs" and the dominance of the city-as-organism metaphor are being complemented by a growing emphasis on biodiversity. This new focus places the cultivation, management, and governance of the city's nonhuman forms of life as a new domain of urban planning. The result is a reversal of the long-standing city-as-organism metaphor; now, nonhuman organisms, from flora to fauna, are understood, planned, managed, and governed as part of the city. Urban biodiversity initiatives have risen to the fore in the wake of the 2010 Nagoya Protocol to a Convention of Biological Diversity and subsequent declaration of a UN Decade on Biodiversity. In response, sustainable urbanism networks were abuzz with new initiatives and activity on this theme in the early 2010s. For example, the ICLEI—through its BiodiverCity Hotspot program—has declared "biodiversity conservation, planning and management" an important area of urban policy.[24] Examples of such programs include the BioCity program in Curitiba, Brazil, which emphasizes riverine ecosystem management and the reintroduction of "indigenous plant species" to promote knowledge and familiarity with regions with indigenous flora and preserve "genetic diversity" with the goal of developing "locally well-adapted cultivars."[25] In another example, the eThekwini region (Durban, South Africa) has focused on the natural ecosystem as a "source of valuable goods and services to its citizens" in numerous forms, including "food production," "natural products," and "genetic resources."[26] Such programs posit the promotion of a vibrant urban ecosystem as both a way of rebuilding damaged ecosystems and a source of human subsistence and survival in a world of increasing economic precariousness.

In both cases, urban policy makers are able to harness powerful concepts of indigeneity linked to the presence of unique niche communities legitimized by environmental science. However, in a neoliberal, neo-Darwinian light, the genetic diversity of local ecosystems is linked not only to the language of adaptation and survival but profit accumulation in a globalized world. The urban biodiversity perspective therefore represents an important shift from neo-Malthusian urban sustainability. If the latter approach emphasized a catastrophist vision of an overconsuming city as the antithesis of natural equilibrium, programs such as ICLEI's "BiodiverCity Hotspots Program" (launched in 2012 in partnership with UN Habitat and in more than 250 cities around the world) view the city as a producer of natural distinctiveness, and hence, capital. Thus, the ICLEI BiodiverCity program focuses on helping cities around the world with what it calls "securing ecosystem services" in the form of freshwater, pollination, and climate regulation, and estimates the value of these services at more than $1.5 trillion a year.[27]

Moreover, an urban ecosystem perspective provides a new way to rescale cities as riverine systems, forests, and other ecological zones that supersede the importance of administrative zones by an authority vested in science. Ecological science is now rescaling the political life and boundaries of municipalities and regions. Biodiversity therefore naturalizes place making by reinventing urban regions as distinctive niche ecoregions in a neoliberal global ecosystem in which the circulation of capital and life itself becomes increasingly difficult to separate. Interurban competition, the shifting of scales, and the transformation of ecosystem processes into a productive economic sector become part of a natural order.

Greening Paris

In the global realm, the green turn in urban policy and planning can often appear extraordinarily diffuse and difficult to define. Agenda 21 and the Aalborg Charter are, after all, both meant to be adaptable to a wide variety of settings. For this reason, a close reading of urban sustainability initiatives from the ground up—such as the contestation over scooter riding—provides a particularly invaluable window on how such projects can even serve to produce new idioms of social exclusion. Another helpful, if somewhat amusing, vantage point on how sustainable urbanism operates at a social, cultural, and political level can be attained by focusing on the mode of travel that might be termed the antithesis of the scooter: Vélib'.

Vélib' (the name is a contraction of *vélo* or "bike" and *liberté* or freedom) is Paris's bicycle-sharing program and one of Mayor Bertrand Delanoë's most widely publicized urban sustainability initiatives.[28] The first time I rode a

Vélib', a few months after the program was launched in 2007, I was more taken by it as a social phenomenon than as a revolution in urban mobility. Biking is, after all, hardly new in Paris, which is a latecomer to bike shares compared to other cities in Europe and even within France itself. Officials from the city of Paris, however, have maintained that their goal was not to innovate by bringing bike share to Paris but to promote sustainability by doing the opposite: bringing the Paris "brand" to bike sharing.[29] In other words, Vélib' was never only oriented toward offering a form of emission-free mobility to Parisians; it sought to use the city's cultural prestige to build up the global visibility of bike sharing, and in doing so attach the idea of sustainability to the Paris "brand" and vice versa. Vélib' is therefore a fascinating example of how an urban project based on hyperlocal experiences— the system is designed for half-hour bike rides—can be part of a much broader global imaginary.

The name Vélib' evokes both the motto of the Republic ("Liberté, Égalité, Fraternité") and the unrestrained "liberty" of being able to travel at a low cost. After paying a €1.70 daily subscription (this cost can be lowered substantially by subscribing on a monthly or yearly basis), the system is free for rides under thirty minutes, though a rider needs a bank account and balance of at least €150 for the system to work. Vélib' is particularly useful for traveling across the city after the metro system has closed for the night, and the system's utility for employers and the city to blunt the effects of labor unrest should not be underappreciated. Indeed, when strikes do occur, the system is utilized to full capacity; during multiple transit strikes between 2007 and 2008, I found bicycles almost impossible to come by. French media outlets report that Vélib' administrators now make special preparations in advance of expected walkouts by transit workers.[30] Indeed, the 1996 transit strike, which did a great service to normalizing bicycle commuting in the Paris region, can be thought of as foreshadowing not only the Vélib' system but the creation of an extensive bicycle infrastructure of paths and trails throughout the Île-de-France region. When viewed in conjunction with the planned Grand Paris Express—an automatic, driverless metro system planned as a key part of the sustainable remaking of the entire capital region—Paris as an emerging ecocity appears as a harsh new environment for organized labor.

At the same time, public discussions related to the bike system's highly publicized problems provide another important site for the drawing of boundaries around the familiar themes of nation and culture. At first, the launch of the Vélib' system was accompanied by jokes regarding "Vélibobos," linking the program to *bobos* (bourgeois bohemians or yuppies) and the *boboïsation* of Paris.[31] Within a short time, however, Vélib' discourse shifted onto a decidedly less populist terrain. The program was barely more than a year old when it became the focus of a moral panic around themes of delinquency and, again, youths of immigrant origin. Media attention was lavished upon self-captured YouTube videos depicting young people subjecting the bikes to destructive stunts and vandalism, and reports of Vélib's stolen, only to be recovered vandalized in "troubled neighborhoods" and the *banlieue*.[32] The ethnic inflection of Vélib' even began to chart a postcolonial geography as media outlets published reports of a Vélib' discovered in North Africa–bound cargo containers and images of a Vélib' "mysteriously" appearing on the streets of Bamako, Mali, circulated widely.[33] These often ethnically tinged public anxieties over the destruction and transcontinental mobility of Paris's new sustainable infrastructure grew so profound that the city began running advertisements on streets and subways castigating would-be Vélib' vandals—presumably male and macho—for cowardice. The Vélib' moral panic of the late 2000s brought renewed international attention to France's politics of national belonging to a degree not seen since the 2005 *banlieue* uprisings. The Vélib' program therefore gave rise to broad social space that transcends the bike system itself and traces the boundaries of the French nation for a domestic and international audience alike.

In this regard, some brief reflections on using the system itself merit comment, as my experience with Vélib' as a casual user led me also to view it as a way in which neoliberal subjectivities can be built into the city. The design of the bikes and the stations themselves function as important signifiers in a spatial vocabulary of power. A great deal of effort was spent by the city in branding Vélib' with a distinct "look" in order to make a statement about biking itself. The system's designers tried to make bicycling appear as futuristic as possible because of worries that bike transit might still be associated with the period of economic hardship during and immediately after the Second World War.[34] The stations feature "pod"-like kiosks equipped with beautiful maps as well as electronic display screens. Everything is painted in a dull grayish-bronze tone, making stations vaguely reminiscent of Apple Computer products.[35]

The bicycles themselves are somewhat awkward. The handlebars are of exaggerated size and the fenders are large as well, making them to easy see and impossible to misidentify. Vélib' also has a distinctive ergonomic feel that many self-styled urban bikers do not always appreciate. During my first ride, I will not forget how quickly my enthusiasm for trying out a Vélib' was replaced by a somewhat self-conscious sensation of goofiness upon my departure. I lumbered down the bike path, ringing the bell to alert pedestrians of my approach, with my back and neck stuck by design at such an upright angle that I could have been seated at a formal banquet; meanwhile, cyclists on their own road bikes zoomed by me on all sides. The eminently civil Vélib' comes across as the opposite of a sleek, specialized, and thus dangerous or exclusive racing bike; it is an accessible, friendly, even welcoming bicycle, though it is common to hear Parisians claim that the bikes are intentionally

A Vélib' station in northeast Paris. Despite media coverage that associates so-called delinquency and vandalism with the system, the bike program has expanded to become the global leader in numbers of bicycles per city inhabitant (one bike for ninety-seven residents).

meant to look silly in order to discourage theft. These features also make the Vélib' relatively heavy, slow, and lacking in maneuverability; the system's administrators eventually had to fall back on a *homo economicus*–inspired strategy of offering extra "checkout time" for riders to incentivize the return of the heavy bikes to stations in hilly neighborhoods. When this measure proved less than adequate, the final resort has been to ferry bikes between stations by truck. In general, symbolic "messaging" has taken a high priority in the system's design; one could say that Vélib' appears to prioritize the bike system's value as a mode of representation over everyday mobility.

As a subjective experience, using Vélib' undoubtedly opens up new ways of inhabiting, feeling, knowing, and relating to the city (and other city dwellers).[36] The swipe of a bank card gives one a sense of membership and the ability to hop on a bicycle anytime. It is one of the more individualistic ways to inhabit and move throughout a city, and, ironically, the "shared" nature of Vélib' actually accentuates this aspect of the experience. On more than one occasion, I have spotted the sole remaining bicycle at a station only to see another would-be rider, who upon seeing me first, quickly picked up the pace to nab it (I confess to having done the same to others). Even when a number of bikes are available, choosing one can become a competition of sorts, because at least one is often damaged and, if a person is in a hurry, a degree of savvy and skill comes into play through his or her ability to quickly "read" the available bikes for problems. In my experience, Vélib' reinforces the competitive aspects of living in the city, despite the images of collectivity that come to mind when one uses the language of "bike share" to describe it.

Once you are off and riding, this aspect of the experience is further heightened for reasons that are more owing to the individualistic nature of bicycling in general, especially when compared to the social experience of traveling by bus or train. As you pedal down the bike lanes (often set in the sidewalks of the boulevards), the crowds lining the boulevards change from multitudes of fellow citizens into a sea of moving obstacles, many of whom tend to wander into bicycle lanes. This sensation—along with sharing the busy streets with cars and buses—reinforces one's awareness of the fragility of one's own existence, and self-preservation becomes a top priority. Still, every once in a while, when one finds just the right vantage point, usually at the centerline of an especially monumental boulevard, one can grasp the perceptive power of bicycling as a way of knowing the city. Once, late at night when traffic had quieted (and only for a few moments), I suddenly realized that the only other time I had ever been directly in the centerline of a Parisian boulevard and had such a perfect sense of the city's monumental symmetry was during a political demonstration. On that occasion—a protest march for the *sans-papiers*—we had chanted that the streets were *ours*. But this time, alone on the bike, I felt a different relationship to public space: the street was *mine*. To inhabit and know the city via Vélib' is to see the city in ways that reverberate with neoliberal individualism, ownership, competition, and, at other times, even a sensation of precariousness. Vélib', it seems, has a way of spatializing and materializing neoliberal experience—that is, for those with bank cards, a bit of time to spare, and no need for a long-distance *banlieue*–city center commute.

Dueling for Scale: Delanoë, Sarkozy, and Le Grand Paris

Throughout the 2000s, the Delanoë administration was far from the only part of the policy establishment planning the sustainable reinvention of Paris. Soon after the rollout of Vélib', President Nicolas Sarkozy of the right-wing UMP proposed the Grand Paris plan. In keeping within a late-twentieth-century tradition in which each president of the Republic bequeaths a monumental megaproject in Paris to posterity, Sarkozy made a characteristically immodest proposal: the reconstruction of the entire metropolitan region. In a speech announcing the plan, he described the project in the following terms:

> How do you invent a sustainable city, a post-Kyoto city, an ecologically sound city, a city that blends with nature instead of fighting against it?
> Voilà! This may be the greatest policy challenge of the twenty-first century. I want France to meet this challenge. I want France to set the example. This is the ambition of Grand Paris.[37]

The original Grand Paris plan called not only for urban reconstruction on a vast scale but for a radical administrative reorganization of the metropolitan area, including the dissolution and integration of numerous, historically Left-leaning suburban municipalities. At a more concrete level, the integrative vision proposed a new suburban Métro Automatique, a driverless, and thus strike-proof, metro of unprecedented size. Grand Paris explicitly invoked Haussmann's restructuring of Paris as a precedent for a needed "response to a vital challenge facing our country: how to sustainably engage France in international economic competition."[38] The multi-municipality project, which included Paris and many of the cities along its outskirts, took aim specifically at London and New York as urban competitors.[39] At a neighborhood scale, the plan consists of 650 district-level projects scattered throughout the metropolitan area, many of which combine an attention to sustainable, or so-called post-Kyoto, urban design, with attention to regional-level integration. Many projects combine the sustainable management of resources and waste with a general aesthetic of greening that often blends the built environment with natural landscapes. Each of the 650 projects is intended to be part of the large whole (Grand Paris), which is in turn meant to place the city (and France) in an advantageous position in a new frontier of international interurban competition: the creation of a "green" global urban center. Sarkozy's Grand Paris vision epitomized his approach toward governance: it was large, almost impossibly ambitious, but ultimately attempted to work through a statist approach to make France competitive within a neoliberal framework.

Grand Paris was widely publicized and controversial from the start. The project is fraught with contradictions, not least of which is the fact that it sought to combine the grandeur of a pharaonic megaproject with the attention to resource scarcity and low consumption that is the hallmark of sustainable urbanism. Among Grand Paris's most vigorous critics was Bertrand Delanoë, who, having his own vision for the sustainable remaking of the capital already under way, saw the project as an attempt by national politicians "to appropriate" the dominant position of the city in the global economy.[40] A less restrained Jean-Paul Huchon, Socialist president of the Île-de-France region, described Grand Paris as an "authoritarian project constructed behind closed doors," resulting in a situation in which a UMP official described as a "total deadlock between the state and region."[41] The surprisingly public and vitriolic debates over Grand Paris between Paris, allied regional politicians, and the president of the Republic provide a vivid demonstration of the way the production of scale can become a source of tremendous tension among policy makers. The question was: who would have access to what might be called the sustainability dividend furnished by the reinvention of the region, and who would receive political capital from the project as well? The episode demonstrates the degree to which sustainable urbanism can become an object of struggle among a political elite factionalized not only across party and ideological lines but, even more significantly, between urban and national positions.

Sarkozy's 2012 electoral defeat by Socialist François Hollande provides the saga with an unanticipated twist. Interestingly enough, with Sarkozy out of the picture, the Grand Paris project not only lived on but has been embraced by the Socialists at every level of government. While this odd situation has led some commentators to try to compare and contrast the Grand Paris of the Left and Right, it appears that the difference is more one of style than of substance.[42] The reinvigoration of Grand Paris, which has been gingerly redubbed Le Nouveau Grand Paris (or simply termed *métropolitanisation* by others), has continued largely because its inspiration and several basic components actually preceded Sarkozy's presidency. Indeed, the over-centralization of the Île-de-France region has long been a preoccupation of Paris planners.[43] The unprecedented two-hundred-kilometer expansion of Paris metro lines and extending commuter rail into the *banlieue* (at a cost of 30 billion euros) remains the centerpiece of the plan, which now emphasizes regional "solidarity" alongside "competitiveness."[44]

While plans to radically reorganize the administrative and municipal districts of the Île-de-France were largely defeated before Sarkozy left office, many of the main subprojects in the plan, which are themselves mega-projects, have long histories, some of which formed part of a 2001 plan called the Grand Projet de Renouvellement Urbain (GPRU—literally, great urban renewal plan) that brought large-scale demolition and rebuilding to the "border" areas between Paris and the *banlieue*. One of the cornerstones of this regional vision is La Plaine Saint-Denis, a four-hundred-hectare urban-renewal project of a large postindustrial area abutting the Canal de Saint-Denis, which is adjacent to northeast Paris and the neighborhood surrounding the Jardins d'Éole. La Plaine Saint-Denis consists of five thousand new housing units and eight hundred thousand square meters of office space,

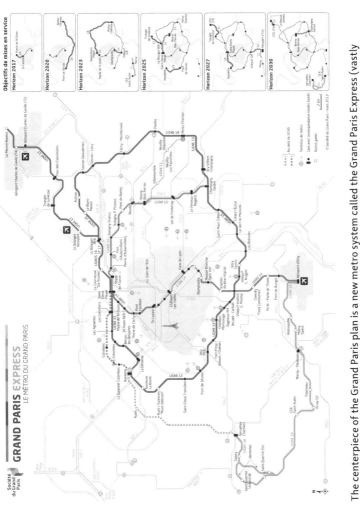

The centerpiece of the Grand Paris plan is a new metro system called the Grand Paris Express (vastly exceeding the size of the original Paris metro). It will provide unprecedented connectivity to—and among—the historically isolated *banlieue* districts. Most of the approximately 650 development projects related to Grand Paris are located along the various lines. Copyright Société du Grand Paris, March 2013.

and a major film studio, designed to be a new "European Movie City."[45] The roots of the project, however, go back to the 1980s, and specifically a two-decade-old regional plan to redevelop the *banlieues* of Saint-Denis and Aubervilliers, centered on the national soccer stadium, the eighty-thousand-seat, $400 million Stade de France, which hosted France's 1998 World Cup win. Grand Paris therefore built upon long-standing efforts to bring Paris in line with other acknowledged "global cities."

For all of the abundant criticism, the most significant effects of the Grand Paris plan have been to make discussions of scale, and specifically the link between globalization and metropolitanization, a taken-for-granted center-piece of multiple urban projects, and to integrate this connection with what Sarkozy called the "city blended with nature."[46] This discursive sea change has transformed the ways the urban is imagined and talked about in Paris as a whole, and not just in the context of the Grand Paris projects themselves. For example, in 2011 the mayor's office released Paris's first Biodiversity Plan. This vision, a veritable production of space appealing to the authority of nature itself, amounts to a reimagining of the metropolitan scale through the lens of environmental science. The parallels between ecological metro-politanization and the Grand Paris plan are striking. Whereas the Grand Paris plan seeks to connect a mosaic of municipalities through political and infrastructure-based transformations, the Paris Biodiversity Plan seeks to connect "fragmented habitats," often by using the vacant rights-of-way of preexisting connective infrastructure.[47] The "margins of railroad tracks and expressways," as well as parks, tree-lined boulevards, and especially dis-used and vacant urban land, is reimagined as greenways enabling the "circu-lation and diffusion of species" at the scale of the Île-de-France.[48] As with the Grand Paris Plan, particular attention is given to railway connections, but this time of a different kind. In the following quote, note the intermin-gling of the urban and the natural, something that suffuses the document as a whole:

> Railroad corridors are of significant potential as ecological corridors by link-ing the center of the urban agglomeration with the great natural spaces of the Île-de-France and the more distant countryside [*campagnes*]. Flora can grow and wildlife can move with ease on the less trafficked [railway] embankments,

rights-of-way, and ballast areas as long as the current usage of chemical herbicides is stopped.

These corridors are also places to breathe in the city. These spaces open onto large landscapes, which as wind corridors are conducive to biodiversity and the movement of species, especially when near gardens, rivers, and canals. In Paris, railways abut several parks (André-Citroën, Martin-Luther-King, Batignolles, Bercy, Éole, Pajol . . .), as well as the Seine to the southeast and southwest, and to the northeast, the canals.[49]

The document is striking for the degree to which it transposes traditional urban planning concerns with movements, flow, and infrastructural connection onto the logic of biodiversity, with its focus on genetic diversity and species interdependence. There is a long history of "city-as-organism" metaphors in urban planning, but here the notion of urban metabolism is far more literal than ever. Nature allows for the redefinition of railway lines as "places to breathe," an ironic observation given the environmental justice issues raised by activists regarding trains and air pollution (see chapter 1). The railroads themselves are redefined as "ecological corridors" and "wind corridors" that facilitate the reproduction of animal, avian, and plant life in the city. Interestingly, the city/country dichotomy remains central to this vision of urban nature: Paris's "urban agglomeration" is juxtaposed against the "great natural spaces of the Île-de-France and the more distant countryside"; it is the liminality of the railroad edges that facilitates the blurring of the boundaries between each.

While in some cases terminology such as countryside (campagne) is deployed to evoke the nation's natural substance, the biodiversity plan overwhelming stresses an embrace of the global. In the report's introduction, Delanoë places urban biodiversity on a par with climate change as an issue to be addressed "at every scale, by citizens of every country."[50] The report historicizes itself as emerging out of discussions at the Earth Summit as well as the Nagoya Protocol in 2010, marking the plan as a global intervention above all else. Throughout the report it becomes clear that this reimagining of Paris is about issues that go far beyond its own boundaries. Rather, Paris is cast as an agent for the global production of biodiversity, a form of inter-urban competition that its leaders hope to define as well as lead.

A Sustainable Northeast Paris—for Whom?

Northeast Paris has been a focal point in these globally focused sustainablity projects for two principal reasons: first, its status as a "border" neighborhood between Paris and the historically disconnected *banlieue* makes it an important point of regional articulation (or 'bridgehead'), to use the militaristic language of one APUR report.[51] Second, its postindustrial built environment, as we have seen, makes it a desirable space for reimagining the urban future along the lines of sustainablity on the part of elite policy makers and residents alike.

Since 2001, after the establishment of the GPRU, the La Chapelle International plan has sought to redefine the identity of a neighborhood that is famously isolated by railway tracks along explicitly globally focused lines. The project focuses on the reconstruction of a railway freight facility into a high-density multitower housing development consisting of nine hundred units, a school, twelve thousand square meters of green space forming a greenway that parallels the neighborhood's historic north–south rail axis, connecting the city center with the banlieue.[52] And this project is only one of nearly a dozen other "sectors" of a massive redevelopment known as Paris Nord-Est that will eventually bring twenty-eight thousand new residents to northeast Paris: Paris Nord-Est is, of course, yet another subcomponent of the larger Grand Paris vision. Paris Nord-Est is the largest urban redevelopment project under way in Paris itself. It consists of more than two hundred hectares of redevelopment (or more than five hundred when one includes the adjacent Plaine Saint-Denis project described earlier), a concert hall for the Paris Philharmonic designed by Jean Nouvel, a new light-rail line, a major commuter station (known as Rosa Parks station), and entire neighborhoods consisting of high-density housing, schools, residential districts, and commercial zones.[53] As to Paris Nord-Est itself, "the project is a unique opportunity to 'make a city' *[faire de la ville]* and constitutes a laboratory in vivo to construct a new generation of attractive and sustainable neighborhoods."[54] Paris Nord-Est is expected to use geothermal power, its buildings are certified for low energy consumption, and it uses a sustainable water-management regime for the entire district. Special attention is given to creation of multiple ecological corridors on the site, including two urban forests that run along each flank of the project area, a small, one-hectare nature preserve, and further greenways along the railways and canals that crisscross the area. The project and various components such as La Chapelle International reveal the magnitude of redevelopment under way in Paris; in some respects the effort even echoes the ambitious goals of Abu Dhabi's Masdar City to function as a "laboratory" of sustainability urbanism and urban planning.

However, the notion of northeast Paris as a "laboratory" and the emphasis on urban visions of the future (with no mention of a past of any kind) suggest that northeast Paris is treated as a blank slate, an empty canvas. It is not. As is often the case with gentrification and redevelopment, the physical renovation of Paris's urban landscape is inseparable from the class-based and ethnocultural remaking of the capital. The geographic scope of Paris Nord-Est and related redevelopment projects in the area is largely coterminous with the city's immigrant neighborhoods.[55] In this regard, the relationship between redevelopment and the housing situations facing immigrant-origin

In the Paris Nord-Est project, landscape design itself conveys an allegory of capitalism's nature: here corporate offices—and a globally competitive Paris—sprout among tall grasses and flowers that evoke the site's history as a postindustrial lot.

Parisians is of crucial importance. Real-estate values in northeast Paris, despite being the lowest in the city, have been among its most rapidly rising. Between 1995 and 2013, apartment values there have risen approximately 347 percent, compared to the rest of the city at 300 percent.[56] At the same time, during a period of severe economic contraction since 2009, in which unemployment rates in Paris increased from 7.7 to 9.1 percent, capital has flooded into northeast Paris, causing land values to skyrocket more than 30 percent.[57] These shifts have occurred in tandem with mass evictions accompanying the demolition of housing in the area; more than 350 apartment buildings have been demolished since 2001 to make way for new development.[58] Residents have responded through protests and housing movements such as DAL and the Mal-logés, whose emergence occurred in conjunction with the remaking of Paris's working-class and immigrant neighborhoods.

The framing of northeast Paris's "sustainable" redevelopment in the media and by policy makers has taken the character of a class-based, ethnoracial, and civilization-based project. As early as 1991, an article in Le Monde lamented the "foreign" character of working-class neighborhoods in northeast Paris. Pointing to development of "black neighborhoods" as well as shops with signs now written in Arabic, the article deployed the language of reconquest (reconquête) in describing efforts by elites to solve the problems of France's emergent "ghettos."[59] The historical and civilization implications of "reconquest," with its reference to the Reconquest of Spain and the shift in power in the Iberian Peninsula from Muslims of North African origin to Christians, may appear extreme, but "reconquest" discourse has become normalized (and thus dehistoricized) in Parisian urban politics. The usage of the term is commonplace when describing the cultural, economic, and social remaking of northeast Paris.[60] In this sense, the sociospatial remaking of the city parallels an established body of Islamophobic discourse rendering European civilization as being in a state of struggle with an internal Islamic other.[61] Paris's ethnoracial and spatial patterns of redevelopment, gentrification, and displacement now reflect France's exclusionary politics of national belonging toward postcolonial minorities.

From this perspective, one must ask whether the green spaces that lay at the center of these redevelopment projects will ultimately be ecological corridors or more akin to the cordon sanitaire of Louis Hubert Lyautey's colonial plan for Rabat, Morocco, which used green spaces among other barriers and buffer zones to segregate colonizer from colonized.[62] Tensions that run across ethnic, class, and gendered lines are particularly visible in the Jardins de'Éole: when the city itself (and not merely the park) is viewed as a "project," the stakes behind the political life of even small green spaces such as this one become quite visible.

The social contradictions raised by ecological urbanism become apparent in the everyday usage of the park. As already mentioned, the architects chose species of plants that would in turn attract birds, which it was thought would give the park an air of vitality and contribute to biodiversity in Paris. This plan rested upon the assumption that birds would nest there at night, when it offered a quiet resting place of refuge. At the same time, however, the city stipulated that a great deal of effort be placed on lighting the park for reasons of security. Unfortunately, the birds have never arrived in the park as hoped, and the reasons for this lack of avian life at night are viewed by the many members of the design team and park employees as a result of noise caused by youths in the park; it is they who have been blamed for the breakdown in biodiversity. In the contested ecological terrain of northeast Paris, even nesting habits of birds can provide a political idiom of exclusion.

At other moments, the confrontation between those who use the park and ecological design can be a far more spontaneous (and therefore revealing) process. Sustainability became a fundamental theme for the design team combining both aesthetic and technical details. A number of symbolic elements such as a miniature wind turbine (a token with a minimal power yield), the use of "natural" materials (meaning wood, millstone, terracotta, and slate), and an overall aesthetic of sparse, resource-efficient minimalism helped to conjure an aura of sustainability through the park's visual composition. Resource efficiency was a theme of particular emphasis: stones from the abandoned railway station were reappropriated in the park's construction, and according to the architects' design proposal, careful attention was paid to using sustainable building materials. In many respects, the park combines recycling and resource efficiency with ambiance to make the space an example of—and an allegory for—environmental sustainability.

Indeed, the park was meant as a medium through which ideals of sustainability could be communicated to northeast Paris residents—a veritable green polemic or allegory inscribed on the northeast Paris landscape. Nowhere was this more clear than with the use of water, which was viewed as an important visual and sensorial element and a symbol laden with connotations relating to resource management. Emphasis was placed on the recycling of rainwater and a self-cycling canal was created, itself host to an aquatic garden and ducks. Nearby, an ingenious "gravel garden" (*jardin de graviers*)—a large open expanse made up of pebbles that resemble railroad ballast—was laid out and designed to spontaneously reseed itself throughout the year. The close relationship between the gravel garden and the plant-filled canal was meant to call to mind a symbolic interrelationship: "the gravel garden evokes vital links between earth, water, and plants, evoking the fragility and scarcity of resources," wrote the architectural team in its design proposal, adding: "In this sense, the garden is a didactic digression of our project."[63] In essence, the canal and gravel garden were meant to coexist in perfect

A plea for sustainability inscribed on the city: the canal and gravel garden (*jardin de graviers*) of the Jardins d'Éole.

harmony, as a self-sustaining, human-made analogy of a naturally balanced ecosystem, and a statement of the imperative for resource conservation. Indeed, the design proposal and related documents are filled with language dwelling on the "didactic" and "pedagogical" aspects of the space.

Ironically, however, when the park opened, responses to the pedagogical aspects of the space proved quite instructive. While puzzlement and indifference were the most common reactions to the gravel garden on the part of adults, which one parent described to me as an "architects' thingy" (truc de les architectes), children engaged it, and the most amusing "critique" of the park's design can be read thorough their play in this tactile environment. Much to the chagrin of park officials, they enjoy tossing the gravel in the canal, a pastime that continually threatens to cause a malfunction of the system's carefully planned simulacra of ecological equilibrium. While this was not the intended use, could one have designed a more apt allegory?

In other moments, however, the park has become a site for far more direct confrontations over the displacement of residents associated with ecological urbanism. Such tensions were on vivid display at the park's inauguration ceremony in May 2007. Northeast Paris residents, Éole activists, Mayor Delanoë, Daniel Vaillant, and the design team saw the proceedings upstaged by a raucous protest. A visibly frustrated Delanoë, whose speech listed and praised the sustainable attributes of the park project, was nearly shouted down by several dozen members of the Mal-logés housing-rights mobilization who had gathered to demand the construction of affordable housing and protest home demolitions in northeast Paris. Riot police were dispatched to form a barricade between the Mal-logés and the other residents attending the event, including the Éole activists. The police detained and arrested the majority of the protesters, many of whom were Maghrebi and West African women. Like their allies in Droit au Logement, many Mal-logés protesters who take to the streets are women with children (and often small babies). In many cases, this was the result of the fact that women (and especially young parents) are disproportionately impacted by housing inequality and many of the economically precarious (especially the undocumented) lack access to even state-provided child care. However, the presence of women with infants protesting at the new sustainable park also made a powerful point about the "nature" of ecological urbanism in Paris: was the city placing a greater value on the reproduction of biodiversity than on the lives of its most vulnerable residents?

Conclusion

Ultimately, it is difficult to understand the ecological remaking of the Paris region without viewing it in the context of a shifting and locally varied global discourse on urban sustainability. From at least the time of Agenda 21 on, sustainability discourse has often provided a way for urban policy makers to reimagine scale in ways that are advantageous for interurban competition; in many respects, the green turn in urban planning and policy merges with neoliberal visions of the global rooted in such competition, networks of cities, and a market-driven imperative for policy makers to build the brand equity of their cities.[64] Since the 1990s, the policy leaders of cities from Barcelona to Paris to Stockholm have proven adept at capitalizing on the "brand" of the European city as a center of green innovation, often with regional twists. In more recent years, elites in cities as varied as New York and Abu Dhabi are again reimagining the role of cities in a competitive global economy driven by sustainable innovation.

However, this global picture becomes far more complex and filled with contradictions when viewed from the standpoint of on-the-ground politics in Paris. The Aalborg Charter appeals to a global humanitarian need as a basis for the redesign of European cities in a sustainable manner. However, in Paris, debates over scooter drivers, Vélib' discourse, and the *reconquête* of northeast Paris's immigrant districts call into question whether city dwellers whose origins lay beyond the traditional boundaries of Europe are included in this vision. Seen from this perspective, the "ends" of urban ecology or the outcome of Lubin and Esty's "sustainability revolution" appear grim: the road to sustainability that Ban Ki-moon described at Rio+20 may ultimately prove to be a private drive for the world's affluent.

But this does not mean that urban ecology ends there. Sustainable designs such as the Jardins d'Éole do indeed have revolutionary environmental potential when scaled up to the level of metropolitan regions, and key tenets of ecological urbanism such as the emphasis on biodiversity are indispensable if we aspire to a future that breaks with the history of globally destructive environmental damage that is the historical hallmark of urbanization.

Any politics oriented toward urban justice must therefore work toward urban ecology and not against it; this is why a political ecology analysis of sustainable urbanism is an important endeavor.

The green turn in urban design may best be understood as the twenty-first-century equivalent of Haussmann's boulevards writ large: it represents a new spatial logic of capital accumulation as well as a new form of social exclusion. But as a veritable school of urban-focused social critique has taught us, such new spaces often contain within them the seeds of transformation.[65] Architecture provides us with a useful political metaphor in this regard, as people rarely conform to such designs as "users," nor do they do the diametric opposite of what the powerful intend. Instead, places often become filled with possibility, spontaneity, and unpredictability. The remainder of this book focuses on how these often creative, varying, and contradictory efforts play out in of everyday life.

5 To Watch and Be Watched

Urban Design, Vigilance, and Contested Streets

A whole problematic then develops: that of an architecture that is
no longer built simply to be seen (as with the ostentation of palaces),
or to observe the external space (cf. the geometry of fortresses) but
to permit an internal, articulated and detailed control . . . The old
simple schema of confinement and enclosure—thick walls, a heavy
gate that prevents entering or leaving—began to be replaced by the
calculation of openings, of filled and empty spaces, passages and
transparencies.

—Michel Foucault, *Discipline and Punish*

The beating was halted by one of our neighbors who saw it from his
window and who, unconsciously certain that even at night he was part
of a web of strong street law and order, intervened.

—Jane Jacobs, *The Death and Life of
Great American Cities*

One of the most significant political implications of northeast Paris's ecological redevelopment was made clear to me during an interview with Matthieu, a DEVE administrator who was charged with managing the park's AAS (Agents d'Accueil et de Surveillance—welcoming and surveillance agents). When I asked him about the suitability of the Jardins d'Éole for securitization, he beamed at me proudly and pointed at his office roughly two hundred meters on the other side of the park from where we were standing. "From the moment I left my door," he said, "I saw you were here and could watch you the entire time I was walking over to meet you."

While many residents (including myself, upon first impression) had found
the Jardins d'Éole somewhat sparsely planted, it quickly became clear to me
that the "openness" of the park was not a matter of mere aesthetics but was
itself a surveillance tool. Indeed, it was a design feature I myself put to use
in my efforts at getting to know the daily routines of residents who used the
park. I learned that I could get a quick "snapshot" of who was doing what
in every section of the Jardins d'Éole in a walk-through of less than ten minutes; there were few nooks and crannies for anyone to hide in. It was clear
that the design team had not only put a tremendous amount of thought into
making the space interesting to look at, but had been equally expert at making the park amenable to the gaze of surveillance, be it that of an ethnographer or a security guard. While reminiscent of the cordon sanitaire, which
mobilizes nature and open space as a measure for security and purification,
the design of the Jardins d'Éole is oriented toward more incipient and com-
prehensive forms of social control based on vigilance and surveillance.

The sight lines of the Jardins d'Éole provide excellent views of what Jane Jacobs called
"the sidewalk ballet," while also situating visitors to the park in a web of mutual
surveillance. Note the number of people who are simply watching others in the picture.

It is tempting to situate the Jardins d'Éole as a powerful metaphor for the remaking of Paris—like many other global cities—into a surveillance city (and to do so would not be entirely incorrect). As this chapter shows, the design is heavily informed by anxieties over "delinquency" and an emphasis on securitization and vigilance. The Jardins d'Éole may have been intended by activists as a park for all of northeast Paris's residents, but it was also an effort to "pacify" the area, specifically by giving drug users and dealers no place to hide and making it too risky for them to operate in the open. It is both a public park *and* a securitization technology; but that is the beginning of the story, not the end.

Most accounts emphasizing the role of urban surveillance have dwelled on the top-down aspect of the "surveillance society."[1] Whether the concern is with technologies like closed-circuit television (CCTV) and biometrics or the urban design of streets and parks, urban surveillance is usually understood in the framework of the omnipotent panopticon, gazing down from the realms of power on high.[2] The boom in urban surveillance has been accompanied by a concurrent outpouring of critical literature detailing its emergence as part of a broader effort by neoliberal regimes to make once restive and impoverished districts safe for the burgeoning iPhone-toting urban middle classes now prevalent in many postindustrial cities worldwide. Urban surveillance intensified under the banner of antiterrorism since 9/11, but it was well under way in the 1990s in leading global centers like New York and, especially, London.

Indeed, in December 2011, Paris joined the growing number of cities employing police-operated open-street CCTV systems. As is in other places, the arrival of so-called *vidéoprotection* produced a litany of protest equating electronic surveillance with the enclosure of the democratic commons.[3] In Paris, concerns over CCTV carry added weight because the streets occupy a symbolic place in a national tradition of radical protest that can be traced from the French Revolution, through the Commune, to the May '68 uprising. However, the outpouring of concern over CCTV belies the fact that other forms of enclosure are well under way in Paris. The installation of cameras is an act of undoubted legal, practical, and symbolic importance, but the neoliberalization of the city is an ongoing social and political process that precedes any one policy.

This chapter takes the focus off of the electronic technologies behind surveillance and instead pulls from an analysis of the Jardins d'Éole's design process, ethnographic accounts of neighborhood activists, and the everyday experiences of residents. It draws a picture that goes beyond top-down notions of urban surveillance, suggesting that the park is only part of northeast Paris's broader transformation into a "surveillance city." This transformation is described less accurately by the commonly invoked panopticon metaphor than it is by Foucault's description of disciplinary architecture's ultimate goal: the making of the disciplined (and disciplining) subject. As Foucault argues, that ultimate project is not only to "render visible" but to "transform individuals," or, in other words, "to carry the effects of power right to them, to make it possible to know them, to alter them".[4] The disciplinary architecture of the Jardins d'Éole is an eloquent example of this process, but it is only part of a regime of vigilance that pervades the daily life of northeast Paris residents, as well as urban design and the political practices of activists.

In the context of vigilance, watching takes place not only from the top down but from side to side, and from the bottom up. In fact, watching and being watched are an indispensable part of daily life in northeast Paris, particularly in the tense atmosphere following the *banlieue* uprisings of 2005 and the subsequent immigration crackdown that began under the administration of Nicolas Sarkozy (a trend that eased under the Hollande administration, only to be replaced by an emphasis on "security zones" in cities).[5] Police, park security, and a host of other government authorities as varied as public-health and urban-planning agencies monitor northeast Paris and its residents, but residents also watch each other.

Power, however, does not flow through subjects so easily without being diverted, and at times subverted. Residents also survey their surveyors and engage in "watching" for a host of different reasons and political projects. For some, this everyday watching is an extension of the efforts of the powerful; for others, it is done to preempt it, or resist it, and for those in the most precarious situations (especially those who are extremely poor or possesses an "irregular" immigration status), it is simply a means of everyday survival. But what this chapter makes clear is that the "surveillance city" is marked not merely by the presence of an electronic surveillance apparatus, mobilized by governing regimes who favor police, CCTVs, and security-oriented urban design. There is, in fact, a deeper, more insidious set of political practices that include a pervasive degree of complicit surveillance. These practices include residents watching residents, but also countersurveillance and watching as a tool of survival that is a crucial part of everyday life in northeast Paris.

Urban design and the emergence of political subjectivities oriented toward watching are linked to the neoliberal remaking of the urban commons. Urban design concerned with what I term "vigilant citizenship" draws from and seizes upon the insurgent tradition of street democracy in Paris. Through the promise of local autonomy and in keeping with an ethos of grassroots civism, vigilant citizenship delegates the managerial responsibility of creating and overseeing a "successful" public space to residents, even though actual political power remains with the state. In Paris, a "successful" public space is subjectively defined by municipal authorities as marked by conviviality and civility and not delinquency.[6] In the climate of contemporary French politics, these are highly loaded ideological terms that pivot squarely around the degree to which a space is perceived as controlled by youths of Maghrebi and West African descent. Such polemics provide an urban counterpart to republican concerns over a supposedly neutral public sphere being appropriated by a particular sect or "non-French" group—the same concerns animating debates over the wearing of Islamic headscarves in schools and the burka in public spaces. Despite the fact that these debates are articulated through the idiom of France's republican cultural politics, the discourse is couched in sociospatial processes of exclusion and enclosure that are symptomatic of neoliberalization in cities around the world. Moreover, these linked shifts in political subjectivity and urban design operate in a more subtle and incipient fashion than mounting cameras on streetlights because the process appropriates a long tradition of radical street democracy.

Vigilant citizenship represents a departure from other established forms of watching and grassroots surveillance. Various types of neighborly vigilance such as Jane Jacobs's famous "eyes upon the street" have probably been vital to urban sociality as long as there have been neighborhoods.[7] However, if neighborhood associations carry out the ideological projects of the state—while explicitly rejecting the authority of the state in favor of local autonomy—a shift in political subjectivities and in the role of the grassroots appears to be under way. As Ida Susser has pointed out, urban movements' orientation toward "collective consumption" and the use-value of urban space is transformed in the context of neoliberalization.[8] One feature of neoliberal governmentality is that "grassroots" organizations are increasingly supplanting the managerial function of states.[9] In this case, residents adopt the language and practice of managerialism and entrepreneurialism to depoliticize a deeply political question: whether immigrant-origin youth have access to Paris's public spaces, and thus whether they are "compatible" with membership in the French republic. This adoption of managerial ideals to depoliticize the political is a microlevel equivalent to an approach used in neoliberal urban policy.[10] Moreover, as a neoliberal "class strategy," vigilant citizenship has the potential to serve as a political wedge between middle-class residents (who make up the majority of association membership) and low-income residents (especially the immigrant-origin youths and their families) who are jointly but unevenly affected by social, economic, and environmental degradations that impact northeast Paris as a whole.[11] As a result, it has the potential to weaken coalitions that are already threatened by a broader ongoing process of dispossession: the gentrification of Paris's formerly working-class districts.

However, neighborhood association members—many of whom are astute lifelong activists—are often highly aware of the political implications of their actions. As residents and association members, they are neither passive "users" of urban design nor mindless appendages of a homogenized neoliberal body politic. Residents often perform a delicate balancing act in which they test the trust of politicians and agencies (who tend to favor more control and repressive measures) and their own confidence in the youths' "civility" (and who respond, in turn, with their own territorial practices) by "managing" space but resisting the obligation to exclude outright. As with other architectural features, a "built-in" political subjectivity can be subverted, changed, and utilized as a means to disrupt the dominant ideology. Paris's urban commons may be subject to varying forms of enclosure, but residents—and neighborhood associations in particular—remain in the role of gatekeeper.

My choice of the term "vigilance" is meant to distinguish between different types of monitoring. If surveillance may be understood as a way to "render visible" certain objects to power, allowing power to "act on" subjects and objects in Foucauldian terms, vigilance is a more vague and undetermined form of social practice. It can be an indispensable part of resisting power through countersurveillance (through the idea of a "lookout"), but to "keep watch" is also to claim territory for any number of projects that can be complicit, oppositional, or ulterior to those embarked upon by agents of "official" surveillance. In contrast to formal surveillance, people remain vigilant for themselves, their friends, and their interests, in pursuit of goals that don't simply further the interests of dominant regimes or diametrically oppose it either. Vigilance is therefore necessary for the reproduction of an urban commons, but it can also erode it if it becomes a means of class-based, gendered, or ethnoracial exclusion.

Northeast Paris's political history during the 2000s suggests that the emergence of so-called vigilance must be contextualized. Around the world, urban areas, especially neighborhoods inhabited by the working class and the poor, have long displayed varying forms of "street-corner" sociality and self-regulatory, territorial surveillance. However, vigilant citizenship in northeast Paris is partially a legacy of the Sarkozy era, which brought with it a focus on an immigrant population, as well as longer-standing efforts to police "youth delinquency" and "quality-of-life"–related crime. Sarkozy's administration set quotas for mass deportations of immigrants in "irregular" status, and over the length of his term the number of expulsions rose rapidly, from 24,000 in 2006, to 28,000 in 2010, to more than 36,000 in 2012.[12] Not only have these measures driven out many undocumented persons, but it has likely increased the number who seek shelter in the "shadow market" of overcrowded, deteriorated apartments in centrally located neighborhoods such as northeast Paris, as the multitude of apartments in older working-class neighborhoods are more difficult to surveil than the commuter lines connecting the *banlieue* to the city center. Northeast Paris has long been subject to pressure by a range of authorities, but these particular measures intensified the extent to which the area became a hotbed of both police surveillance and suspicious countersurveillance and territoriality by residents seeking to protect themselves and their friends and kin. The surveillance of persons in "irregular status" is concurrent and overlapping with a less publicized but significant push to evict and clear residences used as squats and "insalubrious housing," as well as with long-standing programs to combat "delinquency" among youths living in such "sensitive urban zones."

As this chapter demonstrates, the streets, sidewalks, and parks that are the focal point of this intensified surveillance are not only passively being watched. Indeed, northeast Paris is actively transformed by vigilant citizenship, as the area becomes host to a range of projects of complicit co-surveillance, countersurveillance, and even divergent alter-surveillances. Its effects are felt not only in the design of the Jardins d'Éole itself but in the way activists claim the "right to the city" and in the everyday lives of a diverse array of inhabitants from café owners to teenagers.

Under the Gaze of Experts:
Architects, Social Scientists, and Surveillance

When Socialist Party candidate Bertrand Delanoë was elected mayor in 2001, one of his first policy changes from the administration of Jean Tiberi was to recognize the Éole mobilzation's demand to build a park at the Cour du Maroc. In what was viewed as a new approach to urbanism in Paris, Delanoë's adjunct mayor of urbanism emphasized neighborhood-scaled projects for the capital over monumental, centrally located landmarks favored by his predecessors. The gesture was as much a symbolic recognition that a new era had arrived in Paris as it was a political calculation. Delanoë, the first left-wing politican to be elected in the city's modern history, owed an electoral debt to left-wing bastions such as the northeast part of the city, and he had begun his own public career in a nearby neighborhood of the eighteenth arrondissement. The Jardins d'Éole represented an ideal project for him to support as it demonstrated a legitimization of grassroots politics in the city's left-leaning neighborhoods, embraced environmentalism and sustainable development, and impacted an area that had been neglected under previous administrations.

Any ideological gestures toward grassroots involvement in this so-called *quartier difficile* did not, however, diminish the questions of security and surveillance that whirled around the project from the start. The site of the future Jardins d'Éole lay at a street corner that authorities regarded as an epicenter of the crack-cocaine economy in the city at the time. The question of how to secure the new park was therefore sensitive. Delanoë held a "pro-camera" position on surveillance in general that was contentious within the left-wing coalition that governed the city's arrondissements and councils. Green Party candidates were already using the issue to threaten to unseat Socialists in the lower echelons of city government (including that of northeast Paris itself). Two other options were settled upon by the mayor's office and the parks department (the DEVE) to manage the space in a social sense. These measures would be the architecture itself, and, to the surprise of many, ethnography, in the form of what would be called a "mission sociologique" or "accompagnement sociologique" (literally, an ethnographic mission, or accompaniment) whose task would be to assist in the process of designing the park for the neighborhood in question.

It is likely that the winning design for the park was chosen in no small measure because of its surveillance-friendly nature. Ultimately, the jury, which, in addition to the mayor's office and DEVE officials, included a sociologist and a member of the Éole mobilization, chose a design that was submitted by a team led by the architecture studio of Claire and Michel Corajoud, Georges Descombes, and the firm ADR (Atelier Descombes Rampini). A number of features of the Éole plan were unique and well liked by the jury. According to one jury member, the first and foremost advantage of the Éole plan (then still called the Parc de la Cour du Maroc) was the "simplicity" of the design. In contrast to complex and intricate pieces of landscaping submitted by several competitors, this plan was easy to read and "legible" from the point of view of jurors and potential users. It divided the park into three easily discernible zones: a great lawn at the park's southern end, a set of terraced paths and athletic areas at the north end, and an esplanade along the Rue d'Aubervilliers. It was not crowded with trees and myriad enclosures but instead favored large, somewhat monolithic expanses granting a large degree of visibility and openness throughout the design. Indeed, the proposal itself often deployed terms such as "simple space" and "open space" as key concepts.

In many respects, the most distinctive aspect of the design was the esplanade. The esplanade operated as the expression of several linked concepts. It was to be an open, concrete-and-gravel expanse that ran along the park's eastern flank. Other than a small booth to sell refreshments and some scattered trees, it offered unobstructed views into the park. This design was at

odds with many plans for the park articulated by residents, who often imagined "lush gardens" full of trees. However, when one strolls by the Jardins
d'Éole as it was built, one finds no lush forest, but instead scattered trees,
which do little to block a wide-open vista across concrete and grass exposing the vast majority of the space. This relative degree of minimalism allows
the passerby, whether a prospective park visitor or a police officer on patrol,
to fully see into and know the space. Most, but not all, activity within the
park is visible from the street.

A more surprising design decision, given the park's location at a street
corner infamous for drug activity, was the choice of leaving the esplanade
ungated (and therefore open at all hours), making it unique in Paris's parks
system. This idea brought together a way of playing with the park's edges
("an edge that is porous and alive," according to an architect) with the idea
of the design as a kind of dialogue with inhabitants. The esplanade was
described as "ultra-public" and "ultra-domestic" because it was open, and yet
it was meant to serve as an extension of the domestic spaces that many of
the crowded dwellings of the neighborhood lacked: this was to be the *espace
de vie* concept (space for living) realized in material form.

The design team found the esplanade to be a way to integrate several key
elements called for by Éole activists. First, the Corajoud-Descombes–ADR
team was the only one of the candidates to pay serious attention to the issue
of lighting, and in fact make use of it in a creative way (using different-
colored lights) that illuminated the area at night. Renderings of the space
depicted a bustling café and space that played host to neighborhood gatherings. This was to be the soul of the park as a "space for living," as it was imagined in the Corajoud-Descombes–ADR concept, but it would also prove to
be the most complicated area of the park to plan and manage, at the political,
social, and administrative level.

The other intervention with regard to questions of security was the role
of ethnographers. Urban sociologists were included as key parties to the
project (along with the DEVE and the architects), meaning that their signature of approval would hold the same degree of legitimacy and authority as
that of the city and the architects. Such a step reinforces the perception that
the city had agreed with one of the Éole movement's key tenets: the building
of the new park was oriented toward the reconstruction of the neighborhood

in social and material aspects. It also indicated a remarkable legitimation of the value of ethnographic knowledge regarding urban design.

However, the unprecedented nature of this arrangement meant that the position of the sociologists in the design process would be somewhat improvised and defined while "on the job." Moreover, a sense of urgency was rooted in political pressures: the mayor's office sought to inaugurate the park at least six months before the next round of municipal elections, to be held in 2007.[13] As a result, the new team of sociologists had to join the planning effort in mid-stride, in a period where debates over the conceptual content of the park were eschewed for progress toward logistical and construction-related planning.

This politically driven reality immediately clashed with the initial goals of the sociologists, who sought an intervention into how the architects "translated the desires of the residents into the technical practices of creating the park." According to both sociologists, they became abruptly aware that a consensus had developed between the DEVE and the architects to move quickly. From the design team's point of view, "the dialogue with the sociologists was before, in the conceptual stage," and now there was a worry about the "risks of putting the project behind," according to one of the sociologists. He continued: "We decided on a strategy to work on the functioning of the park, and not on the design, because they wouldn't let us." A combination of chance and political developments thus produced a situation where formal ethnographic practice, already extraneous to an established process of design, was in danger of being pushed aside despite its official legitimation at the project's outset. The sociologists therefore found themselves in a less than enviable position: devising a novel form of intervention in a politically charged process that had already built momentum without them.

However, there was one section of the park that generated enough worry among planners that ethnographic knowledge was deemed conceptually and practically necessary. The esplanade was already, at a conceptual level, a difficult space for both the DEVE and the architects. It crossed a line that was rare in the Parisian tradition of public gardens: by being ungated, and open to the street at all hours, it violated norms common in every other Parisian park. But far more worrisome than any conceptual ambiguity (though perhaps not divorced from it, either) were the strong reservations voiced by some planners and policy makers based on the public presence of a drug economy (and specifically crack cocaine) here. The creation of an open, ungated plaza at this very spot would therefore be a surprising move for any city parks department, but especially for the DEVE, for which the boundaries between park and street are so crucial to the definition of urban parkland in Paris, and which had already encountered difficulties managing a nearby park in the area, the Square Léon (see chapter 3).

It was therefore in the context of security that the sociologists found themselves able to intervene with some undeniable effects, despite the rigid timetable. As one sociologist involved in the design stated:

At that point, everything I could say was a potential risk for questioning at least the design. I remember one time, at a meeting, I pointed to a mistake, and [one of the architects] was not happy that I saw that! It was on the esplanade ... in the design they had originally put the gate further into the park, and there was this dead space that was invisible from the street, but closed from the park at night. I pointed at that spot and I said to him, "If there is trouble, this is where it's going to start with drugs in that park." I thought I was playing my part around the esplanade because that's how I thought I had an "in." You wanted to keep it open, but everybody was scared. Everybody was afraid it was going to be a drug spot. The DEVE prepared small walls, so if there was a problem they could put up a chain-link fence in one night. So, I told him: "Well, if you want to make sure the space stays open and you want to make sure this is a safe space, one way for it to be safe is, first, don't create nooks and crannies, but also, let the people of the neighborhood be involved in the day-to-day workings of the space."

The esplanade revealed itself to be an opening for the sociologists to address the social concerns that seemed to defy easy architectural or administrative control. The esplanade was arguably the most public space in the Jardin d'Éole, and therefore it most represented the ideals of the campaign for the park. It was also, by no coincidence, the area least controlled by the DEVE, which was reluctant to completely relinquish it to "the public" by ungating it: thus the DEVE went so far as to build a foundation for a chain-link fence so that the area could be enclosed in short notice. The sociologists' recommendations were to make the area a gathering space for neighbor-hood residents and allow them to be involved in its day-to-day workings. This would be accomplished by creating a *buvette* (concession stand) man-aged by neighborhood associations, which would sell inexpensive drinks and food as part of an effort to animate the esplanade. Such measures would complement already-established modes of surveillance of parks that are orthodox in Paris, namely, that of the AAS (see chapter 6) and the special nature of parks as codified in formal rules of usage (see chapter 3).[14]

The DEVE and local politicians viewed the park with trepidation because the esplanade was directly adjacent to a street corner that was infamous for illegal drug peddling. However, it was the design team's contention that this vulnerability necessitated a radical rethinking of how to secure the space, given the failures of the nearby Square Léon. This argument, led by the design team and residents, ultimately prevailed, though the city of Paris's parks department (at that time known as the DPJEV) required that the foundation for a fence be added so that the area could be quickly sealed off if needed.[15] Residents argued that fencing would not be needed, as they would secure the space by "animating the esplanade" or organizing events there. This aspect of the design was supported by the sociologists as a way of retaining a tradition of popular control of the streets in the city's working-class neighborhoods, and it honored the spirit of the park mobilization by making it a "park for the residents." The design team also followed a logic adapted from Jane Jacobs's famous "eyes upon the street" argument: if resi-dents (instead of outside agents such as park guards or police) successfully populated and inhabited the space, they would create a social center that would displace "negative uses" (e.g., illegal drug activity). Thus, the plan for the esplanade combined what Jacobs called "do-it-yourself surveillance" with the ethos of the grassroots mobilization that had successfully won the park for the neighborhood.[16]

This gesture to local democracy and residents' autonomy also has the effect of building in a political subjectivity for residents as regulators of public space. Typically, the DEVE alone has been tasked with watching over and controlling the public in city parks. The Jardins d'Éole would only succeed as a social project if residents adopted this vigilant role. In Paris, where the urban fabric and the city's streets, sidewalks, and public spaces are routinely conflated with national space, "delinquency," and "civility," and are often viewed as threatening the republican order, "built-in" vigilance has an important bearing on the ways that citizenship and national belonging are practiced, articulated, and defined.[17] The question that remains is how well residents would play the role of vigilant citizens and how their actions would impact the youths who actually used the park the most.

Thus, the most important design feature of the Jardins d'Éole was the idea of "built-in" vigilant citizenship that focused on the esplanade. It is a radical departure from the DEVE's traditional emphasis on gating and temporal control, as it gives residents both freedom and responsibility with regard to boundary making.

Vigilance as Neoliberal Citizenship Practice

Over the course of my fieldwork, I attended numerous meetings with association members and spent hundreds of days on the esplanade in the company of both activists and the young people who are the primary users of the space. I observed how the micropolitics of the urban commons became a way that ordinary Parisians intervened in national belonging and the redefinition of citizenship, in a manner that followed a neoliberal logic. The mechanism by which residents are tasked with vigilance is an extension of an established "citizenship practice": engagement with neighborhood associations.[18] The Jardins d'Éole demonstrates that this role of citizenship can be "built into" an urban park in an attempt to control the urban commons in several ways.

First, vigilant citizenship is articulated through language and practices emphasizing urban managerialism and entrepreneurialism. Indeed, residents sought to "manage" the urban commons as a business through a plan calling for the establishment of a resident-operated *buvette* (concession stand) in the esplanade. The *buvette* was intended by the architect as an activity center to attract users into the park, create a social center, and give neighborhood associations a well-defined role in the everyday operation of the park. Initially, association members embraced the plan as a way to attract residents to the park, employ youth from the neighborhood, and involve residents in the life of the space. However, the logistical demands and financial strain of running the *buvette* proved difficult, even for the national-level NGO that

Friday afternoon at the Jardins d'Éole esplanade.

ultimately funded and organized the actual operation. In the first two years of the park's existence (2007–9), meetings to address the *buvette*'s struggling finances became an unexpected and demanding commitment as well as a source of tension and disunity between the neighborhood association's members. While the *buvette*'s survival remains uncertain, it undoubtedly immersed association members in the language and logic of management in a broader sense. Members spoke about their roles using the language of investment *(investir)*, management *(gérer)*, and self-management *(auto-gérer)* to describe their relationship to the space. Thus Paul once explained the Éole activists' constant emphasis on holding events by saying that "managing this open space is a very, very important issue." This language of entrepreneurialism and business permeates association members' articulations of their civic responsibilities. In Paris, where parks have been historically managed by the DEVE, the notion that the civic responsibility of citizens includes "managing" parks is a radical idea that threatens a core republican notion: public space as a common good furnished to all by the state. As in other neoliberal regimes, the language of management depoliticizes the redefinition of public space by rendering it a technical process that does not involve a change of power or control.

The notion of vigilance is central to understanding why managerialism is required of citizens: it is tied to a sense of urgency borne by threats. The great irony of the Jardins d'Éole esplanade is that citizens become "managers of space" to preempt the state from imposing its own forms of social control, which are perceived as drastic and unjust. In other words, the predominant residents must surveil their less privileged neighbors (and in particular the youth) in order to guarantee everyone a right to access the space. In the esplanade, the threat of enclosure from the DEVE literally came with a concrete reminder: a short one-meter-high mini-wall ran the perimeter of the space, to be used as a foundation for a fence that could be quickly installed if deemed necessary. Thus Tomi once described the "little wall" in starkly antiauthoritarian terms. During an interview held on the esplanade itself, he beckoned toward it, saying:

> Notice this little concrete wall there. Up until the last minute [before the inauguration of the Jardins d'Éole], that was the last big struggle we had, over the creation of that fence . . . after all, this is a neighborhood reputed for drug addiction and dealers, so it's a worry of certain people.

The threat of "that fence" was of tremendous importance to the association members, and resisting it was deemed the last "big struggle" of the campaign to build the park. That the residents imbued the fence with such deep political meanings is suggestive of multiple issues running to the heart of the contradictory social position of vigilant citizens. As already mentioned, the DEVE had been hesitant to leave the esplanade open because this was a break with a standard policy dictating how parks were controlled *and* the space was located next to a known hub for illegal drug sales. For residents, the fence symbolized the official distrust of city officials toward the "public" of northeast Paris; it was viewed as physical evidence of the neighborhood's reputation for having a disorderly urban commons. It was a political barrier as well as a symbolic one because it would literally place the esplanade under the firm control of the DEVE, erasing the Jardins d'Éole's exceptionalism as a residents' park brought about by grassroots mobilization. The underlying danger, lurking behind the threat of top-down enclosure (and the symbolic erasure of street democracy) was the potential for "delinquency." This left the onus for preserving and controlling the urban commons on residents, and as a result, keeping the esplanade "open" became a secondary mobilization itself, an outgrowth of the original movement to build the park. Several members of the Éole mobilization now continued their work by addressing the threat of "drug dealers" by organizing events at the space and constantly socializing there on informal occasions as well. During a conversation about this offshoot of the original mobilization, Rachael once stated that construction of the Jardins d'Éole "is like a birth, in fact, the park is only just beginning." Her counterpart, Tomi, continued, "The preoccupation is not only the garden, in general, it is social; the inauguration of the new park was not the end for us." Seen in this light, the Jardins d'Éole takes on the air of a political project concerned with creating, regulating, and shaping a commons.

As a result of these concerns, a "collective" of associations was formed to discuss ways to "animate" the esplanade, with monthly children's activities and seasonal festivals for children being a central focus of the project. Although the organizers of these activities were predominately of French descent, a multiethnic collection of families often attended the events. Events catering to youth draw particularly large crowds of teenagers, a reflection of the high number of residents under the age of twenty-five. Association leaders often strove to maintain social inclusiveness while making sure there was a full agenda so that the esplanade was always buzzing with controlled activities. Instead of merely watching the space for "undesirables," residents practice vigilance by struggling in often tiresome and time-consuming efforts to conjure an idealized public to fill the space, month after month, lest "delinquents" appropriate it instead.

Many young people who find themselves the objects of this vigilance respond with their own practices of watching and territoriality, though the differing sociopolitical position of youths and association members marks this reciprocity as unbalanced. Regardless of the activities planned by the associations, young men of Maghrebi and West African descent are the main people who use the space on a day-to-day basis. While there are frequently fewer than a dozen youths present during weekdays, on weekends (especially

during the late hours) a large groups of friends more than twice that number
gather at the space on many nights. Many youths would gather after association events had ended, and sit side by side along a wall affording them an
expansive view of the adjacent street. These late-night gatherings, which are
typically marked by little more than loud joking and the consumption of large
amounts soft drinks and cigarettes, nonetheless trigger suspicions and unease
by many residents and local shop owners. Police drive by the esplanade on
roughly half-hour intervals. The friends who spend time at the esplanade are
an informal social network who, like the associations, practice their own
forms of vigilance and territoriality. Despite the degree of suspicion that is
directed at these youngsters, it is likely that their nocturnal gatherings at the
park displace drug activity even more effectively than the daytime activities
of the associations and park guards. Nevertheless, vigilance takes on a far
more expansive meaning for many of these young men and boys, whose
compatibility with reified notions of French culture and republican citizenship is constantly being questioned and scrutinized (see chapters 4 and 6).

Children's activities at the Jardins d'Éole esplanade.

Surveillance and Ethnographic Encounters:
Everyday Life on the Rue d'Aubervilliers

Yet another layer of "street-corner" surveillance was revealed by my presence in northeast Paris. Interestingly, my position as an ethnographer often meant that encounters began by my having to explain my own obvious surveillance practices to residents. More than the presence of a notebook or camera, it seemed that the most disconcerting aspect of my presence to residents was that I had no place in certain contexts other than practicing surveillance in one form or another. This detached state, which was primarily a problem early in my fieldwork, attracted obvious attention in a community that was already vigilant because of immigration raids, police operations, and criminal activity. Being marked as white, middle-class, and male potentially led to skepticism by a few residents; but what led to far more difficult situations was simply a classic ethnographic practice: jotting in a notebook, asking questions, and being curious. As the following anecdotes show, all of which were collected on one block, I learned that it was possible to use my outward identity in a number of ways to "trip" alarm bells and elicit forms of territoriality that were both revealing and varied.

Although I often restrained myself from overly intrusive observations, I had a series of encounters provoked by my own ethnographic practices (i.e., surveillance), which in turn revealed the informal, street-corner surveillance of residents themselves. Many residents or local business owners appeared at first to embody what Jane Jacobs termed "eyes upon the street." But, in contrast to Jacobs's argument, I found that such watching is not simply an enactment of "neighborliness" or careful "looking out" for fellow members of a community. Numerous sociopolitical and often deeply ideological factors shape the meaning of watching as it is practiced by individuals. In some cases, these practices seemed to give the impression of agency by granting not only control of a territory but possible interventions in much larger issues.

At times, my appearance could elicit trust from French residents of European descent who held deep and angry prejudices against their Maghrebi and West African neighbors. Anthropologists, and in particular Verena Stolcke, may be right that culture has replaced race in many "official" discourses of difference and exclusion in postwar Europe.[19] However, in everyday life in northeast Paris, I found that my own phenotypic markers of "European" descent (despite being non-French) led several residents to reveal their xenophobic sentiments before they even knew my name, background, or political sentiments.

Indeed, it appeared that the willingness of such individuals to place their trust in me was directly related to a kind of weariness brought about from their own compulsions toward the surveillance of "others" in their midst. Claude, the French proprietor of a café on the Rue d'Aubervilliers appeared to be an extreme case of such paranoid watching. He frequently seemed overly happy to see me waiting at the polished zinc counter of his otherwise poorly kept establishment. A thin, wiry man who often appeared nervous and worried, he spoke of his business with great dread, fearing that he would be unable to make the payments to keep his café open for the remainder of the year. He had, in fact only been in northeast Paris for three years, having sold a previous establishment in Saint-Denis because, he said, the neighborhood had become too dangerous. Lured to northeast Paris by municipal subsidies for businesses in the area, he now felt that not only his business but the entire neighborhood was under threat by "delinquents" and "drug dealers." As a response, he had a battery of security cameras installed in the café and had himself taken to perching nervously behind his cash register; often warily eying the street even as he poured beers, coffees, and spoke to customers.

This constant surveillance was rooted in a venomous hatred of his Maghrebi and West African neighbors, despite the fact that he needed more of them as customers to survive. In fact, he constantly appeared to be on the verge of alienating the few immigrant-origin customers who did patronize his café, mostly for cigarettes, as his was the only licensed *tabac* or cigarette vendor on a block in a large *cité*. On occasion, he would greet my arrival with tirades of disparagement against "immigrants" and Muslims. More than once he said such things to me literally while serving Maghrebi and West African customers coffee or cigarettes (I thought it surprising he had any customers). His favorite refrain was "People say it is the extreme right who are racists, but really, the immigrants are the racists"—a quote borrowed from Jean-Marie Le Pen. He often assured me that I only disagreed with him because I had not spent enough time "in this neighborhood." He reserved particular animosity for teenage boys and young men.

On one memorable day, Claude seemed given to an almost pathological state of paranoia. I arrived to find him fixated on the sidewalk and passersby with a particularly acute level of worry and fear. Presently, a young West African teenager of about eighteen or nineteen years of age came strolling down the street dressed in a black leather baseball hat, leather jacket, and the designer jeans that were at their peak of popularity among Parisian youths at the time. Claude stared at the young man with suspicion; he even seemed to physically tense up as the youth stepped through the door and up to the register. He was, of course, buying cigarettes, and Claude indulged him. But when the young man casually stepped back outside in front of the café and with the habitual nonchalance of any smoker, tapped his fresh pack of Marlboros on the end and paused for a light, Claude lost it. Crying out to me, "Look! Now it is starting again!" he ran outside, and confronted the youth with the question: "What are you doing!?" The young man, who seemed neither surprised nor particularly threatened by Claude's inquisition, simply responded with a question: "Am I bothering you?" To this Claude responded angrily: "Get out of here!" And so off the young man walked, aloofly smoking his cigarette, having apparently cultivated a level of resilience to such treatment that I found difficult to fathom. Claude returned in a state of fury: he stated that it was the third time he had to chase away "drug dealers" on that day alone.

By this point in my fieldwork I had become very familiar with which street corners and at what times groups of men sold crack cocaine and heroin in this area, and I knew upon first glance that this young man was not involved in the drug economy. But I remained silent, nodded, and even got Claude to illustrate the northeast Paris he inhabited, as twisted as it may have been by paranoia, delusions, and gendered, ethnoracial, and class-based anxieties. "The police do nothing," he said, "and the people at the arrondissement say, 'Just wait, the neighborhood will improve.' But I won't last another year here." Still, after this incident, I found it increasingly difficult to visit Claude's establishment; and I worried that if others saw me with him or at his café, my relationships with them could be jeopardized. Nonetheless, his café did stay open, and upon my return trips to northeast Paris in later years, I noticed that the opening of the Le Centquarte contemporary art center on the Rue d'Aubervilliers had furnished him with nearly too many weekend customers to adequately serve. Apparently, he is now in northeast Paris to stay.

A few addresses down from Claude's café is a West African restaurant owned and operated by a woman named Aminata and her eldest daughter, Binata, who arrived from Senegal in the mid-1980s. Like Claude's, their establishment is in an ill state of repair, except that care has been taken to keep it clean and ordered; pictures almost conceal the cracked sections on the walls and vibrant dyed fabrics are draped over torn vinyl seats. Frequently, it too seemed empty; I never saw more than three of the dozen tables occupied in the small restaurant. And here too I was overcome by the role of watching in everyday life, but in a very different manner than that seen at Claude's. Aminata often stands beside the nearly always open door of the restaurant (frequently with a cigar in her mouth and clothed in a colorful caftan), greeting passing neighbors and watching the children of her friends and relatives play across the street in the esplanade of the Jardins d'Éole.

In many respects, she and her daughter fit the Jacobsian notion of "public characters" for the Rue d'Aubervilliers, but this watching is not simply about preserving "social harmony," nor is it tied to "law and order," at least not in any conventionally understood sense. Nor did their concerns, despite their restaurant being located directly on a corner associated with drug trafficking, have much to do with fears of "dealers" and drug users. Indeed, as Binata once told me when describing growing up in the restaurant, "I was scared of the 'druggies' as a little girl, but when I grew older I realized some of them were nice people, and some became our customers." The manner of watching practiced by Aminata is best illustrated by a second anecdote.

Early in my fieldwork, when I decided to stop in and eat at Aminata's restaurant for the first time, I became aware of the fact that it, like many other spaces associated with transient and poor populations, could quickly become one of tension, suspicion, and paranoia. I visited the restaurant soon after it opened for the day, right after sundown, as it was common for Aminata's to open late in the day and stay open into the early hours of the morning. That night, I would later learn, would be a typical one for the restaurant. When I arrived, there were only a half-dozen other people there, all of whom were together at a table in the rear of the restaurant watching a televised *laamb* wrestling match live from Dakar via satellite.

Aminata was very friendly upon my arrival but had no menu to offer me. She seemed genuinely surprised that I intended to order a meal and offered "meat and rice" as the sole dining option before sending a somewhat annoyed-looking Binata away from a table full of friends into the kitchen to prepare me dinner. Despite her outward hospitality, I had the distinct feeling she would not mind my leaving at all. I then noticed a lanky middle-aged man of West African descent in jeans and a T-shirt take a step up to the door, see me, awkwardly stop short, and step back toward the curb in a poorly executed act of fake nonchalance. He stayed outside for a while, peering in toward Aminata until they made eye contact. One of the men with Aminata then rose from his table, went outside, had a lengthy discussion with the man in front of the restaurant, and then returned to retrieve a brown paper bag from the back of the restaurant, which he delivered to the man outside. More people, all of whom were Wolof speakers, came into the restaurant through-out the night, with the vast majority not staying but nervously waiting about while Aminata gave them brown paper bags, or merely saying "hello." Despite Aminata's friendliness, I knew my presence generated suspicion—and even stress. Even though people seemed to relax later in my stay—a bottle of liquor and a pack of cigarettes was produced from one of the brown paper bags in front of me—I felt dismay at my having disrupted a clandestine routine.

Over time I would learn that Aminata's was less a restaurant in the classic sense than a gathering place for a network of West African, and specifically Wolof-speaking, migrants. It survived, despite elevating rents, not by serving food but by illegally selling cigarettes, single drinks, or the occasional bottle of rum or whiskey to a clientele who resided in the apartment buildings nearby. Indeed, Aminata's place was something like a collective living room and dining room for an overcrowded, exhausted group of migrants, many of whom were men. More than a few of the regular clientele, like Moussa, the man who was too paranoid to enter the restaurant the first time he saw me in it, share single studios with as many as half a dozen roommates and relax at Aminata's table after their late shifts have ended, while waiting for room-mates to leave a bed free for them to sleep in. The watching, nervousness, and paranoia are partially to safeguard the "informal" sale of cigarettes and alcohol that permits survival of the restaurant. But an even greater source of tension comes from the fact that places like Aminata's are nodes serving as an indispensable, but hidden and carefully watched and guarded, type of "commons" for individuals in irregular immigration status whose movements are increasingly at risk. Indeed, local associations of *sans-papiers* report an arrest of a local worker nearly once a week. More than ever, as France continues to deport scores of immigrants, the undocumented live under the constant threat of detention. For several people I met, even the fact that I was non-French did little to alleviate their suspicion of me, so great was their vulnerability. Aminata herself is a naturalized French citizen, as is her daughter. But individuals such as her function as "eyes upon the street" *against* the forces of "law and order," on behalf of their neighbors. Strictly speaking, she and her daughter are the matriarchs and custodians not so much of a city block, but of a network of transient, precariously employed, and mostly male workers.

Yet another example of such encounters occurred the first time I met three young men: Ziad, Danko, and Munir, who would later become acquaintances. I had just left an interview in a building nearby, and while running through details of the meeting in my head, I decided to pause on the Jardins d'Éole to write down my thoughts. I began jotting in my notes feverishly, hoping to make sure I recorded several key impressions, and then hurry home for dinner. After a few moments, I became aware that someone was standing over me. Without realizing it, I had sat down directly across from a couple of young men who had been sitting on the inside wall of the esplanade, probably watching the street. They likely had watched me scribble notes, and perhaps vacantly stare at the street in thought, for several minutes. One of them, a very youthful-looking teenager of Maghrebi descent, abruptly asked me: "What are you writing?" I tried to answer the question as if it was posed casually, or out of curiosity, but it was in fact put forward quite aggressively, almost as a challenge. I said that I was writing notes about my work and I that was a researcher. The next question was—as is often the case—about my accent ("Yes, it's American, not English"), which led to a domino-like series of further interrogations. The questions were aggressive enough to make me uncomfortable—otherwise I would have welcomed our discussion. Taking my notebook from me, one of the young men flipped through it, and then began to scribble in it, while he related to me a bit about himself. This was Ziad, twenty-one years of age, born in Morocco, and he lived with his mother and younger sister directly across the street. Just when I thought he was feeling more comfortable with me, however, he abruptly showed me what he had drawn: an unflattering portrait of me, wearing a hat marked "FBI." "Voilà!" he said. "This is you." The implication was clear: I was a cop, or worse, a kind of unspecified American agent.

At this point he beckoned other young men about his age to come over and join us—his brother Munir and Danko, who was of Serbian origin (he had arrived with his family as war refuges in 1994). Both were a little wary of me but clearly lacked his sense of dissatisfaction at my presence, and told me about where their families were from upon hearing that I was writing about the neighborhood. Ziad then grew angrier, and in an animated, gesturing performance in front of his friends, he began to pepper me with condemnations of the American invasion of Iraq. It mattered little to Ziad that I expressed agreement with most of what he said. The point was that he had caught me here, in the esplanade, a territory that was definitively his. For him, I was American Empire in person—the flesh-and-blood representation of something he clearly harbored a deep disgust for but had apparently only known until now in an abstract form. At one point, when a tall, bearded Maghrebi man, wearing a *taqiyah* and flowing robe passed us by, it prompted him to yell out, mockingly, "Look! There is Osama bin Laden! That's incredible! Go back and tell the Americans that Osama is in Stalingrad!" Then, in his most intense expression of his aggressiveness toward me, he produced a small pocketknife and said, "I detest your president, Bush." He made a swiping gesture in the air, adding, "I will cut your Bush/mouth" ("Je vais vous couper la Bush")—a pun that switched the word *mouth* or *bouche* with "Bush." While doing this, it was clear, he was strutting the stage, so to speak, in front of his friends. After about ten minutes of my trying to defuse the situation with a combination of calm reassurance and somewhat forced humor, he closed the folding knife and then, in a strange gesture that combined intimidation with a sense of trust, handed it to me (not to keep, just to "hold" and "see"). Ziad and Danko would end up being the local esplanade youths whom I knew best, though his pocketknife gesture defined our relationship. We trusted each other in the area when it was otherwise filled with strangers, but because of Ziad's mercurial personality, I never felt fully at ease with him, and I suspect he was never certain that I was an entirely benign presence, either.

What is clear in hindsight, however, is the ease in which highly localized, individual expressions of territoriality and surveillance can lead to articulations of resistance against incredibly global geopolitical regimes such as the war on terror. Simultaneously, the same encounter seemed to betray the emotions of helplessness and frustration of individuals who feel oppressed by such powers, who are left literally swiping the air in futile anger. Ziad's vigilance, though articulated through a highly localized encounter in the esplanade of the Jardins d'Éole, was nonetheless mobilized to represent a global community of Muslims who are united not by a theological orthodoxy or shared degree of piety (Ziad enjoyed alcohol, for example), but rather by their status as subjects of Islamophobic suspicions and surveillance. Vigilance is thus not only about the maintenance of urban commons in a localized sense, but about the protection of much broader communities as well.

Conclusion

Urban surveillance does not merely have the effect of making contested spaces more closely watched; it can fundamentally alter social relations in such places as well. Indeed, my experience in northeast Paris suggests that watching begets watching. From the design of urban parks to everyday life in its cafés and squares, interactions in Paris are deeply shaped by vigilant citizenship as a form of a social practice. Jane Jacobs's "eyes upon the street" idea is a widely embraced notion for what constitutes everyday vigilance in dense urban settings like Paris, but her explanation—an essentially functionalist theory based on the maintenance of social equilibrium—misses an obvious aspect of such practices in northeast Paris. People, it turns out, watch each other from socially asymmetrical, historically rooted, and often deeply ideological positions. These highly varied forms of vigilance are arguably more pervasive than the mere presence of security cameras, two of which were installed on streets adjacent to the Jardins d'Éole in 2011 and which few people ever seem to mention or acknowledge.

However, another even more incipient form of spatial control has been incorporated in the grassroots political landscape of northeast Paris with the construction of the Jardins d'Éole. In the context of urban neoliberalization, neighborhood movements often take on ambiguous political implications compared to urban movements of previous eras.[20] The mobilization to build the Jardins d'Éole captures the uncertainty of grassroots politics in the neoliberal era. In one respect, the protest movement sought to create a space of collective consumption for northeast Paris and reverse a land-use pattern toward use-value rather than exchange value. At the same time, the design of the park implicated residents' associations in processes of social control previously associated with the state. Under the guise of grassroots democracy, what Jacobs called "do-it-yourself surveillance" requires that residents take part in the reproduction of a spatial regime of control and assume responsibilities normally associated with the state, which in this case involves defining and delimiting the proper public in a city park.[21] Vigilant citizenship substitutes one of the key tenets of republicanism, namely, the state as a guarantor of equal rights for the public, and places a privileged, exemplary set of citizens in that role instead. This idea threatens a cornerstone of republicanism (the idea of the state as arbiter of the public) and suggests that a neoliberal logic is gaining ground in France and is redefining how the (re)public is constituted and reproduced.

Thus, the redesign of urban public space can be used to cultivate a form of "vigilant citizenship" in the context of urban neoliberalization. Struggles over the control of urban commons are probably as old as the city itself, but this particular form of contestation is steeped in neoliberal ideals: the creation of a managerial, vigilant citizenry that assumes the social responsibilities of the state while still being subject to its oversight and power. Numerous methods of enclosure mark the era of the neoliberal city, including the legal redefinition of public space, the creation of gated communities, and the power of electronic surveillance to enable the social "sorting" of access to urban space. The role that regular citizens play in this process has been generally assumed either to be passive recipients of surveillance or to protest against it. The idea that citizens, as well as the institution of citizenship itself, could become incorporated into processes of neoliberal enclosure in the city has been less explored; vigilant citizenship captures the ambiguous role that residents play in this process as gatekeepers. While contestation surrounding the Jardins d'Éole is immersed in the ethnoracial and class-based politics of urban France, the increasing involvement of residents in "managing" parks and public spaces in other cities leads to the open question of whether vigilance as a form of citizenship can be seen in other contexts.[22]

This should not be surprising given what is known about the relationship between neoliberalism, cities, and citizenship. In urban contexts, neoliberalization is often thought about as a repressive force associated with militarized policing, surveillance, the penal state, gated communities, and other forms of enclosure. As dramatic as such demonstrations of power may be, we must also remember to emphasize the capacity of many regimes to create while—and perhaps through—enacting forms of enclosure. Citizenship is one of the most important forms of enclosure available to the modern state, and its redefinition has already been crucial to the neoliberal project in other contexts.[23]

The esplanade maintains its inclusive quality at the discretion of neighborhood associations. Young people contest the association's control of the esplanade indirectly through claiming it as their own territory, but if the relationship between the predominately middle-class activists and the youth soured, their right to simply be in public space could be infringed.[24] Vigilance is a privilege and a burden: the middle-class residents' right to the city is subject to a logic of accountability in controlling the rights of less privileged subjects; their own freedoms rest on their careful surveillance of others.

It is tempting to view the 2011 arrival of CCTV as the start of a brave new world, spelling the end the urban commons in Paris. But the struggle over the right to the city has long been central to a dialectical process of capitalist urbanization, and contestations over the urban commons change form as quickly as the city itself.[25] The image of the partially built wall that encircles the Jardins d'Éole esplanade is an instructive one in this regard. In the process of neoliberalization, residents become compelled to become part of an extension of a disciplinary apparatus through a reworking of citizenship responsibilities. It would, however, be a mistake to assume that they are a mere component of disciplinary architecture. As the case of the Jardins d'Éole shows, city dwellers possess the power to reimagine and reappropriate the function and meaning of the city merely by occupying and using it. Regardless of what technologies are appropriated to subdivide, control, and enclose, residents remain the gatekeepers to the urban commons.

6 The Political Life of Small Urban Spaces

Fear proves itself.

—William H. Whyte, *The Social Life of Small Urban Spaces*

The global economic crisis that began in the United States in 2008 and reverberated throughout the EU in the early 2010s has severely impacted France, where unemployment rose from 7 to 10 percent between 2008 and 2013.[1] The everyday reality of this downturn is especially visible in the Jardins d'Éole. The park increasingly functions as a shelter for the homeless as well as for international refugees, a place of respite for the unemployed, and an important node in a growing informal economy, the participants in which range from rag sellers to crack-cocaine dealers. An end result of these transformations has been the unraveling of the uneasy détente that seemed to exist between residents, the diverse groups of people who use the space, and those charged with its social control, a group that includes both the state and, as mentioned in the last chapter, residents themselves. Increasingly, public authorities including the DEVE and the police play a heavy-handed role in regulating space through conspicuous displays of force and surveillance, as well as the occasional clampdown.[2] This contestation, which often entails competing efforts to reframe the meaning of the boundaries between public and private, illustrates much about the political life of urban spaces as a form of commons.

In many respects, these dynamics were under way before the crisis "officially" began. I begin by recounting an incident that occurred during an early part of my fieldwork in 2007. On a cold day in December, about fifty protesters gathered in the esplanade of the Jardins d'Éole for a demonstration. Most were women of West African and Maghrebi descent, and several carried or wore infants. They had arrived to call public attention to the plight of those affected by unjust housing conditions, and in particular the situation at an *hôtel meublé* (single-room-occupancy hotel) called the Hôtel Chartres, which had recently caught fire, injuring two people, one seriously.[3] After the fire, the occupants of the hotel, who included forty-three adults and ten children, were evacuated by the city. For a day, the families were caught in a bureaucratic quagmire waiting to be rehoused. Many had little choice other than to wait in the cold December rain on the Jardins d'Éole esplanade until, in a vivid display of the Janus-faced qualities of the welfare state, they were forcefully evacuated by a combination of social workers and riot police. Because the vast majority of the families were part of the clandestine world of undocumented migrants and refugees, the fire had the effect of rendering visible the often hidden victims of social suffering. As a result, protesters affiliated with the national-level housing rights movement called DAL (Droit au Logement) arrived at the esplanade days later to renew the visibility of this often private form of suffering as part of their broader call for political change throughout France.

The Hôtel Chartres fire was anything but exceptional in Paris's recent history. Fires in the city's numerous *hôtels meublés* had begun to take on added meaning in the mid-2000s following a horrendous tragedy in which twenty-three people died (ten of whom were children) in the Hôtel Paris Opéra. Despite its location in one of the city's fashionable districts, the "hotel" was part of large network of domiciles used by social-service agencies to house refugees and undocumented people awaiting the outcome of deportation and asylum hearings. The tragedy therefore shed light on two ironic and important facts. First, France's most impoverished and precarious families were housed in scandalous conditions, just out of sight of wealthy neighbors in the heart of the capital, and in growing numbers.[4] Second, the state was complicit in this social suffering by relying on (and therefore aiding the reproduction of) this shadow economy of often poorly regulated hotels. As a social space, the hotels function as temporary zones of social abandonment, and are evidence of the socially unsustainable production of gendered, class-based, and ethnoracial inequalities within Paris that marked the period "before" the officially declared crisis started, and foreshadowed what soon came to pass.[5] The protest at the Jardins d'Éole was part of a series of demonstrations carried out by DAL. The demonstrators carried signs demanding justice for housing and a DAL organizer delivered a speech in which he described the horrid conditions in the hotel and the exploitative rents of more than five hundred euros a month that the residents paid. In one respect, the speeches, chants, and signs gave the action the appearance of a "traditional" protest that used public space as a site of political expression. At the same time, like many housing-rights protests, including a similar one held at the Jardins d'Éole inauguration, the sight of numerous women taking care of infants within the protest itself made it a spectacle of displaced, unhoused bodies. By literally placing what is often viewed as the domestic "nonpublic" work of child care in the street, the protest also sought to politicize the personal and render visible a private, gendered, and often individualized form of suffering experienced by families.

Because the protest took place on a Saturday afternoon, many people from the surrounding apartments and businesses were out and about and had gathered on sidewalks, doorstops, and glared down from windows at the demonstration. I was at the esplanade at the time, and along with a few other bystanders, walked over to the edge of the protest, "waiting in the wings," so to speak, but not joining outright. No one in this tight-knit community was acquainted with the protesters, and the individuals who had been affected by the fire were not present; the demonstrators were mobilized by DAL largely from outside of northeast Paris, and they arrived as a group. This created a curious juxtaposition in that many of the spectators were acquainted with the victims of the fire, but no one knew the demonstrators who had come to protest on their behalf.

On the other hand, nearly everyone who lives in this neighborhood knew the owners of the Hôtel Chartres. In contrast to their tenants, for whom transience is a condition of social precariousness, the owners are a couple who had lived in the hotel for nearly forty years. As with many owners of *hôtels meublés,* Tariq (who goes by the de-Arabicized moniker Ricky) and his spouse Fauzia were part of an earlier, now more economically established wave of immigrants who leveraged networks in Paris and the home country (in this case, Algeria) to draw income from new migrants as well as those being processed by public agencies. The austere first-floor lobby of the Chartres was a popular pseudopublic space in the neighborhood where many Maghrebi residents (tenants and nontenants alike) gathered to watch Arabic-language soap operas and soccer matches on satellite television. Ricky also fancied himself as informal "proprietor" of the neighborhood's public spaces and sidewalks (he is quick to inform anyone he meets that he has extensive training in karate). He often passed the days at his front-door entrance, keeping an eye on the street at all times, functioning as a classic example of a Jacobsian "public figure" on the Rue d'Aubervilliers.

However, when Ricky and Fauzia came to their front window and saw the protesters angrily shouting at them from across the street, none of these many acquaintances and neighbors came to offer them support. Everyone appeared to gather along the sidewalks or around the esplanade. A number of people found the most comfortable vantage point to be from nearby the protest, and some, including Tomi and several Éole activists, appeared to orbit it nervously, while trying not to appear part of it. Certainly, nobody made the important gesture of crossing the street to Ricky and Fauzia's side. It seemed that everyone wanted to be privy to what we all sensed was about to occur but no one wanted to be publicly seen expressing outright allegiance. And from here we watched a drama unfold that demonstrated the ways activists manipulate the boundaries of public and private as a form of direct action, which in this case led to the closing of one of northeast Paris's oldest and longest-running *hôtels meublés*.[6]

At first, the demonstrators' speeches and chants appeared to be largely directed toward their fellow protesters and perhaps us bystanders. But after a DAL activist had spent several minutes decrying the "inhumane" conditions at the Chartres, Fauzia emerged from inside with her sister and crossed the street to confront the crowd. The dynamic changed irrevocably and the atmosphere boiled with a sense that anything was possible. A loud face-to-face shouting match ensued. Suddenly, in a fast blur of movement, a younger man from the protest, his arm raised high above his head, flew through the crowd directly into the two women from the hotel. The entire gathering of demonstrators surged forward with his motion, seemingly in a kind of collective reflex, and then listed backward. I had difficulty seeing clearly what happened next; the protest transformed instantly before my eyes from people standing around chanting and holding signs to a tangle of arms and legs, contorted faces, watery eyes, and crying voices. There was much pushing and shoving. Some of the women with infants managed to extract themselves from the scrum, but otherwise the mass of bodies grew more compact and tense. Ricky appeared from the hotel, ran across the street and into the maelstrom of bodies. Just when I was certain a horrendous melee would ensue, he reappeared, now with Fauzia and her sister, and the three moved quickly across the street looking utterly broken, and retreated back into the Hôtel Chartres. The demonstrators quickly returned to form, and their leader—who I would soon learn was one of DAL's highest-ranking organizers—called on the group to march to the *mairie* of the nineteenth arrondissement. Away they went, chanting, clapping, and singing. A moment later, the esplanade and surrounding streets were calm and quiet, as if nothing had happened.

In fact, something momentous had just occurred. When I turned to leave after the confrontation, I saw Tomi, Paul, and many of the Éole activists. Aminata, Binata, and numerous teenagers and young people had also gathered to watch. Nearly everyone who lived and spent time on the Rue d'Aubervilliers had been there. It was the eyes of all these neighbors that ultimately proved the most damaging to Ricky and Fauzia. Interestingly, until then their status as owners of an *hôtel meublé* had never proved controversial and had been effectively normalized as a taken-for-granted, if somewhat regrettable, institution of a kind that had defined the neighborhood for ages. DAL had succeeded, however, in forcing what had long been a hidden private issue of the tenants' exploitation into the open in such a spectacular fashion that Ricky and Fauzia's social position as exploiters of vulnerable families now overshadowed their public persona. A permanent stigma was now attached to the hotel and, by extension, to them. The Chartres fell under regulatory scrutiny from the city and soon closed. Ricky and Fauzia would ultimately try to reinvent it as a tourist hotel, though it struggles to garner bookings. The protest succeeded largely because the activists had called attention to the social suffering of the tenants and their exploitation by the owners, and they did so by disrupting the boundaries of public and private that structured the everyday tolerance of social suffering in the neighborhood.

The DAL protest provides an extraordinary—and one could say classic—example of the political life of the city's spaces, streets, and infrastructure. As it demonstrates, access to formally defined public spaces plays an important and even essential role in the ability of residents to demand rights and achieve change. But one must be careful not to oversimplify the scope of urban politics along the lines of a public/private dichotomy in which "public" is equivalent to "the people or society" and "private" equals neoliberal enclosure or spaces that are subject to the logic of accumulation. Indeed, the existence of the very dichotomy itself is part of the capitalist production of space. Rather, elements of the "public" and the "private" are incorporated into the process by which residents demand the right to the city.

The Jardins d'Eole is a perfect example of the contradictory nature of the city as a form of commons. One of the ironies of the Jardins d'Éole (and the sustainable urbanism of which it was a part) is that it was implicated in the ethnoracially charged "reconquest" of northeast Paris. However, the DAL protest also demonstrated the usefulness of the Jardins d'Éole as a public space in the most classic democratic sense: public space as a "stage" of political expression and interventions. Indeed, one could argue that the design of the esplanade—which resembles more of a square or a forum than a classic public garden—made it particularly effective as an important political site. It is precisely this muddling of the private/public dichotomy that had been an important demand of the Éole mobilization for the sake of asserting more residents' control.

The paradoxical notion that this new park—despite being successful as a public space—was also part of an emergent geography of dispossession is by no means limited to the Jardins d'Éole itself. Public spaces have political lives and uses that are deeply intertwined and inseparable from their social ones. Indeed, the very nomenclature of public/private is a component of this political life, and it is a point of important contention. At times, residents mobilize in ways that strategically erode the boundaries of public and private; at other moments, they seek to redefine these divisions in ways that are more rigid than those defined by public regimes and hegemonic notions of property. However, my main point regarding an urban commons is not that such a space is characterized by an absence of such partitions or categories, but rather that the boundaries are defined and controlled by differing groups of residents for their own needs. As this chapter demonstrates, the crucial question is not always how "public" or "private" the streets, sidewalks, and squares of the city might be, but who decides the boundaries between public/private, and whose needs such divisions serve.

The Right to the City: Beyond Public and Private

For several decades, a range of commentators have sounded the alarm on the impending "end of public space." In cities around the world, in a wide variety of national, cultural, and political contexts, one can point to a combination of coercive, even violent means, including policing, surveillance, architectural strategies of gating, and the creation of fortresslike residential and commericial developments, to say nothing of economic transformations by which the poor or otherwise "undesirable" are excluded from the city, and hence from democratic citizenship.[7] One potential problem with such otherwise cogent analyses is a tendency to reify public space as a clearly bounded, static "thing." In other words, public space is understood broadly as a form of space for everyone's use, and is thus equated with justice, while private space is unjust because it entails the exclusion of nearly everyone for the enrichment of a few. However, a range of empirically grounded examples for a variety of political, economic, and cultural contexts suggest that the categories of public and private are themselves culturally and historically contingent, and in many cases there are multiple publics of concern in cities—and multiple types of "private" space as well.[8]

Ethnographic work that focuses on the contested spaces of Paris's working-class and gentrifying neighborhoods—by me and a host of fellow researchers—has highlighted the degree to which the politics of public space entails a far more complex set of interactions than one characterized by struggles *between* the private and public.[9] The streets of northeast Paris (and many other cities) are host to not only multiple "publics" but a complex mosaic of territorial practices that call into question the public/private dichotomy altogether. A range of people with different social positions—from youths, to middle-class activists, to street vendors and police—constantly engages in practices that negotiate, mediate, and play with the boundaries of public and private, as opposed to representing one side of the dichotomy against the other. As the DAL protest showed, even urban social movements—the actors most often associated with the struggle for public space—do more with public space than merely "occupy" it as a stage for protest. The DAL protest shows how activists fold the public/private dichotomy into their own political narrative, strategically deploying themes of public and private as part of their political practice.

From this perspective, the intricate territories and publics of street life, despite being sometimes conceived of as microsociological phenomena, are in fact revealed to be sites where processes of macro-level significance become manifest. In this regard, the complex and contested arena that is often ethnographically understood as the "social life" of streets is in fact the linkage between the immediate everyday life of individual streets and scales that bridge cities, nation-states, and continents.[10] Whether a protest is occurring or not, it is in this important context that the right to the city is often claimed in everyday life. To understand how this is the case, it is worth looking carefully at two of Lefebvre's central themes: the city as *fête* (a party or festival) and the city as *œuvre* (a work or project). For Lefebvre, cities

> are centres of social and political life where not only wealth is accumulated, but knowledge (*connaissances*), techniques, and oeuvres (works of art, monuments). The city is itself "*œuvre*", a feature which contrasts with the irreversible tendency towards money and commerce, towards exchange *products*. Indeed, the *œuvre* is use value and the product is exchange value. The eminent use of the city, that is, of its streets and squares, edifices and monuments, is *la Fête* (a celebration which consumes unproductively, without other advantage but pleasure and prestige and enormous riches in money and objects).[11]

The *œuvre*, which could be understood as the concretization of surplus wealth in the form of monuments and the built environment, has a dual role. It is at once a product—a commodity—that is produced and traded to create wealth and an object and tool with use-values that can be planned or spontaneous. For Lefebvre, this inherent ambiguity makes the city as oeuvre an inherently unstable and uncontrollable site of political possibility, the meaning and use of which is continually being redefined and negotiated. The intended use of boulevards, streets, squares, and monuments may indeed have been for symbolic, economic, and even forceful domination of the city by elites, but there is always the possibility that the oeuvre in its concrete, realized form can be used in ways different than those intended, and even retaken, allowing streets, squares, edifices, and monuments to be appropriated, reclaimed, and redefined.

This process of contestation and reappropriation, which could be understood as the creation or negotiation of an urban commons, is the realization of the oeuvre's value in use as opposed to exchange. Some might use the term "public space" for this idea, but to do so naturalizes the capitalist production of space that gives rise to the public/private binary in the first place. Hence, Lefebvre's interest in *la Fête*, which is a celebratory collective reclamation of the city that would overturn the opposition between public and private, work and leisure—in short, the spatial logic of capitalism itself. Thus, Lefebvre writes, "the problem is to put an end to the separations of 'daily life—leisure' or 'daily life—festivity.'"[12] *La Fête* largely represents the celebration of the right to the city as a collective and shared project: an oeuvre.

But what are the politics of *la Fête*? In other words, how do people in a city's often deeply divided neighborhoods realize "their right to the city"? One can find interesting parallels between Lefebvre's notion and the *manif-festives* organized by the Éole mobilization, for example, and in many other instances of street protests. However, *la Fête* is based on a notion of recovering a distant, if not mythical past, rooted in the precapitalist, medieval origins of the European city and rural life. Lefebvre writes that the "rural society was (still is) a society of scarcity and penury . . . It was also the society of *la Fête* (or festivities). But that aspect, the best, has lost."[13] Such a vision seems to elevate an idealistic image of a much more simple, albeit parochial and impoverished, France, which seems very distant from the globalized, culturally diverse, and economically stratified society that marks Paris in the present moment. In many respects, *la Fête* is, for Lefebvre, what the idyllic prewar Greenwich Village street of neighbors and small merchants is for Jane Jacobs: instantly recognizable in the mind's eye as an urban ideal, but mirage-like in its resistance to empirical verification, in either the present or the past.

However, *la Fête* and *œuvre* contain within them the powerful notion that urban spaces—especially so called public spaces—remain incomplete social projects that often elude the control of any one person or group. This seemingly perpetual quality of becoming is the basis for my understanding of the city as a form of commons. Sometimes the "commons" are somewhat simplistically glossed as spaces that are "truly public" or controlled by the "people." However, because the "people" are a heterogeneous category, often riven with social contradictions, a commons is anything but a harmonious space. Indeed, a commons is defined by conflict, or at the very least mediation. The moment the contestation or negotiation ends is frequently the moment a space becomes "fixed" or "determined" or fully under the control of one group, be it the state, private property owners, or, for that matter, a particular group of residents. Whether such a space is ultimately defined as public or private, it is not likely to be vibrant, energetic, and heterogeneous; nor will it likely give rise to insurgent forms of belonging or creative possibilities for social change.

The Commons and Enclosure: DAL on the Rue de la Banque

Indeed, some commons defy the often presumed expectation of inclusivity and "publicness" nearly altogether. There are times when the preservation of a commons appears to require a degree of enclosure or pseudoprivate qualities. This aspect of "commons-ing" was vividly on display in DAL's nearly five-year occupation of an abandoned Crédit Lyonnais bank branch on Paris's Rue de la Banque.[14]

I visited the occupied bank shortly after the Hôtel Chartres protest. The "requisition" of the bank, to quote one of the banners, which hung from a window, was part of a long-standing direct-action strategy by DAL that entailed the occupation of abandoned buildings in Paris, and employing them as shelter for those who lacked housing. The group's primary goal is to pressure government officials to recognize housing as a "basic right," though it is engaged in a broad spectrum of housing-rights work, from lobbying politicians for legislation to aiding individual families who have been displaced. The group has always been active in France's immigrant communities by virtue of immigrants' often precarious housing situation throughout France; its protests and public demonstrations are some of the most visible demonstrations by Maghrebis and West Africans in France. However, in what might be considered "good republican" fashion, DAL does not position its demand as related to immigrant rights. Instead, its political identity is dedicated to struggling for the citizenry as a whole to enjoy housing as an inalienable right. DAL typically picks buildings for occupation in areas rich with symbolic importance: the requisition of the former bank branch, located on Rue de la Banque (Bank Street), directly across the street from the Paris Bourse (stock exchange), could not have provided a more obvious symbol of the group's demand that housing be provided to people as a right rather than as a function of profit accumulation. At Rue de la Banque, the activists hung a gigantic banner over the front of the bank emblazoned with the words "Ministry of Housing Crisis," the invocation of crisis providing a poignant foreshadowing of a word that would be widely associated with Rue de la Banque later in 2008—but for very different reasons.

The "ministry of housing crisis" may have been "requisitioned" as a commons of sorts, but there was nothing public about it. DAL's leaders took careful procedures to assure that the space was secure from police, journalists, and anyone who could be a source of potential harm. It took me several minutes of wandering around the outside of the abandoned bank to find the new entrance, as many of the windows and former entrances were barricaded or covered with blue tarp. When I found a side-door entrance, two women of Maghrebi origin, wearing headscarves and in their early twenties, confronted me. I was stopped and questioned, firmly but cordially: I was fully expecting to be immediately turned away. As was often the case, my reply that I was an anthropologist never produced the level of surprise or confusion that I had expected. In fact, because I was also asking for information about the protest outside of the Hôtel Chartres, my being an anthropologist appeared to be just random enough to temporarily assuage suspicion that I was a journalist, which would have resulted in my being redirected through different channels. I waited outside in the January cold for what felt far longer than the several minutes it actually was, as one of the women passed on word of my arrival. I learned the name of a woman who kept me at the front door (Aïcha) but little else. She politely told me that she could not say much more and spent most of her time carefully watching the street, and carefully moving between the doorway and the interior. Again, I was surprised to find that I was allowed inside, though I had to follow her companion, who served as a runner between the front door and the main office inside.

Farah, who told me little beyond her name, led me into what once had been the bank's main lobby. In the office and work areas that had once adjoined it, were at least two dozen women and children surrounded by inflatable mattresses, linens, pillows, open suitcases, toys, and all manner of personal belongings: the bank was repurposed as a shelter. The lobby, though poorly ventilated and musty, was frigid. We passed offices where children played quietly and women rocked infants, and soon arrived near what had once been a glass-walled conference room. Nearby, DAL staff with clipboards conducting "intake" work collected information from a few of the women who appeared to have just arrived. Ironically, in this largely female space, I was being immediately taken to see another man, an organizer named Guy, who was also one of the few people of French origin in the bank. He had long graying hair and wore a black leather jacket—I recognized him from the protest. As we discussed the protest at the Jardins d'Éole, and compared the frequency of fires in northeast Paris's long-stay hotels to Rome under Nero and underlined the importance of public space for demonstrations, he described the "street" as the "only place of communication not manipulated" by the media or the state.

However, as the process of merely entering the repurposed bank shows, the careful maintenance of boundaries and even enclosures is just as crucial. At the "ministry of housing crisis," a careful distance was maintained at all times between outsiders and the families who sought shelter there, as many were undocumented (in addition to being unhoused and impoverished). Movements that represent the socially precarious are forced to create safe zones or spaces of enclosure within commons; vulnerable individuals can often not even take to the streets or risk arrest the way more privileged activists might.[15] As a result, the spatial politics of such movements becomes a complex process of renegotiating the boundaries of public/private while demanding access for housing as a public good.

Between Public Space and Urban Commons: The Jardins d'Éole

Activists such as those in DAL are not the only people who attempt to redefine boundaries of the public and private. The everyday politics of the Jardins d'Éole itself plays out along similar tensions, but the dynamics are complex: residents do not simply push against the DEVE to make space more of a commons, and the DEVE does not simply push back against these efforts with its often restrictive notion of what public space entails. Indeed, over the course of my fieldwork, I found that DEVE staff in the Jardins d'Éole played a particularly interesting and unexpected role in maintaining the status of the space as a commons. In contrast, I found that residents sometimes adopted the formal roles of the DEVE in their attempts to regulate a carefully circumscribed, disciplined definition of the public.

For this reason, the Jardins d'Éole presents an interesting view of the everyday political life of a vibrant urban space. As it turns out, what might be called the space's "vibrancy" is not the result of one particular group successfully "fixing" the space according to its vision, but the constant, ongoing negotiation between groups. Ultimately, the biggest threat to this vibrant commons emerged in the context of the economic crisis, and specifically in the efforts of public agencies to securitize the space. This entailed several public agencies putting an end to—or attempting to curtail—the highly negotiated, mediated quality of street life as commons, and replacing it with qualities emphasizing predictability, surveillance, and the careful control of movement and behavior.

At a formal level, those officially designated with overseeing the social life of the Jardins d'Éole are the AAS (Agents d'Accueil et de Surveillance— welcoming and surveillance agents), who have been described by Pierre Sansot as the "master and servant of the public garden."[16] The "guards" or "guardians" (as they are often known in colloquial terms) have a formal job title that itself embodies the paradoxical relationship between the state and the "public." In one respect, their role is coercive: AAS personnel wear uniforms, patrol the space, keep an eye on the "users," and are responsible for enforcing the *réglementation générale* of Paris's public gardens. Their responsibilities also include opening and closing the gates of the garden each day and keeping a careful watch over users to make sure that no party interferes with another's ability to enjoy the garden. Overall, they ensure the republican ideal of equal access for all and privileged treatment for none. Thus, they not only enforce the rule of law and ensure everyone's safety, but, more profoundly, guarantee that a certain "civism" holds sway in the space.[17] In short, they literally embody the state's agency to delimit and define the public.

At the same time, the guardians embody a more benevolent "welcoming" vision of power. Guardians are decidedly not police. They are almost always unarmed (save for whistles) and are expected to summon law enforcement for any incident beyond a minor disturbance of the peace. They are expected to be a cordial, even "friendly" face of the public garden (and the state that it represents) to its users (the citizens). Because guardians spend every day with the public, they become neighbors to the residents who routinely visit, as well as guides and sources of aid to visitors and tourists, and to some extent even parents and teachers for youths and children who use the parks. In this sense, guardians must balance their coercive role as "keepers of order" with their paternalistic role as caretakers. Moreover, they face an inherently contradictory role at multiple levels. Not only must they balance coercion with compassion, but they must essentially represent the public to the public itself.[18]

As I grew closer with the AAS staff as well as the horticulturalists, I noticed that this process of social control unfolded in interesting ways and with unexpected results. Guardians are not assigned to a single park; they rotate through a set of posts, usually delimited by arrondissements. At the Jardins d'Éole, Gérard was an amicable veteran guardian in his forties with more than ten years of service who would often lecture children for breaking rules while slightly cracking a smile. Despite his "official role" as the keeper of order of a relatively staid public institution, I was always amused by the fact that he seemed to make sure that a T-shirt emblazoned with either a heavy metal band or with cannabis leaves was clearly visible under his uniform, and he sported multiple piercings. Suzelle, who occasionally worked alongside Gérard, was of Antillean origin and always was quick to invite me for lunches with her and her colleagues. She was lively, gregarious, warm, and particularly well known and liked by many of the parents and families who frequented the park. Soon after I entered into a more familiar *tutoyer* relationship with the AAS, the gardeners became friendlier to me as well. Among them was one of the lead gardeners named Simone, a woman of French descent in her fifties who would often make a point of showing me "hidden" gems of the garden's natural realm, varying from bird's nests to in-season fruit trees and berry bushes. It was clear to me that the gardeners viewed knowledge of such things as a form of privilege afforded by their métier, and I always considered it a compliment to be let in on such secrets. Despite constant rotations between parks, the staff at the Jardins d'Éole often came across as a "crew" or "team." They especially liked to throw parties for each other and came across not as stern "guards" but as a lighthearted group of colleagues. Their relationship with the public could best be described as cordial and pedagogical.

I was very interested in the manner in which the DEVE staff at the Jardins d'Éole went about enforcing rules. Whistles were only blown when some-one appeared to be in imminent danger, such as when a person rode a bicy-cle too close to an area where small children were playing. Otherwise, the enforcement of rules seemed to be mediated with the public to a surprising extent. The playing of a ball game outside of designated areas could be toler-ated as long as players kept a safe distance from plants and, if present, small children. Sometimes, significant ground was even ceded to the public. The AAS soon stopped bothering to tell children and parents to not throw stones in the canal because it was such a common practice; they became far more forgiving about sports outside of the athletic area because the park could get

The DEVE largely tolerates—and at times even endorses—an insurgent identity at the Jardins d'Éole: here, local graffiti artists provide their retort to Occupy Wall Street (with the permission of the DEVE).

so overcrowded. A group of Sri Lankan youth who traveled to the park from a large Tamil neighborhood near the Gare du Nord were unofficially allowed to play cricket on the lawn on certain evenings because the guardians knew that this was the only open space to which they had access. The entire place operated on the basis of a constant negotiation of limits rather than imposition of them.

The exception to this rule, however, was the closing of the park each night. On several occasions, the AAS at the Jardins d'Éole had to call for "backup" from other AAS teams in the arrondissement, including on one occasion when a group of teenage girls simply refused to stop playing a ball game and go home for the night. Closing hours were one of the sole absolute rules, and there was no room for negotiation around this important ritual that conveys, quite literally, that at the end of the day the park belongs to the DEVE (i.e., the state) and not to its users. The closing of the park is therefore a moment when the fiction of the state's self-identification with the public is revealed.

My discussions of closing time with AAS revealed the ways in which they articulated their role toward the public in stark terms. During an interview with Gérard and Suzelle in 2009, when I asked what situation is the most difficult to address with users, Suzelle quickly said, "Definitely the closing time." And Gérard then put forward an explanation that added a further layer of complexity to the relationship between these guardians of the public and the public itself:

> During the day, people are usually pretty respectful of the site, but the one moment you get a little issue is when you tell people to leave, at closing time. You see, this place has only been open for a couple of years; before that it was not a green space, or really a regulated place, with an opening time and a *closing time* [Suzelle says these words with him, nodding]. Before that it was, if you will, a wasteland [*terrain vague*]. So, for the people—and especially the kids who used the wasteland before—for them—there was never a time to leave the site.

Several aspects of Gérard's statement warrant special mention. First, the professional self-identification of the AAS with the space itself—"the site"—is significant in that it illustrates the ways in which the AAS constructs "respect" for the rules (and for themselves) as respect for the public garden as an institution. Laxity or strictness on the part of the AAS personnel is therefore understood to be a quality of the public garden itself, not of the individual guardians; indeed, his professional sense of self is integrated with the public garden as a social space.

Moreover, Gérard's explanation for why people, especially young people and children, are not as "respectful" of the public garden at closing time is illuminating as it is constructed as a unique legacy of the period when it was a *terrain vague*—the Cour du Maroc. According to him, because of this history, people are not yet accustomed to a public garden. The wasteland was a place of complete freedom for the "kids," whereas the public garden is one of regulation, respect, and, in short, civility. The implication, then, is that the public of the Jardins d'Éole needs to be taught how to be a respectful public. From this standpoint, the paradoxical roles of the AAS (welcoming and surveillance) merge: they are not as much guardians as teachers with the goal of helping to "produce" a public. Thus, the mediations with park users, many of whom are, after all, children, are best understood as a form of pedagogy, and the garden itself can be viewed as a social mission. In a fashion that carries multiple analogies with the work of the gardeners, the AAS's mission in the Jardins d'Éole is imagined as one of cultivating a public.

This notion has significant ethnoracial implications because many users of the park are people culturally and ethnically identified with groups that have long been imagined as in need of a civilizing mission on the part of the French state. Nevertheless, the expectation of the public as being in a state of becoming has the everyday effect of making the Jardins d'Éole operate in a pedagogical manner in which it is a space of flexibility, most of the time. Ironically, this negotiated status has the effect of making the Jardins d'Éole closer to a commons than a true public garden, as it is viewed as still retaining the more permissible qualities of the old "wasteland" in some respects.

As a result, the actions of the "vigilant citizens" on the esplanade were especially important because they effectively became regulators of the space when DEVE guardians left for the night. In many respects, the residents' nighttime approach parallels that of AAS in that they seek to embody an attribute of the space itself, in this case by manifesting an idealized form of sociality. In order to accomplish this, Éole activists resurrected the *manif-festive* concept: in the evenings, "parties" were thrown that included spreads of homemade food, wine, and dozens of guests.[19] Often, the Éole activists were effective in involving a diverse group of residents in terms of ethnicity, age, and gender. The parties were some of the few places, for example, where I saw young French-origin, middle-class professionals intermingle with residents of Maghrebi, Antillean, and West African origin. And in keeping with their typical style, the group was effective in bringing officials from the local arrondissements to these soirées, as I saw Mamadou, as well as a Green Party elected official from the nineteenth arrondissement, attend one such gathering in his official capacity. Beyond having a good time, the goal of these events was to provide a defining form of sociality for the esplanade, stressing a jovial but decidedly civil, middle-class atmosphere. This display was meant for both the residents and the elected officials who may have the power to "enclose" the space, as well as to displace any potential "undesirable" activities—principally drug dealing—from the esplanade.

Breaking the Ramadan fast at the Jardins d'Éole. Public gardens are popularly imagined as secular spatializations of the Republic itself. Here, a collective *iftar* on the esplanade—which raised no eyebrows in northeast Paris—demonstrates the degree to which the space can operate as an inclusive commons amid a national political climate in which any public manifestation of Islam is a cause for scandal.

By 2012, however, the atmosphere of these gatherings began to change. Tomi—doubtlessly influenced by events that had recently unfolded in New York—used the term "occupying space" to describe the purpose of the parties, which had grown smaller but now occurred more regularly and seemed to take on more of a sense of "duty." Although the atmosphere of the parties had seemed enjoyable, increasingly a sense of worry was in the air.

At this time, the sense of crisis in northeast Paris was palpable. Far more people were being forced to sleep in public spaces at night, including in the Jardins d'Éole. In many places, various types of informal market activity—typically the selling of clothes, used CDs, and other items—were becoming an increasingly common sight on the street. There was a great deal of dread about the future of the park, and concerns about what transpired there at night. However, when I asked for examples of specific crimes or incidents, no one could mention any event out of the ordinary; rather, there was a general level of anxiety over what might occur. Many residents began carrying cards newly supplied by the city and customized for the Stalingrad

Residents begin an evening party at the Jardins d'Éole.

neighborhood with phone numbers for "mediators" who negotiate disputes between residents at night, most of which involve noise-related issues.

In this atmosphere, some of the Éole activists involved in the esplanade "parties" decided to take matters into their own hands and began playing a role similar to that performed by the AAS. On one occasion, a friend of Ziad and Danko who regularly came to the esplanade on his scooter was performing tricks. Along with a female companion, he began executing "donuts" in the middle of the esplanade, causing the vehicle and its unhelmeted occupants to skid recklessly about the concrete plaza, kicking up clouds of dust, and eliciting roars of shock and approval from the young bystanders gathered nearby. The noise and spectacular disregard for personal safety were too much for some of the association members gathered at the picnic, whose long resentment of "scooter battles" on the esplanade finally came to a head. Two female Éole activists of French origin approached the youths and told them that scooters "were forbidden on the esplanade." Because this was technically the park, the DEVE rule against motorized vehicles was indeed in effect here, though the DEVE guardians had long departed for the day. It should also be noted that the rosé that was being consumed by the two women was also technically banned in this space. Even though the negotiation involved two women confronting roughly a dozen young men whose public presentation of self involves a good deal of swagger, the youths listened, and the daredevil rider and his companion roared off, though he would later return after the adults had gone home for the night, but keeping a noticeably lower profile.

Why did the young people obey? The negotiation between the women and the teenagers was essentially a mapping out of networks in which both parties smoothed over the tense situation by searching for mutual connections that bridged the social gap and broke down the discrete categories differentiating "youths" from "association members." In this case, a link was found through a young man's grandparent who was acquainted with the association member. This linkage was made possible by the local school, which is the place where residents from across the neighborhood's social divisions are most likely to interact and work together. Interestingly enough, the negotiation of the commons in this context was indirectly facilitated by another "public" institution: the school. In sharp contrast to the guardians, however, Tomi and his neighbors were not interested in "cultivating a public." Instead,

they acted because their own right to access public space rested on their willingness and ability to control the usage of their less privileged, typically low-
income and immigrant-origin neighbors.

Ironically, my observations of the everyday life of the space suggested
that despite the esplanade's being a fixation for activists and the DEVE alike,
it was not the "problematic" part of the Jardins d'Éole. As early as 2007, soon
after the park first opened, I noticed that a section consisting of terraced
rows of grass alleyways enclosed by hedges appeared underutilized. This
area was one of the most "traditional" parts of the design, as it consisted of
three perfectly aligned pathway-like lawns, an allusion to symmetrical alleys
found in many French formal gardens, each enclosed by hedges. This gives
the area the feeling of being a relatively quiet, contemplative space. The terraced nature of the area—each alleyway was placed a step above the other—
was not a choice of the architects. Originally, it was supposed to have been
placed above a facility operated by the Tafanel beverage distribution company, a zone that it and the SNCF had retained until the final moment of
negotiations over the site's future. Because the design process was already
well under way, and the need to promote the completed park in time for an
electoral campaign was viewed as vital by elected officials, a redesign was
ruled out. As a result, the park would bear the "imprint" of the former plan
to make the Cour du Maroc a trucking facility, despite the activists and their
allies having ultimately secured the entirety of the space for public use.

As a result of this hurried, but far from insignificant, design change, the
terraced area never drained properly. The grass is often flooded or damp, and
even on days when the playgrounds and main lawn are over capacity, this section of the park is nearly always empty, with only occasional use during sum-
mertime, primarily by picnickers and sunbathers. It therefore became a place
where one could reliably expect to not encounter others, making it a favored
spot for a range of "private" activities conducted in public: it served as a living
space for the homeless, a quiet, secluded place for drinkers, and, over time, a
rendezvous for crack-cocaine and IV drug users. This social pattern developed early but was never raised as an issue by residents or the DEVE, even
as the esplanade remained an important space of anxiety. Many people who
visited the park were either unaware of what happened in the terraced paths
or saw such "undesirable" uses as effectively contained and not impeding on

the rights of other park visitors or the ability of the staff to do their jobs. The park therefore continued to function as a type of commons, and these otherwise unwelcomed uses of the space were given tacit approval.

As the crisis wore on, tensions surrounding these varying uses of the space intensified. More people began to arrive in the park to actively seek shelter during the day and at night. The Jardin d'Éole's proximity to a global transport network meant that it became an important gathering site for successive waves of displaced persons, including Kyrgyz, Roma, and Syrians. In addition, more people began to make use of northeast Paris's sidewalks and other public space for street vending. At the same time, the uneasy détente that existed between drug dealers, residents, and other participants in the informal economy throughout the neighborhood was being overturned by redevelopment and gentrification. In particular, the redevelopment of the Place de la Bataille-de-Stalingrad (recall that real-estate values in northeast Paris were booming even while the economic crisis worsened) displaced and dispersed a network of IV drug and crack-cocaine users who began to appropriate the alleys of the Jardins d'Éole in larger numbers than before. These new arrivals in turn displaced many families with children who were refugees, forcing them to seek shelter in the more open visible spaces near the Jardins d'Éole's main lawn. As it often had in the past, the Jardins d'Éole became a place where often hidden forms of social vulnerability were rendered visible.

As these signs of the crisis became increasingly apparent in all of northeast Paris's public spaces and in cities throughout France, the Hollande administration reacted with the establishment of the Zone de Sécurité Prioritaire (ZSP—priority security zone) program. Established in July 2012, the program created fifteen priority security zones throughout the country, with the Goutte d'Or placed at the top of the list, followed by a second wave of zones in November, one of which included the Jardins d'Éole, Stalingrad, and the Cité Michelet. The zones were designed to coordinate efforts between national and local police forces to create "specific patrols" to address a range of issues, including

[t]he underground economy, arms and narcotics trafficking, violence, burglary, gatherings in the common areas of residential buildings, as well as nuisances and general incivility in the public thoroughfares.[20]

In short, the ZSP targets all of the visual manifestations of the economic crisis in public spaces, including not only drug traffickers but street vendors and
anyone who is viewed as a "nuisance" or source of "incivility," a label commonly applied to youths and refugees alike.[21] As research in Paris has shown,
these policing efforts effectively criminalize the most socially vulnerable victims of the crisis.[22] The ZSP strategy, which aims to eliminate the symbols of
social insecurity rather than its underlying causes, amounts to a symbolic
cleansing of northeast Paris's public spaces. Moreover, Éole activists argued
that the policy actually led more drug users to take refuge in the Jardins
d'Éole because the enforcement has the effect of moving the targeted populations throughout the city, (instead, activists have urged the city to adopt a
containment strategy by creating designated safe zones for IV users). Such
initiatives reveal the deeply political and symbolic link between the economic crisis and the streets as an urban commons that always seems to elude

Despite the worries over drug dealing on the esplanade, it was this problematic section
of the park (it had long been prone to flooding owing to a design compromise for the
Tafanel company) where participants in the illegal drug economy ultimately sought
refuge during the economic crisis.

the control of the powerful. In other words, the Hollande administration has resorted to clamping down on (or attempting to "fix") the unruly commons as a demonstration of its efficacy in the face of economic catastrophe.

This crackdown in the face of crisis was joined by DEVE. By the summer of 2012, a new set of management practices and attitudes were adopted by DEVE staff and administrators. Most tellingly, the entire "ritual" for closing the park had changed. What had once been a relatively uncomfortable procedure that typically consisted of four or five AAS blowing whistles and admonishing teenagers to stop playing basketball or soccer was now a more aggressive operation involving twelve AAS accompanied by a German shepherd on a leash. At times, special security patrols consisting of unfamiliar, mostly male DEVE personnel with nightsticks and more militaristic uniforms would appear in the park. These "special" AAS were cordial when I spoke with them, but they would never say why they were there.

At the same time, the security crackdown seemed to be reshaping the internal culture of DEVE at the Jardins d'Éole. By 2012, the days of casual gatherings with residents and impromptu socializing with staff seemed to be gone. While AAS staff such as Suzelle remained outwardly as friendly as ever, everyone became far more tight-lipped about the status of the park; in general, staff members began to fall back on official protocol in all manner of communications, suggesting that they perceived a level of professional insecurity and that there was internal surveillance from the organization that had not been in place before. Even the gardeners had become more closed off; Simone began referring me to her superior more often when we talked, and when I asked her about how things were in the park, she said: "The garden is great, it's the people that are the problem!" Most tellingly she repeated the complaints that had once been voiced by gardeners who worked at the "failed" Square Léon years before: the garden's flowerbeds were impossible to maintain because drug traffickers would not let her near them. The Jardins d'Éole was becoming another spatial and ecological metaphor for the breakdown of the republican social order.

Then, in spring 2013, the City of Paris announced that the Jardins d'Éole would be temporarily closed. Although the closure was for a period of only two weeks, it represented a frank admission by the DEVE that it had lost control over the space. Closing and reopening the park also had the effect of "starting a new chapter" in the park's public identity, which by early 2013 had received a great deal of negative coverage.[23] As has happened in the case of other "problematic" public spaces, the DEVE resorted to a series of spatial "fixes," and on this occasion ecological interventions as well. First, bamboo plants that had originally been envisioned by the design team as a semi-opaque "screen" at the park's northeastern side would be cut back, allowing police patrols to survey the park from the outside. This move is a significant symbolic step, as it essentially amounts to the DEVE requesting help from the police and thus extends the impact of the ZSP program into the park. Second, steps would be taken to fix the drainage problems that made the terraced paths unappealing in the first place. In addition, an ecologically managed area of tall grass and flowers known as the *prairie fleurie* (the grassland or flowery meadow), where many displaced persons had gathered during the daytime, was mowed. Nature therefore became the site for intervening in the social, which for the DEVE meant reasserting the public's—or at least the state's—control over the commons.

Conclusion

In the annals of scholarship on everyday life in cities, William H. Whyte's *The Social Life of Small Urban Spaces* represents a well-known effort to determine what constitutes a "successful" urban space. But Whyte's innovative methodological approach, along with his broader view of the social realm, has glaring blind spots. What are the political lives of small urban spaces? Can politics even be thought of as "contained" within small spaces, or do small public spaces happen to have a special use for very large political projects? The social life of the Jardins d'Éole from the DAL protest in 2007 to its temporary closure in 2013 demonstrates the relationship between "small" urban spaces and "big" political processes. My project was not conceived from the start as a rejoinder to Whyte, but engaging with his approach provides a useful way to address a profound issue facing cities: the political importance that is often attached to everyday life in streets and public spaces.

The political life of the Jardins d'Éole has several important things to teach us about the relationship between the right to the city, urban social movements, and the everyday life of contested neighborhoods. First, the value of "public space," while of vital importance for social movements like

DAL, cannot be theorized as simply being a "container" for their protests. Indeed, DAL provides an example—at the Jardins d'Éole and the Rue de la Banque—of how mobilizations claim the right to the city by strategically deploying the public and the private, and manipulating the boundaries between the two. At times, this redrawing of boundaries is done for self-preservation, as in the case of DAL's "security" practices at the "ministry of housing crisis." At other moments, protests can expose private and gendered forms of suffering and exploitation—with profound consequences—as occurred at the protest over the Hôtel Chartres fire.

Second, it isn't only protesters who redraw the boundaries between public and private. This ethnography, as well as the work of a number of ethnographers who have focused on Paris, underlines the ways that the everyday life of streets and sidewalks is divided into a contested series of territories, and that which is public or private is continually up for renegotiation.[24] This process is driven by quotidian forms of political contestation, which plays out in the Jardins d'Éole between residents, youths, storekeepers, and the park guards. Moreover, as the establishment of the ZSP demonstrates, law-enforcement agencies become important players in this process as well. Because the signs of large-scale political and economic crisis become all too evident in the contested commons of streets and parks, the signifiers of crisis—who are often its most socially vulnerable victims—are frequently targeted in efforts to define a zone as secure. Thus, one could say that small urban spaces like the Jardins d'Éole have political importance (and uses) far exceeding their size.

Like any number of things, urban spaces have "lives." Although I am wary of indulging in what Ida Susser has termed "magical urbanism," if urban spaces have lives (social and political), it is the constant process of contestation and renegotiation that makes them vibrant.[25] In this regard, the Jardins d'Éole serves as a demonstration of how an urban space can work as a commons on a quotidian basis, and it just as vividly reveals the inherent fragility of such spaces. A commons, which is always in a state of becoming, is what give spaces their sense of liveliness and vibrancy: the pleasure of never knowing exactly what you will find, as the city itself becomes a vehicle for human creativity in a political, artistic, or other sense. Whyte, of course, was not incorrect when he defined what made a public space "work": many of the attributes of a successful public space are also those of a successful commons.

However, the question that always needs to be asked is "successful for whom?" Unlike a "public space," a commons defies any attempt to "reify" it in the name of an externally defined public. Whyte made the important point of demonstrating that public spaces may be built by architects and planners, but they are finished by residents (Jane Jacobs said essentially the same thing about cities as a whole). A focus on the commons pushes that logic a few steps further: spaces may be built by architects, and varying groups of residents may attempt to complete it, but a commons defies efforts at ever being "finished" by anyone. Ultimately, because a commons belongs to everyone and no one, it is therefore an object of mediation and even a degree of conflict. Indeed, the moment that such exchanges are finished— or put to a stop—so is the commons.

CONCLUSION

My last experience in the Jardins d'Éole before completing this book was not a positive one. The evening before my flight back to Detroit, I decided to take advantage of a beautiful sunset to take photographs for the manuscript, so I lingered on my own in the park until closing time. As I stood at the top of an artificial hill, snapping pictures of the mostly empty garden below, I heard the voices of two young men, who sounded barely old enough to be teenagers.

"Mister! Mister!" called one of the youths. I had seen the two around the neighborhood before, but I didn't know them. They were riding bicycles in the park (and therefore being ever so slightly transgressive), and one of them, after pulling up next to me, asked, "Mister, could you take a picture of me doing a wheelie?" I had barely started to respond when we suddenly heard the punitive tweet of a whistle being blown, causing all three of us to start with surprise. A large group of nearly a dozen DEVE guardians had descended on us seemingly out of nowhere. These were not the typical guardians who worked at the Jardins d'Éole on a regular basis, but a special detail made up of personnel who were unfamiliar to me, and who were mobilized to close parks viewed by the DEVE as having security issues. They were equipped with nightsticks, a muzzled German shepherd, and produced a decidedly unfriendly impression. "Get away from the man," ordered one of the guardians to the youth nearest me. The men were wearing all-black, military-style fatigues with vests and combat boots. One of them stepped in between me and the youth. "It's OK, sir," he said to me. "*You* can go." Although phrased as if it was a recognition of my own freedom of movement—as opposed to the youths, who were now being surrounded—his statement was unmistakably an order to leave.

"But, there's no problem here," I said. The guardian gave me a look of partial surprise and definite annoyance: the issue of whether something was in fact wrong was apparently not up for discussion. He then lectured me about how these kids, who were of West African origin, would steal my camera and be gone on their bicycles before I knew it, and it happened all of the time in Paris. I could tell he was assuming that I was a tourist.

Resisting the impulse to argue, I nodded as if I was listening, but instead watched over his shoulder as the rest of his team corralled the youths. "The garden is closed, let's go!" the guardians repeated to the two boys. They were made to dismount their bikes and were being escorted to the exit. I made eye contact with the youth who had initiated our conversation, and he turned back toward me, prompting one of the guardians to place a firm hand on his shoulder. Then he shouted directly to me as he was hurried along: "I'M NOT A THIEF! Mister! Please! Believe me! I'm not a thief!" He looked on the verge of tears. Like me, he knew exactly what the guardians were thinking, and why. The problem was not that he was being kicked out of the park (it was closing anyway), but rather the symbolic violence of having just been reduced by the authorities to an ethnoracial abstraction of a "delinquent."

My train of thought was interrupted by "my" guardian's terse voice: "The nearest exit is behind you, sir." He was sending me out on the opposite side of the park as the two boys, with the goal of keeping us separated, ostensibly for my own good. "The garden is closed," he said.

That was my last moment at the Jardins d'Éole as of this writing. It seemed oddly apropos: like so many other meaningful moments in fieldwork, the episode was so brief as to be an impression, so quotidian that it could be a nonevent, and yet it provides an invaluable window into how power, space, and ethnographic privilege operate. I felt a sour sense of guilt afterward: by simply taking photographs in such a contested space, I had inadvertently made myself into the locus of a micropolitical storm that brought the youths and guardians into contact with one another. My own privilege as an ethnographic researcher, materialized in the form of a new SLR camera was the premise for the entire encounter—it had caught the attention of the youths and guardians alike. While such moments of discrimination occur all the time, my simply "being there" was incorporated into the guardians' ongoing project to secure a key part of Paris's natural infrastructure and control "delinquency" in the city's public spaces.

In the end, the stakes for the two boys being kicked out of the park were nowhere near as serious as they might have been, as the two appeared to be about the same age as Zyed Benna (seventeen) and Buona Traore (fifteen), whose deaths during a pursuit by police in 2005 by electrocution in an electrical substation in the suburban commune of Clichy-sous-Bois sparked three months of civil unrest in France. As an ethnographer, it is possible to write about incidents like this in a way that exposes an important and meaningful irony in the way we seek to build "just" cities: in this case, the creation of a new park, despite being demanded by residents to address ethnoracial, environmental, and class-based inequalities, can become a site for reproduction of inequality and exclusion.

The episode only highlighted the degree to which the Jardins d'Éole is marked by deep contradictions that reflect those of the broader society. However, it remains a space of hope and possibility as well. As I left that night, I knew that these or other young people would keep returning to the space and claiming it as their own, but the security officials from the DEVE would only be there until this, the latest crackdown in northeast Paris, subsides.

The Nature of Exclusion and Belonging in Urban France

Political belonging and exclusion in today's globalized, multiethnic French society are articulated, reproduced, and transformed in a manner that is at once urban and ecological. Northeast Paris's political and ecological history highlights the connections between the infrastructure, networks, and material/organic spaces that make up the city. Both before and during the arrival of West African and Maghrebi immigrants to northeast Paris, the flows of money, ideas, and people that constituted the French empire shaped northeast Paris into a "hinterland" behind the *portes* of Paris, separate from both the capital's opulent center and the working-class *banlieues* to the north and east of the city. This leads me to challenge the center/periphery framework that has long been overstated in discussions of Paris and its *banlieues,* in which being on the spatial periphery is tied neatly to economic and social marginality. At the same time, the social and political marginality of northeast Paris's residents within the capital is reproduced and naturalized by ecological representations in literary, environmental science, and activist discourse, which reinforces its status as a zone that is liminal and dangerous.

Although it is important to establish that social and political marginalization in France has an urban-ecological component, this book's primary focus lies in the ways people bring their own ideas of nature to address these multifaceted inequalities. These approaches need not invoke "nature" or "ecology" explicitly to be examples of everyday political ecological critiques: struggles for justice and inclusion are associated with the urban environment and the messy amalgam of nature and culture that the city itself represents. From everyday gardening to environmental justice activism, what all of these diverse efforts have in common is the attempt to reappropriate the ecology of the postindustrial city as a medium of social, cultural, and national transformation. This form of urban political vibrancy is the basis for an urban commons and is at once creative, and often insurgent. It is the product of tensions, differences, and contradictions that can have spontaneous and unpredictable results, making the area a place where the city always seems "up for grabs." The Éole mobilization provides an example of one such emergent movement, which drew on the idiom of nature and ecology to transform the city into a less toxic environment for the reproduction of human and nonhuman life alike. The demand for a park was not merely the goal of the movement; it was an ecological critique of a political regime that consistently reproduced gendered, ethnoracial, and class-based disparities in the urban fabric, and would have otherwise created a diesel-truck depot or waste-processing facility at the site.

I have also shown how articulations of the city, including both its natural spaces and infrastructure, gain a special and often unacknowledged importance in the context of France's contemporary politics of cultural belonging and ethnic diversity. Again, the materiality of the city itself and concepts of nature provide an important idiom for change and transformation, but this time in the context of cultural inclusiveness and citizenship. Urban gardens tended by residents, as well as park design and management, provide their own idiom to speak about assimilation and articulate new forms of belonging. The words and actions of a variety of individuals in this book demonstrate that a quiet but significant cultural pluralism is alive and well in northeast Paris. In the wake of the *Charlie Hebdo* attacks, in which northeast Paris itself is frequently cast as a menace to the Republic, it is important to emphasize that the multiethnic politics that thrives in these neighborhoods is neither sectarian nor an imported version of American or British multiculturalism; it is a republican vision of unified belonging grounded in universal notions of human "nature"—reminiscent of what Gary Wilder has termed colonial humanism—that erode even the boundaries of the "French nation" itself.[1]

I describe this pluralistic approach as "actually existing republicanism," building on an argument made by Mustafa Dikeç.[2] This notion of belonging might be understood as oppositional to the "mythic" republicanism articulated by politicians and major newspapers, which emphasizes assimilation and a view of France's culture as static, ahistorical, homogeneous, and otherwise "billiard-ball-like."[3] Like the social world of the streets themselves, republicanism is a dynamic field that is always subject to mediation, contestation, and negotiation; most of all, the meaning of it is lived and fought over in a multiethnic, urban context. Even more important, this insurgent pluralism is not a local aberration. Ironically, it is thoroughly enmeshed in, and an essential part of, the power structure of the Socialist Party in Paris, with implications for national-level politics, even though many high-level "official" discourses formulated by the Left and Right alike are often hostile to such radical forms of humanism.

Green Designs: The Anthropology of the City in the Era of Urban Sustainability

As an ethnography focused on the politics of the green turn in urban design, this book forms part of a scholarly effort to blend the hitherto separate but vital spheres of urban and environmental anthropology.[4] Anthropology has been a relative latecomer to an interdisciplinary focus on "urban nature" that has called into question the foundational city/nature dichotomy in urban studies.[5] This book has shown the value of an ethnographic approach to this literature, which has been more theory- and history-based than empirically grounded, with a few prominent exceptions.[6] Just as important, by engaging anthropology with broader debates on the "nature" of the city, this ethnography has sought to rescue "urban anthropology" from taking its object of study for granted: while a few ethnographies challenge the rural/urban dichotomy, the nature/city binary remains largely unquestioned.[7] My focus on urbanism as a productive and contested process in which the material realms of the city and nature are intermingled is meant as an ethnographic intervention in a theoretical quandary that has haunted ethnographers since the term "urban anthropology" gained common currency in the context of mid-twentieth-century rural to urban migration.[8] Thus, by focusing on ideas of nature and the environment, this book is a step toward an anthropology of the city that does not reify the urban.

Anthropologists' increased attention to infrastructure has important implications for scholarship on cities and urban ethnography, with insights that are more profound than simply calling attention to the "materiality" of the social.[9] In many respects, this emphasis on the networks of pipes, power lines, roads, canals, railways, and other types of socioarchitectural linkages recalls an assertion made by Bruno Latour about the fundamental qualities of networks: "They are connected lines, not surfaces."[10] The provocative shift toward the line and away from the space as a key ethnographic metaphor offers important theoretical response to some of the problems that seem inherent to spatial thinking: lines, after all, always emphasize flows, process, and movement, while connecting multiple spaces.[11] Indeed, to draw a line or trace an infrastructural connection is to engage in an act of synthesis that transcends multiple scales and situates different places in relationships that are correspondingly social and political. In this regard, to think in terms of lines (particularly regarding urban infrastructure) is to break down dichotomies between bounded places, types of places, and scales, such as local/global. In the case of parks and greenways, this also includes revealing the blurred boundaries between nature/culture and nature/city. Most important, this approach moves the anthropology of cities away from the notion of the urban as a reified type of space.

Cities are—at a material level or on a planner's map—an assemblage of lines and spaces that are mutually constitutive. Each gives form to the other, and the many constitutive parts that make up a city, such as its greenways and streets, can be theorized as lines or spaces with differing consequences.

It is important to remember that no line originates from a truly arbitrary point in space, and linearity is itself a historically, culturally constituted logic that is inseparable from—but not wholly determined by—the production of space. Here, Lefebvre's decidedly organic metaphor that space is "secreted" by practice is instructive: space has a fluid and indeterminate quality even when it is organized according to the often brutal logic of capitalist accumulation.[12] As the hotly contested history of northeast Paris's streets and parks shows, what may appear solid, flat, or static is only in a state of temporary suspension, at a material or social level. Indeed, as I have shown, urban contestation is often tied to different actors trying to "fix" such fluidity, frequently in vain. It is therefore up to ethnographers to better understand the relationship between these spaces and lines that constitute the city in terms of social practice; hence my emphasis on design.

In Paris, policy elites have embraced sustainable city design as a form of what Neil Smith termed "nature as accumulation strategy," while simultaneously contributing to ethnoracial inequalities.[13] A range of ecological urbanism discourse, from urban biodiversity to the Aalborg Charter and Agenda 21 guidelines on sustainability, provide a way for policy makers to reimagine cities on a regional and global level, at times in competition across scales, as demonstrated by the visible spat between Bertrand Delanoë and President Sarkozy. The Jardins d'Éole, Vélib', and overarching Grand Paris proposal are just some examples of the variety of ways these globally focused plans are materialized to reconstruct the city and neighborhood scales. In some cases, such as the mass demolition and "reconquest" associated with the remaking of Paris Nord-Est—and even the stigmatization of scooter riders as environmental menaces—the green turn in urbanism is tied to forms of displacement and exclusion that are class-based and ethnoracial. Indeed, even a grassroots strategy to confront ecological, gendered, and ethnoracial inequalities such as the Éole mobilization resulted in the creation of a space that enabled surveillance and exclusionary practices such as the incident described at the start of this chapter. My approach demonstrates how the globally diffuse, and not altogether coherent, set of ideas that some have termed "sustainable urbanism" can only be holistically understood when materialized in a specific historical and social context—in this case, twenty-first-century Paris.[14]

Ironically, as the green turn in urbanism has gained hegemony, such innovations are misleadingly discussed as a neutral body of technical knowledge, thus concealing the way that sustainable design can materialize—and naturalize—social inequalities. It seems that the price that has been paid for the mainstream acceptance of sustainability in urban policy is that an emphasis on justice has been stripped away from many ecological urbanism projects, in both practice and discourse. Now that the issue of whether cities should be built in a sustainable manner is closer to being settled (at least within the urban-planning world), the question that needs to be asked without delay is, What is being sustained, and, in a manner following Heynen, Kaika, and Swyngedouw, for whom?[15] It would be tragic if all of the promise inherent in ecological urban design was of no social consequence other than to reproduce existing inequalities, and yet this is precisely the danger we face.

The Commons: A Basis for a Radically Vibrant Urbanism?

Fortunately, as this ethnography has shown, sites such as the Jardins d'Éole may be marked by intense contradictions, but social life in them is anything but determined, even in periods of crisis when security concerns are invoked to justify a crackdown on public space. This is why the question of the urban commons demands our attention.

Throughout much of my time in the field, I was impressed by the degree to which the streets of northeast Paris appeared to belong simultaneously to everyone and to no one. The City of Paris may technically "own" the pavement, and the DEVE may open and close the gates of Jardins d'Éole each day (other than the esplanade), but a diverse array of residents populated, animated, and defined the space as their own—often in opposition to efforts by the authorities, and sometimes each other. Areas such as this one—and they need not be cities—have a spontaneous quality to them; in the case of northeast Paris, the irrepressible creativity of the inhabitants has historically given rise to myriad political and cultural movements, many of which can be characterized by their insurgent qualities. Building on others, and in particular David Harvey, I ascribe this spontaneous quality of constant exchange, mediation, and even conflict to northeast Paris's status as a kind of urban commons.[16]

As I have shown, a vibrant commons often requires access to a public space, but the politics of the commons is not always focused on freedom of access. As the example of DAL showed, social movements even make use of varying forms of enclosure at both symbolic and practical levels. Moreover, the commons of northeast Paris's streets, sidewalks, squares, and parks is reproduced by numerous, often microlevel practices of territoriality described by me and other ethnographers.[17] Street life is marked by continual negotiation, contestation, and redefinition of the boundaries between public and private, more than a struggle to resist the privatization of the public. In contrast to Jane Jacobs's traditionalist vision, an ideal picture of a city block that superficially resembles a commons, residents do not place their "eyes upon the street" to maintain a harmonious, functionalist fantasy of public space governed by law and order.[18] Instead, people often watch each other in the streets—at times, in an extension of xenophobic ideologies and other moments to protect vulnerable, undocumented friends and neighbors. What Jacobs calls "do-it-yourself surveillance" is an inescapable part of life in northeast Paris because the commons is a highly contested zone of constantly renegotiated boundaries, as opposed to being part of an orderly, self-regulating system.

In many cases, this vibrant but unruly quality of the commons is oppositional to hegemonic notions of public space imposed by the state; this is evident in the way DEVE staff spoke of continually attempting to transform the users of the park into a public in an almost pedagogical, even civilizing manner. Frequently (as discussed in chapter 6), the AAS have little choice but to give up and let residents do what they please, indeed, the most turbulent part of their work is often the closing time, when the DEVE *must* claim the space back from the commons in the name of the "public" for the sake of its own legitimacy as a state institution. As I have shown, a commons should therefore not be equated with a romantic, harmonious picture of public space; rather, an urban commons is by definition an often anarchic site of convergence between conflicting interests, projects, and mediations that can even be marked by acrimony as the boundaries between public/private are blurred.

At the same time, one must be cautious of ascribing a "vibrant urban commons" an agency all its own; a commons is maintained by people and subject to their own intentions and projects. The "esplanade" of the Jardins d'Éole was designed to be a type of commons; that is, it was essentially meant to be regulated by residents as opposed to the DEVE. In this sense, the City of Paris sought to employ a neoliberal logic of control that appropriated and materialized a long tradition of Parisian street democracy. This design featured a built-in form of "vigilant citizenship" by a relatively privileged set of middle-class residents whose own access to the commons depended on their control over less privileged neighbors, and in particular immigrant-origin youths. These vigilant citizens, many of whom are the same Éole activists who fought for the park in the first place, are not unthinking extensions of this neoliberal design. They play a careful balancing act, trying to avoid interventions by the police and other city agencies while also watching, and occasionally intervening in, the activities of young people, and not always in a fair or just manner. The residents have what could be described as a delegated function as gatekeepers of a fragile commons that remains as such because no group truly controls it: once the adults have gone to bed, the streets typically belong to the kids again, but only until the DEVE shows up in the morning.

Everything about the Jardins d'Éole can sometimes seem contradictory and contingent; the status of such spaces as a commons hangs in a delicate balance. At times, like the anecdote recounted at the start of this chapter, it even appears to be "shut down" or curtailed altogether. Readers may wonder if a better example of an urban commons could be found in "liberated territories" such as Freistadt Christiania or those that emerge in the midst of mass protests as in Cairo's Tahrir Square in January 2011. Such political landmarks doubtlessly come closer to a neat and tidy definition of an urban commons: improvised, mostly egalitarian systems of self-governance that persist despite challenges from the outside.[19] But my goal here was not to find the "best example." Instead, my interest has been to look at a site such as the Jardins d'Éole and demonstrate that even here, in fact, space is negotiated, contested, and reappropriated all the time. Places like the Jardins d'Éole are an important reminder that smaller, less spectacular sites of creativity, possibility, and even potential transformation emerge around us all the time, even if they often pass by unseen, unnoticed, and unacknowledged.

ACKNOWLEDGMENTS

Anthropologists have long cultivated an image of our work as a solitary enterprise. My experience with this project dispelled that idea as a myth from the very start. I can only hope that the following comments do some justice to the talents and generosity of many wonderful colleagues, companions, and friends.

I owe my deepest thanks to the numerous residents of northeast Paris, whom I cannot name but whose gracious hospitality still humbles me. I have no words to express my gratitude for the invitations to numerous meetings, planning sessions, and dinners, and for the hospitality I received in many homes. I could never truly express my thanks for all the time that many people set aside from their work and families to sit for interviews or simply explain the "basics" to me (I played the part of the blindly groping ethnographer only too well).

Time and time again, I found my bearings only because of an amazing group of colleagues in France: to Michèle Jolé, the leader of our team (then based at the Institut d'Urbanisme de Paris), I owe an immeasurable debt for welcoming me to an inspiring, interdisciplinary group that included Irene d'Agostino and Sophie Koch, who supported me the whole way through. Ellen Hampton and MICEFA (Mission Interuniversitaire de Coordination des Échanges Franco-Américains) helped me as I settled into Paris. Special thanks go to a great mentor and fellow team member, Stéphane Tonnelat, for sharing his brilliant ethnographic instinct as well as his incredible knowledge of Paris.

Thanks to the diligent work of Michèle and Stéphane, our group was able to secure an invaluable and much appreciated research grant from the Bourse de Recherche de la Ville de Paris. Research for this project was also funded by a doctoral dissertation writing grant from the National Science Foundation and by the Department of Anthropology at Wayne State University. My writing was supported by an Instructional Technology Fellowship at the Macaulay Honors College of the City University of New York (CUNY), as well as a CUNY Graduate Center Writing Fellowship.

I owe a very old debt of gratitude to the faculty at Bard College. It is now obvious to me that this project was born from the intellectual creativity I encountered in the classrooms of Marina van Zuylen, Alan Klima, Michèle Dominy, and Diana Brown. Mario Bick is an especially gifted teacher and undergraduate adviser who shepherded me through an early ethnographic exploration of Houston that led me, improbable as it may seem, straight into Paris.

The energetic and generative intellectual climate of the Department of Anthropology at the CUNY Graduate Center is responsible for helping to turn a fanciful idea into the project that became this book. An amazing group of fellow students taught me more than they know: Vivian Berghan, Julian Brash, Rebecca de Guzman, Abou Ali Farman Farmaian, Yizhou Jiang, Amy Jones, Banu Karaca, Jamie McCallum, Joshua Moses, Andrea Morrell, Nada Moumtaz, Jeremy Rayner, Ted Powers, and Ted Sammons. Many of these students participated in a dissertation writing group led by Julie Skurski; if it wasn't for her keen advice and support, this book (and, likely, a few others) might still be an incomplete dissertation. I was fortunate at CUNY to participate as a fellow at the Center for Place, Culture, and Politics under the continually inspiring direction of David Harvey and the late Neil Smith. Neil was an unshakable pillar of support, and I can only hope this work does justice to his great instruction. I thank Donald Robotham for teaching me to make sense of political machinations, Gary Wilder for helping me think through republicanism, and Setha Low for teaching me how to read the city and its spaces. Along with Neil and Ida Susser, these committee members kept me (and the project) moving forward through thick and thin. To Ida Susser, my visionary adviser, blessed with an irrepressible imagination and keen critical instinct, I reserve a special gratitude: she first urged me to work in Paris.

I owe special thanks to everyone involved in the Quadrant program at the Institute for Advanced Study at the University of Minnesota and the University of Minnesota Press. Thank you to all the participants in the Quadrant seminar, including John Archer, Sian Butcher, Ursula Lang, Stuart McLean, Jason Weidemann, Margaret Werry, and Holly Wlodarczyk. I especially thank Susannah Smith for supporting me as Visiting Quadrant Scholar and Anne Carter for all her invaluable help. At the University of Minnesota Press, this book benefited immeasurably from the help of Kristian Tvedten and the keen eye of David Thorstad. A special thanks goes to my editor, Pieter Martin, who has the gift of being able to see what an author is writing before she or he does. During the development of this work, Paul Silverstein, Cindy Isenhour, Melissa Checker, Gary McDonogh, Jennifer Mack, Michael Herzfeld, Julie Kleinman, and a number of anonymous readers all left an indelible mark on my thinking about various parts of this project, and I thank them for their help and insights. I owe a special thanks to Olivia Dobbs and Tim Stallmann for their work on the maps included in this ethnography.

I'm deeply appreciative to have such a supportive group of colleagues in the Department of Anthropology at Wayne State University. Thanks to Allen Batteau, Tamara Bray, Sherri Briller, Stephen Chrisomalis, Yuson Jung, Julie Lesnik, Mark Luborsky, Barry Lyons, Todd Meyers, Guerin Montilus, Jessica Robbins-Ruszkowski, Krysta Ryzewski, and Teddi Setzer. Special thanks go to Sue Villerot, Deb Mazur, and Uzma Khan, as well as to Tom Killion for continually being a strong advocate and to Andrea Sankar for her tireless help as a mentor. A number of faculty provided invaluable support for the project, especially Walter Edwards, whose Center for Humanities offered an interdisciplinary space for Krysta Ryzewski, Tracy Neuman, Jennifer Hart, Rayman Mohammed, David Fasenfest, Jerry Herron, George Galster, and me to exchange ideas. I thank them for their feedback on this project. I also acknowledge Kami Pothukuchi, Linda Campbell, Shane Bernardo, and Sara Safransky: your warm welcome to Detroit has given me a prism through which to better understand Paris.

I reserve special thanks to dear friends whose words inspire me and on whose shoulders I have leaned while undertaking this work. Thank you,

Darren Flusche, Alex Forrest, Ariel Grossman, David Homan, Liz Homberger, Peter Kileff, Christa Rutt Kileff, Nick Kramer, Monte Large, Ken MacLeish, Moira McCauley, Ruqqayya Maudoodi, Andy O'Neill, Rachael Pomerantz, Dana Resnick, David Resnick, Alex Richards, Brandon Smith, Robyn Smith, Lily White, Sandy White, Ling Yacoub, and Mark Yacoub.

I do not know how to begin to express my deep appreciation to my family, who have supported me through this project's many twists and turns. Thank you, Moaiz, Nurjehan, Khalil, Kirran, Hana, and Maya for making sure I did not forget the joys of life even in the most hectic periods of this project. I have been lucky to benefit from the constant and tireless support of Susy, Dad, Lena, Mom, and Tom—I am able to write these words today only because of all of your many years of loving encouragement. The word *gratitude* doesn't quite seem a worthy descriptor of the profound love and appreciation I feel for my partner in life, Shaira, and our son, Shane Ali. Shaira has been inspiring me and ceaselessly helping me toward the best path forward from the start, and Shane Ali has brought his beautiful heart into our lives.

NOTES

Introduction

1. Reed, *Groundswell*, 16. The 2005 MoMA exhibition took place in the context of growing interest in landscape urbanism, which seeks to rethink the relationship between city and nature in architecture and urban design. See also Balmori and Sanders, *Groundwork*; Brantz and Dümplemann, *Greening the City*.

2. Lefebvre, *The Production of Space*.

3. Because of northeast Paris's long history as a destination for migrants from France's former colonies, most people assume that the Cour du Maroc was named for the neighborhood's Moroccan population. However, the owner of the site since the mid-twentieth century, the French National Railway or SNCF (Société Nationale des Chemins de Fer Français), has a long but informal tradition of naming its facilities after nearby streets. In this case, the nearby Rue du Maroc dates back to the nineteenth century, before the first colonial migrants from the Maghreb began to arrive in the area. It is no small irony that the area's century-old street names (Rue de Tanger, Rue du Maroc, Rue Caillié) also carry the legacy of French empire in North and West Africa. For more on the *terrain vague* as a theory of urban space, see Mariani and Barron, *Terrain Vague*; de Solà-Morales, "Terrain vague"; Gandy, "Marginalia."

4. See Brosius, "Analyses and Interventions." For an in-depth account of the political dance between politicians and environmentalists that is specific to contemporary France, see Bess, *The Green-Light Society*.

5. Gramsci, Hoare, and Nowell-Smith, *Selections from the Prison Notebooks of Antonio Gramsci*.

6. Sarkozy, "Le Grand Paris."

7. See Lefebvre, "The Right to the City"; Harvey, *Rebel Cities.*

8. Harvey, *Rebel Cities,* 4.

9. Biehl and Locke, "Deleuze and the Anthropology of Becoming." There is some common ground between Biehl and Locke's Deleuzian approach, on the one hand, and a view of the city as in a state of becoming that has been theorized by French urbanists and ethnographers in the present and past alike, on the other. See Gatta, "Temporality of Physical and Political Liminal Spaces in the Urban Transformations of the Greater Paris"; Jolé, "Le destin festif du Canal Saint-Martin"; Joseph, *La ville sans qualités;* Joseph, *L'espace du public;* Lefebvre, "The Right to the City"; Milliot, "Pluralistic Ambiance and Urban Socialization"; Milliot and Tonnelat, "Contentious Policing in Paris"; Palumbo, "Figures de l'habiter"; Tonnelat, "Out of Frame."

10. Low, *Theorizing the City.* See also Harms, *Saigon's Edge;* Holston, *The Modernist City;* Kanna, *Dubai, the City as Corporation;* Low, *On the Plaza;* McDonogh, "Discourses of the City"; Rotenberg, *Landscape and Power in Vienna;* Silverstein, *Algeria in France.*

11. Anand, "Pressure"; Appadurai, "Deep Democracy"; Carse, "Nature as Infrastructure"; Chalfin, "Public Things, Excremental Politics, and the Infrastructure of Bare Life in Ghana's City of Tema"; Graham and Marvin, *Splintering Urbanism;* Larkin, "The Politics and Poetics of Infrastructure" and *Signal and Noise;* Latour, *Aramis, or the Love of Technology.*

12. Mairie de Paris, *Plan Biodiversité de Paris,* 11.

13. Carse, "Nature as Infrastructure."

14. Lefebvre, *The Production of Space,* 364, 41.

15. See Stanek, *Henri Lefebvre on Space.*

16. Lefebvre, *The Production of Space,* 38–39.

17. Ibid., 362.

18. Ibid., 364–65.

19. Gramsci, Hoare, and Nowell-Smith, *Selections from the Prison Notebooks of Antonio Gramsci,* 9.

20. See Ingold, *Making.*

21. Brantz and Dümplemann, *Greening the City,* 1.

22. See Anand, "Pressure"; Carse, "Nature as Infrastructure"; Chalfin, "Public Things, Excremental Politics, and the Infrastructure of Bare Life in Ghana's City of Tema"; Kane, *Where Rivers Meet the Sea;* McDonogh, "Mediterranean Reflection"; McDonogh, Isenhour, and Checker, "Introduction"; Rademacher, *Reigning the River.*

23. Balmori and Sanders, *Groundwork;* Brantz and Dümplemann, *Greening the City;* Cronon, *Nature's Metropolis;* Farr, *Sustainable Urbanism;* Gandy, *Concrete and*

Clay; Harvey, *Justice, Nature, and the Geography of Difference;* Heynen, Kaika, and Swyngedouw, *In the Nature of Cities;* Reed, *Groundswell;* Ross, *Bird on Fire;* Swyngedouw, "The City as a Hybrid"; Haas, *Sustainable Urbanism and Beyond;* Williams, *The Country and the City.*

24. See Kaika and Swyngedouw, "Cities, Natures, and the Political Imaginary"; Latour, *Politics of Nature;* Smith, "The Production of Nature."

25. Kaika and Swyngedouw, "Cities, Natures, and the Political Imaginary," 25.

26. See, for example, Kane, *Where Rivers Meet the Sea;* Murray, "The Presence of the Past"; Peet and Watts, *Liberation Ecologies;* Rademacher, *Reigning the River;* Wolf, "Ownership and Political Ecology."

27. See Kane, *Where Rivers Meet the Sea;* Rademacher, *Reigning the River.*

28. Meadows, *The Limits to Growth.*

29. Harvey, *Population, Resources, and the Ideology of Science;* O'Connor, *Is Capitalism Sustainable?;* Swyngedouw, "Impossible Sustainability and the Post-Political Condition."

30. Checker, "Wiped Out by the 'Greenwave'"; McDonogh, Isenhour, and Checker, "Introduction"; Swyngedouw, "Impossible Sustainability and the Post-Political Condition."

31. Lubin and Esty, "The Sustainability Imperative."

32. See McDonogh, "Learning from Barcelona."

33. See Graham and Nordin, "From the Real to the Virtual."

34. Spirn, *The Granite Garden,* 4.

35. Beatley, *Green Urbanism;* Cervero, *The Transit Metropolis;* Giradet, *Creating Sustainable Cities;* Newman and Kenworthy, *Sustainability and Cities.* The concept of "metabolism" is a central theme in Marxist theories of nature; see Harvey, "The City as Body Politic"; Schmidt, *The Concept of Nature in Marx;* Smith, *Uneven Development.*

36. See McDonough, Isenhour, and Checker, "Introduction."

37. See Biehl, *Vita.*

38. Clichy-sous-Bois is infamous as the site of the tragic deaths of two youths in 2005 that sparked weeks of civil unrest in *banlieue* districts throughout France, its overseas territories, and in Belgium and Switzerland.

39. See Body-Gendrot, "Paris"; Sassen, *The Global City;* White, "Old Wine, Cracked Bottle?"; and Brenner and Theodore, *Spaces of Neoliberalism.*

40. Carpenter and Lees, *Gentrification in New York, London and Paris;* Chalvon-Demersay, *Le Triangle du XIVe;* Pinçon and Pinçon-Charlot, *Sociologie de Paris;* Smith, "New Globalism, New Urbanism."

41. Paris—and France in general—might best be described as in the process of a hybrid-style of neoliberalization in which the state directs restructuring of urban space

as part of an effort to maintain global competitiveness. See Visser, *Union Membership Statistics in 24 Countries*; Schmidt, "French Capitalism Transformed, yet Still a Variety of Capitalism"; Prasad, "Why Is France So French?"; Jobert and Théret, "France."

42. See Dikeç, *Badlands of the Republic*; Fassin, *Enforcing Order*; Wacquant, *Deadly Symbiosis*.

43. Epstein, *Collective Terms*.

44. Beriss, *Black Skins, French Voices*; Bowen, "Does French Islam Have Borders?"; Epstein, *Collective Terms*; Silverstein, *Algeria in France*; Selby, *Questioning French Secularism*.

45. Bowen, *Why the French Don't Like Headscarves*; Dubois, "La République Métis-sée"; Fassin, "L'intervention française de la discrimination"; Fernando, "Exceptional Citizens"; Hargreaves, *Multi-Ethnic France*; Jennings, "Citizenship, Republicanism and Multiculturalism in Contemporary France"; Silverstein, "The Context of Antisemi-tism and Islamophobia in France"; Terrio, *Judging Mohammed*; Ticktin, *Casualties of Care*; Wilder, *The French Imperial Nation-State*.

46. See Arkin, "Rhinestone Aesthetics and Religious Essence"; and Bunzl, *Anti-Semitism and Islamophobia*.

47. See Dikeç, *Badlands of the Republic*. See also chapter 3.

48. Pinçon and Pinçon-Charot, *Sociologie de Paris*, 58.

49. APUR, "La politique de la Ville à Paris," 67, 58.

50. Pinol, *Atlas historique des villes de France*, 62–63.

51. APUR, "Paris et ses quartiers: 18e;"APUR, "Paris et ses quartiers: 19e."

52. See www.ateliergrandparis.fr.

53. See Clerval, *Paris sans le peuple*. Data on prices obtained from the Chambre des Notaires de Paris (available online at Paris.notaires.fr); APUR, "La politique de la Ville à Paris," 67, 58.

54. If so, the underrepresentation of low-income vis-à-vis middle-class residents would be anything but a new phenomenon in France's public-housing sector: see Duclaud-Williams, *The Politics of Housing in Britain and France*.

55. De Rudder, "Immigrant Housing and Integration in French Cities."

56. The same term is used to describe the Reconquista, or shift in control of the Iberian Peninsula from Muslim to Christian control. For examples of the usage of urban reconquest discourse, see Ambroise-Rendu, "La Goutte d'Or devient un modèle de reconquête urbaine"; Ambroise-Rendu, "Paris part à la reconquête de ses quartiers difficiles"; Garin, "Les élus parisiens planchent sur les nouvelles règles d'urbanisme"; Boccara, "Les portes de Paris changent de visage."

57. APUR, "La politique de la Ville à Paris," 67, 58.

58. Harvey, *Rebel Cities*. See also Juris, "Reflections on #Occupy Everywhere."

59. Davis, "Fortress Los Angeles"; Iveson, *Publics and the City*; Low, *Behind the Gates*; Low, *On the Plaza*; Low and Smith, *The Politics of Public Space*; Mitchell, *The Right to the City*; Sorkin, *Variations on a Theme Park*; Shepard and Smithsimon, *The Beach beneath the Street*; Smith, *The New Urban Frontier*.

60. See Building Movement Project, "On the Commons"; Klein, "Common Frame for Social Justice"; Harvey, *Rebel Cities*; Hardt and Negri, *Commonwealth*; Susser and Tonnelat, "Transformative Cities"; Holston, *Insurgent Citizenship*; Lefebvre, "The Right to the City"; Mitchell, *The Right to the City*.

61. Whyte, *The Social Life of Small Urban Spaces*.

62. Harvey, *Rebel Cities*, x; Zukin, *Naked City*, 220; Jacobs, *The Death and Life of Great American Cities*, 50; Lefebvre, "The Right to the City," 150.

63. Jolé, "Le destin festif du Canal Saint-Martin"; Milliot, "Pluralistic Ambiance and Urban Socialization"; Milliot and Tonnelat, "Contentious Policing in Paris."

64. Burdick, *Blessed Anastácia*; see also Edelman, "Social Movements, Changing Paradigms and Changing Forms of Politics."

65. Our team was composed of two sociologists, Michèle Jolé and Stéphane Tonnelat, me, and two doctoral candidates in Urban Planning, Irène d'Agostino and Sophie Koch, and was based at the Institut d'Urbanisme de Paris, Université de Paris-Est.

66. See Ingold, *Making*, on framing the pedagogical aspects of anthropology, that is, the ethnographer as learner.

67. Lefebvre, *The Production of Space*, 365.

68. See Pétonnet, "L'observation flottante."

69. See, for example, Biehl, *Vita*; Bourgois, *In Search of Respect*; Duneier, *Sidewalk*.

70. See Burawoy, "The Extended Case Method"; Ferguson, *Expectations of Modernity*; van Velson, "The Extended Case Method."

71. See Wilder, *The French Imperial Nation-State*.

1. Poets and Locomotives

1. Simon, "Tour de Babel."

2. For an excellent of analysis of the fascination with the *terrain vague* concept, see Gandy, "Marginalia"; Silverstein, *Algeria in France*.

3. Harvey, *Rebel Cities*, 4.

4. Rademacher, *Reigning the River*.

5. Gatta, "Temporality of Physical and Political Liminal Spaces in the Urban Transformation of the Greater Paris."

6. De Rudder, "Immigrant Housing and Integration in French Cities."

7. Silverstein, *Algeria in France*, 4.

8. See Noiriel, *The French Melting Pot*.

9. APUR, "La politique de la Ville à Paris," 58, 60, 66.

10. Jobert and Théret, "France"; Clift, "The Changing Political Economy of France."

11. Fysh and Wolfreys, *The Politics of Racism in France*; Hargreaves, *Multi-Ethnic France*.

12. Prasad, "Why Is France So French?"

13. Silberman and Fournier, "Les secondes générations sur le marché du travail en France," 3; Simon, "France and the Unknown Second Generation," 1112.

14. The generation-centered narrative of immigration—which is the dominant framework in France—obscures much of the deeper historical importance of migration to the nation even as it reveal the inequalities of the present. Since the area's railroad terminals (Gare du Nord and Gare de l'Est) were built in the nineteenth century, northeast Paris has long been a destination for migrants from rural provinces whose cultural alignment with the French nation—as well as with other parts of Europe— were very much in question at the time. There are a multitude of accounts of various groups of North Africans residing in the neighborhood from shortly after World War I onward. See, for example, APUR, "Les hôtels meublés à Paris"; Aymé, *Across Paris*; Fargue, *Le piéton de Paris*; Massignon, *Annuaire du monde musulman*.

15. Agence France Presse. "Le maire du 19e Roger Madec s'addresse aux fidèles de la mosquée Adda'wa"; Marchand, "Après l'attentat de la rue de Tanger."

16. See Heynen, Kaika, and Swyngedouw, *In the Nature of Cities*. See also Schmidt, *The Concept of Nature in Marx*; Smith, *Uneven Development*.

17. See Chadych and Leborgne, *Atlas de Paris*.

18. Ibid., 12.

19. Ibid., 150.

20. See http://www.104.fr.

21. Aymé, "Rue de l'Évangile," in *Across Paris*, 17.

22. Ibid., 24.

23. Ibid., 17.

24. Aymé, "Rue de l'Évangile," in *Derrière chez Martin*, 129.

25. Ibid.

26. See Didier, "Un quartier empoisonné"; Hurin, "Fûts toxiques."

27. AIRPARIF, "La pollution atmosphérique d'une gare parisienne," 2–3. Subsequent references are given in the text.

28. AIRPARIF, Modélisation de la dispersion des émissions polluantes dans le quartier de la Gare de l'Est," 15; AIRPARIF, "La pollution atmosphérique d'une gare parisienne," 3.

29. AIRPARIF, "La pollution atmosphérique d'une gare parisienne," 2.

30. AIRPARIF, Modélisation de la dispersion des émissions polluantes dans le quartier de la Gare de l'Est."

31. Ibid., 6.

32. See, for example, Blecher, "Face à face tendu entre jeunes et policiers à la Gare du Nord"; Le Monde, "Heurts entre jeunes et policiers à la Gare du Nord." For an especially cogent analysis of these anxieties over the train station in particular, see also Kleinman, "The Gare du Nord."

33. APUR, "Quartier des gares du Nord et de l'Est," 1.

34. See Lefebvre, The Production of Space, 38.

35. APUR, "Quartier des gares du Nord et de l'Est," 5. Subsequent references are given in the text.

36. Smith, The New Urban Frontier.

37. See http://www.mon-grandparis.fr and http://www.ateliergrandparis.fr.

38. See APUR, "Quartier des gares du Nord et de l'Est," 9.

39. Residents' associations are eligible for state subsidies, but many activists argue that accepting one might compromise political independence.

40. Magnon and Mangeney, Atlas de la santé en Île-de-France, 46.

41. APUR, "La politique de la Ville à Paris," 58, 67; APUR, "Quartier des gares du Nord et de l'Est," 40.

42. Quoted in Stéphane Legras, in the newsletter Pajol: 10 ans de concertation.

43. Ibid.

44. See http://www.semaest.fr/article/zac-pajol-18e.

45. Fargue, "Mon quartier," in Le piéton de Paris, 28.

46. Lefebvre, The Production of Space, 38.

47. Reed, Groundswell, 16.

2. Space, Style, and Grassroots Strategy in the Éole Mobilization

1. Susser, Norman Street; Katz, "Vagabond Capitalism and the Necessity of Social Reproduction"; Susser and Tonnelat, "Transformative Cities."

2. Wolff, "The Invisible Flâneuse."

3. The literature addressing ecological or green gentrification is large and rapidly growing. See Dooling, "Ecological Gentrification"; Dooling and Simon, Cities, Nature and Development; Pearsall, "Moving Out or Moving In?"; Quastel, "Political Ecologies of Gentrification."

4. Graeber, Direct Action. I prefer to use the term "activist style" over "activist culture"; for more on this distinction, see Ferguson, Expectations of Modernity; Hebdige, Subculture.

5. Pinçon and Pinçon-Charlot, *Sociologie de Paris*. For a discussion of the May '68 generation and its cultural legacy, see Ross, *May '68 and Its Afterlives*.

6. See Bullard, *Dumping in Dixie*; Checker, *Polluted Promises*; Sokolovsky, "Civic Ecology and the Anthropology of Place"; Tidball and Krasny, "From Risk to Resilience."

7. Their activism related to the park obviously held social, environmental, as well as financial benefits for them.

8. De Rudder, "Immigrant Housing and Integration in French Cities."

9. APUR, "La politique de la Ville à Paris."

10. Sanjek, *Gray Panthers*.

11. See Jacobs, *The Death and Life of Great American Cities*.

12. In this regard, my evidence supports Sanjek's argument that the presence of elders in protest movements is an important source of intergenerational alliance building and idea sharing. See Sanjek, *Gray Panthers*.

13. See Beriss, *Black Skins, French Voices*.

14. See, for example, Simon, "Tour de Babel."

15. Sokolovsky, "Civic Ecology and the Anthropology of Place."

16. See Ross, *May '68 and Its Afterlives*

17. On "signifying practice," see Hebdige, *Subculture*.

18. Pinçon and Pinçon-Charlot, *Sociologie de Paris*.

19. *Le Parisien*, "Fête du Printemps pour les Jardins d'Éole."

20. Du Martera, "Oui au futur jardin; non à seringues."

21. The Éole activists attempted to manipulate the political system to meet their interests, as opposed to transforming the system along radical lines. Yet its discourse was infused with utopianism; at times, the mobilization appeared to be working "within the system" with the hope of producing the park as a mini-utopian space. See Jacoby, *Picture Imperfect*.

22. Hurin, "Fûts toxiques."

23. Didier, "Un quartier empoisonné."

24. See Smith, *Uneven Development* and "The Production of Nature."

25. Schneider and Susser, *Wounded Cities*.

26. See Gramsci, Hoare, and Nowell-Smith, *Selections from the Prison Notebooks of Antonio Gramsci*.

27. See Ross, *May '68 and Its Afterlives*.

3. Cultivating the Republic?

1. APUR, "La politique de la Ville à Paris," 15.

2. See Dikeç, *Badlands of the Republic*.

3. See Bowen, *Why the French Don't Like Headscarves;* Hargreaves, *Multi-Ethnic France;* Jennings, "Citizenship, Republicanism and Multiculturalism in Contemporary France"; de Rudder, Poiret, and Dewitte, "Affirmative action et 'discrimination justifiée.'"

4. See Beriss, *Black Skins, French Voices;* Dubois, *Soccer Empire;* Epstein, *Collective Terms;* Fernando, "Exceptional Citizens"; Fernando, "Reconfiguring Freedom"; Selby, *Questioning French Secularism;* Silverstein, *Algeria in France;* Terrio, *Judging Mohammed;* Wilder, *The French Imperial Nation-State.*

5. See Arkin, *Rhinestones, Religion, and the Republic.*

6. Bunzl, *Anti-Semitism and Islamophobia.*

7. See Bowen, *Why the French Don't Like Headscarves;* Newman, "Seeing the Republic in a Park."

8. Erlanger, "Parliament Moves France Closer to a Ban on Facial Veils."

9. Dikeç, *Badlands of the Republic;* Donzelot, Mével, and Wyvekens, *Faire Société;* Epstein, *Collective Terms;* Silverstein, *Algeria in France.*

10. See Castells, *The City and the Grassroots.*

11. Duclaud-Williams, *The Politics of Housing in Britain and France,* 125. Castells, in his research on social housing in the Paris area, also points out that that almost 9 percent of the population had no regular home (14 percent for blue-collar workers), 17 percent of families were forced to cohabit with others, and 55 percent of dwellings lacked bathrooms (Castells, *The City and the Grassroots,* 75). *Bidonvilles* refers to informal, "shantytown" settlements surrounding postwar Paris.

12. Silverstein, *Algeria in France.*

13. Dikeç *Badlands of the Republic.*

14. Bordier, "Logement social."

15. Bacqué and Fijalkow, "En attendant sa gentrification, discours et politiques publiques à la Goutte d'Or (1982–2000)."

16. There is a significant formal difference between the definition of a park (which is perhaps the most general way of describing an open, green space set aside for public use or conservation) and a public garden (which typically refers to a green space that has been laid out according to one of the many traditions of landscape or garden design). In practice, however, both the DEVE and my informants use the terms interchangeably, and therefore, to avoid confusion, so will I.

17. The axis of power is also known as the *axe historique parisien* (historical Parisian axis) or the *voie royale* (royal way). The axis historically began at the Louvre Palace and Tuileries Garden. It follows the Champs-Élysées westward, through the Arc de Triomphe. Since the 1980s, it was extended through the Arche de la Défense, located at La Défense, France's symbolic center of corporate globalization. See Pinçon and Pinçon-Charlot; *Sociologie de Paris.*

18. See Bowen, *Why the French Don't Like Headscarves.*

19. Official title: "Réglementation générale des promenades appartenant à la Ville de Paris y compris les bois de Boulogne et Vincennes."

20. Tonnelat has described this as a form "civism" in parks (Tonnelat, "Paris' Parks").

21. The full list of rules is available at available online at http://www.paris.fr/pra tique/parcs-jardins-squares.

22. See http://equipement.paris.fr/parc-monceau-1804.

23. APUR, "Paris et ses quartiers: 8e," 17; APUR, "Paris et ses quartiers: 18e," 17.

24. Jolé, Tonnelat, and Newman, "Le public des jardins de Paris, entre observation et action."

25. The AAS are uniformed, but are not police; they have no weapons, only whistles.

26. Tonnelat, "Paris' Parks."

27. APUR, "Paris et ses quartiers: 18e," 17.

28. See Jasanoff, *States of Knowledge.*

29. See Mostafavi and Doherty, *Ecological Urbanism.*

30. Mairie de Paris, *Plan Biodiversité de Paris.*

31. See http://eluesrepublicainessocialistes.unblog.fr.

32. See Holston, *Insurgent Citizenship.*

33. The word *bande* can mean either "gang" in a criminal sense or a simply a group of friends. In the context of hip-hop in France, *bande* is more akin to a "crew" or group, though the boundaries between these types of *bandes* are at times ambiguous.

34. Favre and Fillieule, "La manifestation comme indicateur de l'engagement politique"; Perrineau, *L'engagement politique;* Waters, *Social Movements in France.*

35. See Beriss, *Black Skins, French Voices;* Epstein, *Collective Terms;* Neveu, *Citoyenneté et espace public.*

36. See Boris, "Esclavage."

37. ibid.

38. Dufay, "Black-beurs."

39. Agence France Presse, "Le maire du 19e Roger Madec s'adresse aux fidèles de la mosque Adda'wa."

40. APUR, "La politique de la Ville à Paris," 57, 66.

41. Erlanger, "Gangland Violence Divides a Paris Neighborhood."

42. Created by legislative decree in 1989, the Haut Conseil à l'Intégration (HCI) is an expert panel overseen by the prime minister and concerned with the cultural integration of immigrants, and in particular the effect of immigration on France's national identity. The HCI, especially in the 1990s, has had a considerable influence in shaping

popular discussions of cultural difference and national belonging in France. See Hargreaves, *Multi-Ethnic France;* Jennings, "Citizenship, Republicanism and Multiculturalism in Contemporary France."

43. Balibar, "Is There a 'Neo-Racism'?," 21.

44. See Anderson, *Imagined Communities.* Wilder has called a similar process the "colonial humanism" of the French empire's interwar period (*The French Imperial Nation-State,* 4).

4. The End(s) of Urban Ecology in the Global City

1. From Ban Ki-moon's "Remarks to 'Cities Leadership Day,'" delivered at the United Nations Conference on Sustainable Development, June 21, 2012, Rio de Janeiro, Brazil. Available online at www.un.org/apps/news/infocus/sgsspeeches.

2. The term is sometimes simply glossed as "conflicts," but the literal translation, "conflicts over usage," is more germane to the urban planning context.

3. APUR, "Quartier des gares du Nord et de l'Est," 7.

4. See, for example, Brosius, "Analyses and Interventions"; Checker, "Wiped Out by the 'Green Wave'"; McDonogh, Isenhour, and Checker, "Introduction"; Tsing; "Nature in the Making"; West, *Conservation Is Our Government Now.*

5. See Harding, "Urban Regimes in a Europe of the Cities"; Logan and Molotch, *Urban Fortunes.*

6. Haut Conseil à l'Intégration, quoted in Hargreaves, *Immigration, "Race" and Ethnicity in Contemporary France,* 184.

7. Association Prévention Routière, "Accident de la route moto et scooter"; Dikeç, *Badlands of the Republic.*

8. Smith, "Remaking Scale"; Tsing, *Friction.*

9. Sassen, *The Global City.*

10. See http://cbc.iclei.org/home; http://www.c40cities.org/.

11. This urban/global–centered reimagining of scale has raised some political hackles (notably in the United States, where an often antiurban Republican Party has managed to ban the adoption of Agenda 21 guidelines by municipalities in the state of Alabama). While such paranoia is driven in no small part by "UN conspiracy theories," it demonstrates the unsettling political effect that can occur when municipal leaders harness the urban scale as a way to reimagine the global.

12. Lefevbre, *The Production of Space,* 38.

13. Veyret et al., *Atlas des villes durables,* 8.

14. Beatly, *Green Urbanism.*

15. European Commission, "Urban Environment—Environment—European Commission," n.p.

16. Ibid.

17. McDonogh, "Learning from Barcelona."

18. Graham and Nordin, "From the Real to the Virtual."

19. Arcology, a concept coined by the architect Paolo Soleri, refers to a utopian vision of a self-contained community, frequently imagined as a hermetically sealed Eden-like setting located in an otherwise inhospitable environment.

20. See http://www.masdarcity.ae/en/.

21. London also beat out Paris, which had been viewed as the favorite for the 2012 Olympics.

22. Harvey, *Population, Resources, and the Ideology of Science.*

23. United Nations, "United Nations Conference on Environment and Development," section 7.1. Available online at http://www.sustainabledevelopment.un.org/content/documents/Agenda21.pdf.

24. http://cbc.iclei.org/hotspots.

25. See "Curitaba" at http://cbc.iclei.org/project.

26. See "eThekwini" at http://cbc.iclei.org/project.

27. http://cbc.iclei.org/hotspots.

28. Although planned by the city and sometimes described as a "community" bike program, the system is in fact operated by an outdoor advertising company, JC Decaux, which receives rights to on-street advertising in exchange for maintaining the system (in addition to a subsidy from the city of Paris itself).

29. Fettig, *Paris.*

30. Couvreur, "Comment Vélib' s'organise face à la grève."

31. Le Gendre, "Pourquoi les Vélib', fétiches des bobos, sont vandalisés." See also: http://blog.velib.paris.fr, "Les Vélib' et les bobos, c'est une grande histoire d'amour!"; Vélib' Officiel, "Vélib'—interview des 'Bobos de Merde.'"

32. Erlanger and de la Baume, "French Ideal of Bicycle-Sharing Meets Reality."

33. Ibid.; Védrines, "Il y a un Vélib' à Bamako."

34. Fettig, *Paris.*

35. Mairie de Paris, "Vélib' fête son 6e anniversaire."

36. See Paquot, "La bicyclette urbaine."

37. Sarkozy, "Le Grand Paris."

38. http://www.mon-grandparis.fr/le-grand-paris.

39. Ibid.

40. Vincendon, "Pour Delanoë, Sarkozy n'est pas propriétaire du Grand Paris."

41. Nunes, "Huchon"; Deprieck, "Le Grand Paris rapproche Sarkozy et Huchon."

42. Slate.fr, "Grand Paris de droite, Grand Paris de gauche?"

43. Savitch, *Post-industrial Cities.*

44. http://www.gouvernement.fr, "Le Nouveau Grand Paris."

45. Lecroart, "Regenerating the Plaine Saint-Denis, 1985–2020."

46. Sarkozy, "Le Grand Paris."

47. Mairie de Paris, *Plan Biodiversité de Paris,* 9.

48. Ibid.

49. Ibid., 15.

50. Ibid., iii.

51. APUR, "Quartier des gares du Nord et de l'Est," 7.

52. Mairie de Paris, "Chapelle International—Paris Nord-Est."

53. Mairie de Paris, "Le project social—Paris Nord-Est."

54. Mairie de Paris, "Un project global—Paris Nord-Est."

55. APUR, "La population étrangère à Paris"; APUR, "La politique de la Ville à Paris." See also Clerval, *Paris sans le peuple.*

56. Chambres des Notaires de Paris—Île-de-France; quarterly real-estate values available at http://www.paris.notaires.fr.

57. Ibid.; Mairie de Paris, "Les chiffres-clés du chômage à Paris."

58. APUR, "La politique de la Ville à Paris," 58.

59. André, "Que faire des ghettos de centre-ville?"

60. Ambroise-Rendu, "La Goutte d'Or devient un modèle de reconquête urbaine dans le dix-huitième arrondissement de Paris"; Ambroise-Rendu, "Paris part à la reconquête de ses quartiers difficiles"; Garin, "Les élus parisiens planchent sur les nouvelles règles d'urbanisme"; Boccara, "Les portes de Paris changent de visage."

61. Bunzl, "Between Anti-Semitism and Islamophobia."

62. Silverstein, *Algeria in France,* 89.

63. Mairie de Paris, "Concours de maîtrise d'œuvre pour la creation d'un parc paysage Cour du Maroc à Paris," 5.

64. Leitner and Sheppard, "'The City Is Dead, Long Live the Net.'"

65. See, for example, Debord, *The Society of the Spectacle;* Harvey, *Rebel Cities;* Harvey, *Spaces of Hope;* Lefebvre, Kofman, and Lebas, *Writings on Cities;* Mitchell, *The Right to The City;* Susser and Tonnelat, "Transformative Cities."

5. To Watch and Be Watched

1. Lyon, *Surveillance Society.*

2. Bennett and Lyon, *Playing the Identity Card;* Coleman, "Images from a Neoliberal City"; Coleman, Tombs, and Whyte, "Capital, Crime Control and Statecraft in the Entrepreneurial City"; Davis, "Fortress Los Angeles."

3. See Paris sans Vidéosurveillance, "La pétition pour un Paris sans cameras de vidéosurveillance."

4. Foucault, *Discipline and Punish*, 172.

5. Termed ZSPs (Zones de Sécurité Prioritaire), the program was launched in 2012 (see chapter 6).

6. Jolé, "Surveiller ou veiller sur le jardin?"; Sansot, *Jardins publics*.

7. Jacobs, *The Death and Life of Great American Cities*.

8. Susser, "Global Visions and Grassroots Movements." See also Castells, *The City and the Grassroots*.

9. Ferguson and Gupta, "Spatializing States."

10. Brash, *Bloomberg's New York*.

11. See Smith, "New Globalism, New Urbanism."

12. Tassel, "Les expulsions de sans-papiers en forte hausse en 2012."

13. After the deadline, elected officials could not legally use a project to promote themselves in an electoral campaign, but in this case municipal elections were later moved to 2008 to avoid overlap with national elections, making the timetable a moot point in the end.

14. Suzelle and Gérard, two AAS personnel with whom I developed a close relationship during the course of my fieldwork, described it as "well made for their professional use" with "excellent visibility."

15. DPJEV (Direction des Parcs, des Jardins et des Espaces Verts) was the predecessor to the administration now known as the DEVE (Direction des Espaces Verts et de l'Environnement).

16. Jacobs, *The Death and Life of Great American Cities*, 39.

17. See Terrio, *Judging Mohammed*.

18. Neveu, *Citoyenneté et espace public*.

19. Stolcke, "Talking Culture."

20. Susser, "Global Visions and Grassroots Movements."

21. See Jacobs, *The Death and Life of Great American Cities*, 39.

22. In the United States in particular, urban park conservancies play an even more formalized role than the neighborhood associations described here in regulating use, management, and even the design of spaces that are still "owned" by the public at large.

23. Ong, *Neoliberalism as Exception*.

24. Mitchell, *The Right to the City*.

25. See Harvey, *Paris*.

6. The Political Life of Small Urban Spaces

1. Mairie de Paris, "Les chiffres-clés du chômage à Paris—juillet 2013."

2. Despite a common association between neoliberal policy and state retrenchment, the 2008 global economic crisis went hand in hand with the "return of the state." See Robotham, "Anthropology of the Present Moment."

3. The name of the hotel has been changed to protect the identities of the persons involved.

4. Although the number of *hôtels meublés* in Paris decreased drastically since the decades following the Second World War, the twenty-first century has seen a large increase in the number of families housed by emergency services for shelter in Paris (from 2,298 in 1999 to 7,671 in 2006). An APUR study found that 96 percent of these families were people who had migrated from sub-Saharan African or the Maghreb. More than a third of the families sheltered in this manner were at hotels in northeast Paris. See APUR, "Les hôtels meublés à Paris."

5. See Biehl, *Vita*.

6. For an extended ethnographic and theoretical meditation on the direct-action concept, see Graeber, *Direct Action*.

7. Caldeira, *City of Walls*; Shepard and Smithsimon, *The Beach beneath the Streets*; Sorkin, *Variations on a Theme Park*.

8. Iveson, *Publics and the City*; Low and Smith, *The Politics of Public Space*; Mitchell, *The Right to the City*.

9. See Gatta, "Temporality of Physical and Political Liminal Spaces in the Urban Transformations of the Greater Paris"; Jolé, "Le destin festif du Canal Saint-Martin"; Joseph, *La ville sans qualités*; Joseph, *L'espace du public*; Milliot, "Pluralistic Ambiance and Urban Socialization"; Milliot and Tonnelat, "Contentious Policing in Paris"; Palumbo, "Figures de l'habiter"; Tonnelat, "Out of Frame."

10. Whyte, *The Social Life of Small Urban Spaces*.

11. Lefebvre, "The Right to the City," 66; emphasis in the original.

12. Ibid., 168.

13. Ibid., 150.

14. See Harvey, *Rebel Cities*.

15. See Graeber, *Direct Action*.

16. Sansot, *Jardins publics*, 143.

17. Tonnelat, "Paris' Parks."

18. See Jolé, "Surveiller ou veiller sur le jardin?"

19. Drinking wine in the esplanade is technically a breach of park regulations, but no one appeared to care.

20. For the full text of the law, see http://www.senat.fr, "Project de loi de finances pour 2013: Sécurité (gendarmerie nationale et police nationale)," article C, part 2.

21. See Milliot and Tonnelat, "Contentious Policing in Paris."

22. Ibid.

23. *Le Parisien*, "Les Jardins d'Éole ferment pour 'réparation'"; *Le Parisien*, "La drogue a vidé les Jardins d'Éole."

24. See Gatta, "Temporality of Physical and Political Liminal Spaces in the Urban Transformations of the Greater Paris"; Jolé, "Le destin festif du Canal Saint-Martin"; Joseph, *La ville sans qualities;* Milliot, "Pluralistic Ambiance and Urban Socialization"; Milliot and Tonnelat, "Contentious Policing in Paris"; Palumbo, "Figures de l'habiter"; Tonnelat, "Out of Frame."

25. Susser, "Magical Urbanism and Rural Resistance."

Conclusion

1. Wilder, *The French Imperial Nation-State.*

2. My use of this term—especially with regard to political implications (see chapter 3)—differs from Dikeç's (in *Badlands of the Republic*).

3. Wolf, *Europe and the People without History,* 6–7.

4. Anand, "Pressure"; Carse, "Nature as Infrastructure"; Chalfin, "Public Things, Excremental Politics, and the Infrastructure of Bare Life in Ghana's City of Tema"; Kane, *Where Rivers Meet the Sea;* McDonogh, "Mediterranean Reflection"; McDonogh, Isenhour, and Checker, "Introduction"; Rademacher, *Reigning the River;* Stoetzer, "At the Forest Edges of the City."

5. See Brantz and Dümplemann, *Greening the City;* Cronon, *Nature's Metropolis;* Gandy, *Concrete and Clay;* Harvey, *Justice, Nature, and the Geography of Difference;* Heynen, Kaika, and Swyngedouw, *In the Nature of Cities;* Meyers, *Disposable Cities;* Ross, *Bird on Fire;* Swyngedouw, "The City as a Hybrid"; Williams, *The Country and the City.*

6. See Meyers, *Disposable Cities;* Heynen, Perkins, and Roy, "The Political Ecology of Uneven Urban Green Space"; Robbins, *Lawn People.*

7. See Herzfeld, "Shaping Cultural Space"; Ferguson, *Expectations of Modernity;* Harms, *Saigon's Edge.*

8. Hannerz, *Exploring the City;* Foster and Kemper, "Anthropological Fieldwork in Cities."

9. Anand, "Pressure"; Appadurai, "Deep Democracy"; Carse, "Nature as Infrastructure"; Chalfin, "Public Things, Excremental Politics, and the Infrastructure of Bare Life in Ghana's City of Tema"; Larkin, "The Politics and Poetics of Infrastructure"; Larkin, *Signal and Noise;* Latour, *Aramis, or the Love of Technology.*

10. Latour, *We Have Never Been Modern,* 118. The following quotation captures the full nuance of Latour's distinctions between network, line, space, and place: "They [networks] are composed of particular places aligned by a series of branchings that cross other places and require other branchings in order to spread. Between the lines of the network there is, strictly speaking, nothing at all: no train, no telephone, no intake pipe, no television set. Technological networks, as the name indicates, are nets

thrown over spaces, and they retain only a few scattered elements of those spaces. They are connected lines, not surfaces" (117–18).

11. See Ingold, *Redrawing Anthropology*.

12. Lefebvre, *The Production Space*, 38.

13. Smith, "Nature as Accumulation Strategy."

14. See Farr, *Sustainable Urbanism*; Haas, *Sustainable Urbanism and Beyond*.

15. Heynen, Kaika, and Swyngedouw, *In the Nature of Cities*.

16. Harvey, *Rebel Cities*. For more on "types" of commons, see Susser and Tonnelat, "Transformative Cities."

17. Milliot, "Pluralistic Ambiance and Urban Socialization"; Milliot and Tonnelat, "Contentious Policing in Paris."

18. However, as Scott Larson pointed out, Jacobs's work has been invoked as part of gentrification strategies. See Larson, *Building like Moses with Jacobs in Mind*.

19. Hardt and Negri, *Commonwealth*; Harvey, *Rebel Cities*; Hess and Ostrum, *Understanding Knowledge as a Commons*; Kohn, *Radical Space*.

BIBLIOGRAPHY

Agence France Presse (AFP). "Le maire du 19e Roger Madec s'adresse aux fidèles de la mosquée Adda'wa." Depêches/Wire release, March 18, 2005.

AIRPARIF (Association Interdépartementale pour la Gestion du Réseau Automatique de Surveillance de la Pollution Atmosphérique et d'Alerte en Région d'Île-de-France). "La pollution atmosphérique d'une gare parisienne." *Airparif Actualité,* no. 19 (July 2003): 1–2.

———. "Modélisation de la dispersion des émissions polluantes dans le quartier de la Gare de l'Est: Influence du traffic ferroviaire Diesel." Paris: Airparif, 2003.

Ambroise-Rendu, Marc. "La Goutte d'Or devient un modèle de reconquête urbaine dans le dix-huitième arrondissement de Paris, élus et associations se sont unis pour restaurer un quartier qui glissait vers le ghetto." *Le Monde,* November 5, 1995.

———. "Paris part à la reconquête de ses quartiers difficiles: Jacques Chirac obtient le soutien de l'opposition dans sa politique sociale." *Le Monde,* February 15, 1995.

Anand, Nikhil. "Pressure: The PoliTechnics of Water Supply in Mumbai." *Cultural Anthropology* 26, no. 4 (2011): 542–64.

Anderson, Benedict. *Imagined Communities: Reflections on the Origin and Spread of Nationalism.* London: Verso, 1991.

André, Jean-Louis. "Que faire des ghettos de centre-ville? Paris, Lyon et Marseille appliquent des stratégies différentes pour la 'reconquête' de quartiers populaires comme la Goutte-d'Or, la place du Pont et Belzunce." *Le Monde,* March 4, 1991.

Appadurai, Arjun. "Deep Democracy: Urban Governmentality and the Horizon of Politics." *Public Culture* 14, no. 1 (2002): 21–47.

APUR (Atelier Parisien d'Urbanisme). "La politique de la Ville à Paris: Observatoire des quartiers prioritaires; Rapport 2010." Paris: Mairie de Paris, 2010.

———. "La population étrangère à Paris." Note de 4 pages, no. 7, 2003.

———. "Les hôtels meublés à Paris." Paris: Mairie de Paris, 2007.

———. "Paris et ses quartiers: 8e." Paris: Mairie de Paris, 2001.

———. "Paris et ses quartiers: 18e." Paris: Mairie de Paris, 2001.

———. "Paris et ses quartiers: 19e." Paris: Mairie de Paris, 2001.

———. "Quartier des gares du Nord et de l'Est: Diagnostic prospectif—dynamique urbaine et évolutions des faisceaux ferrés." Paris: Mairie de Paris, 2012.

Arkin, Kimberly A. "Rhinestone Aesthetics and Religious Essence: Looking Jewish in Paris." *American Ethnologist* 36, no. 4 (2009): 722–34.

———. *Rhinestones, Religion, and the Republic: Fashioning Jewishness in France.* Palo Alto, Calif.: Stanford University Press, 2013.

Association Prévention Routière (APR). "Accident de la route moto et scooter." http://www.preventionroutiere.asso.fr/Nos-publications/Statistiques-d-accidents/Accidents-moto, n.d. Accessed 2013.

Aymé, Marcel. *Across Paris: And Other Stories.* New York: Harper, 1958.

———. *Derrière chez Martin.* Paris: Gallimard, 1938.

Bacqué, Marie-Hélène, and Yankel Fijalkow. "En attendant sa gentrification, discours et politiques publiques à la Goutte d'Or (1982–2000)." *Sociétés contemporaines* 3, no. 63 (2007): 63–84.

Balibar, Étienne. "Is There a 'Neo-Racism'?" In *Race, Nation, Class: Ambiguous Identities,* ed. Étienne Balibar and Immanuel M. Wallerstein, 17–28. London: Verso, 1991.

Balmori, Diana, and Joel Sanders. *Groundwork: Between Landscape and Architecture.* New York: Monacelli Press, 2011.

Beatley, Timothy. *Green Urbanism: Learning from European Cities.* Washington, D.C.: Island Press, 2000.

Benjamin, Walter. "Paris, Capital of the 19th Century (1939)." In *The Arcades Project,* trans. Howard Eiland and Kevin McLaughlin, 14–16. Cambridge, Mass.: Harvard University Press, 1969.

Bennett, Colin J., and David Lyon. *Playing the Identity Card: Surveillance, Security and Identification in Global Perspective.* London: Routledge, 2008.

Beriss, David. *Black Skins, French Voices: Caribbean Ethnicity and Activism in Urban France.* Boulder, Colo.: Westview Press, 2004.

Bess, Michael. *The Light-Green Society: Ecology and Technological Modernity in France, 1960–2000.* Chicago: University of Chicago Press, 2003.

Biehl, João, and Peter Locke. "Deleuze and the Anthropology of Becoming." *Current Anthropology* 51, no. 3 (2010): 317–52.

Biehl, João. *Vita: Life in a Zone of Social Abandonment.* Berkeley: University of California Press, 2005.

Blecher, Ludovic. "Face à face tendu entre jeunes et policiers à la Gare du Nord." *Libération,* March 27, 2007.

Boccara, Laurance. "Les portes de Paris changent de visage." *Les Echos,* October 26, 2006.

Body-Gendrot, Sophie. "Paris: A 'Soft' Global City?" *New Community* 22, no. 4 (1996): 595–606.

Bordier, Philippe. "Logement social: Politique et objectifs dans le 18e arrondissement— L'actualité du 18e arrondissement de Paris." June 21, 2009. http://www.dixhuitinfo .com. Accessed 2011.

Boris, Thiolay. "Esclavage: Les devoirs de l'école." *L'Express,* March 14, 2005.

Bourgois, Philippe. *In Search of Respect: Selling Crack in El Barrio.* Cambridge: Cambridge University Press, 1995.

Bowen, John R. "Does French Islam Have Borders? Dilemmas of Domestication in a Global Religious Field." *American Anthropologist* 106 (2004): 43–55.

———. *Why the French Don't Like Headscarves: Islam, the State, and Public Space.* Princeton, N.J.: Princeton University Press, 2007.

Brantz, Dorothee, and Sonja Dümpelmann, eds. *Greening the City: Urban Landscapes in the Twentieth Century.* Charlottesville: University of Virginia Press, 2011.

Brash, Julian. *Bloomberg's New York: Class and Governance in the Luxury City.* Athens: University of Georgia Press, 2011.

Brenner, Neil, and Nikolas Theodore. *Spaces of Neoliberalism: Urban Restructuring in North America and Western Europe.* Malden, Mass.: Blackwell, 2002.

Brosius, J. Peter. "Analyses and Interventions: Anthropological Engagements with Environmentalism." *Current Anthropology* 40, no. 3 (1999): 277–309.

Building Movement Project. *On the Commons.* http://buildingmovement.org. Accessed 2013.

Bullard, Robert D. *Dumping in Dixie: Race, Class, and Environmental Quality.* Boulder, Colo.: Westview Press, 2000.

Bunzl, Matti. *Anti-Semitism and Islamophobia: Hatreds Old and New in Europe.* Chicago: Prickly Paradigm Press, 2007.

———. "Between Anti-Semitism and Islamophobia: Some Thoughts on the New Europe." *American Ethnologist* 32, no. 4 (2005): 499–508.

Burawoy, Michael. "The Extended Case Method." *Sociological Theory* 16, no. 1 (1998): 4–33.

Burdick, John. *Blessed Anastácia: Women, Race, and Popular Christianity in Brazil.* New York: Routledge, 1998.

Caldeira, Teresa P. R. *City of Walls: Crime, Segregation, and Citizenship in São Paulo.* Berkeley: University of California Press, 2000.

Carpenter, Juliet, and Loretta Lees. *Gentrification in New York, London and Paris: An International Comparison.* Oxford: Blackwell, 1995.

Carse, Ashley. "Nature as Infrastructure: Making and Managing the Panama Canal Watershed." *Social Studies of Science* 42, no. 4 (2012): 539–63.

Castells, Manuel. *The City and the Grassroots: A Cross-Cultural Theory of Urban Social Movements.* Berkeley: University of California Press, 1983.

Cervero, Robert. *The Transit Metropolis: A Global Inquiry.* Washington, D.C: Island Press, 1998.

Chadych, Danièle, and Dominique Leborgne. *Atlas de Paris: Évolution d'un paysage urbain.* Paris: Parigramme, 1999.

Chalfin, Brenda. "Public Things, Excremental Politics, and the Infrastructure of Bare Life in Ghana's City of Tema." *American Ethnologist* 41, no. 1 (2014): 92–109.

Chalvon-Demersay, Sabine. *Le Triangle du XIV e: Des nouveaux habitants dans un vieux quartier de Paris.* Paris: Maison des Sciences de l'Homme, 1984.

Checker, Melissa. *Polluted Promises: Environmental Racism and the Search for Justice in a Southern Town.* New York: New York University Press, 2005.

———. "Wiped Out by the 'Greenwave': Environmental Gentrification and the Paradoxical Politics of Urban Sustainability." *City and Society* 23, no. 2 (2011): 210–29.

Clerval, Anne. *Paris sans le peuple: La gentrification de la capitale.* Paris: Éditions la Découverte, 2013.

Clift, Ben. "The Changing Political Economy of France: *Dirigisme* under Duress." In *A Ruined Fortress: Neoliberal Hegemony and Transformation in Europe,* ed. Alan W. Cafruny and Magnus Ryner, 173–200. Lanham, Md.: Rowan and Littlefield, 2006.

Coleman, Roy. "Images from a Neoliberal City: The State, Surveillance and Social Control." *Critical Criminology* 12, no. 1 (2004): 21–42.

Coleman, Roy, Steve Tombs, and Dave Whyte. "Capital, Crime Control and Statecraft in the Entrepreneurial City." *Urban Studies* 42, no. 13 (2005): 2511–30.

Couvreur, Olivier. "Comment Vélib' s'organise face à la grève." *Le Figaro,* September 22, 2010. http://www.lefigaro.fr. Accessed 2013.

Cronon, William. *Nature's Metropolis: Chicago and the Great West.* New York: W. W. Norton, 1991.

Davis, Mike. "Fortress Los Angeles: The Militarization of Urban Space." In *Variations on a Theme Park: The New American City and the End of Public Space,* ed. Michael Sorkin, 154–80. New York: Hill and Wang, 1992.

Debord, Guy. *The Society of the Spectacle.* New York: Zone Books, 1994.

Deprieck, Matthieu. "Le Grand Paris rapproche Sarkozy et Huchon." L'Express.fr. June 9, 2010. Accessed 2013.

de Rudder, Véronique. "Immigrant Housing and Integration in French Cities." In *Immigrants in Two Democracies: French and American Experience*, ed. Donald L. Horowitz and Gérard Noiriel, 247–67. New York: New York University Press, 1992.

de Rudder, Véronique, Christian Poiret, and P. Dewitte. "Affirmative action et 'discrimination justifiée': Vers un universalisme en acte." In *Immigration et intégration: L'état des savoirs*, ed. Philippe Dewite, 397–406. Paris: Éditions La Découverte, 1999.

de Solà-Morales, Ignasi. "Terrain vague." *Quaderns d'Arquitectes i Urbanisme*, no. 212 (1996): 34–43.

Didier, Caroline. "Un quartier empoisonné." *France Soir*, March 17, 1999.

Dikeç, Mustafa. *Badlands of the Republic: Space, Politics and Urban Policy*. Malden, Mass.: Blackwell, 2007.

Donzelot, Jacques, Catherine Mével, and Anne Wyvekens. *Faire société: La politique de la ville aux États-Unis et en France*. Paris: Éditions du Seuil, 2003.

Dooling, Sarah. "Ecological Gentrification: A Research Agenda Exploring Justice in the City." *International Journal of Urban and Regional Research* 33, no. 3 (2009): 621–39.

Dooling, Sarah, and Gregory Simon. *Cities, Nature and Development: The Politics and Production of Urban Vulnerabilities*. Farnham, Surrey, England: Ashgate Publishing Company, 2012.

Dubois, Laurent. "La République Métissée: Citizenship, Colonialism, and the Borders of French History." *Cultural Studies* 14, no. 1 (2000): 15–34.

———. *Soccer Empire: The World Cup and the Future of France*. Berkeley: University of California Press, 2010.

Dubost, Michel. "Rencontre de l'autre croyant, rencontre de Dieu," *Corbiniana*, no. 471 (December 2008), http://evry.catholique.fr. Accessed 2013.

Duclaud-Williams, Roger H. *The Politics of Housing in Britain and France*. London: Heinemann, 1978.

Dufay, François. "Black-beurs: La montée des minorités." *Le Point*, May 12, 2012.

du Martera, Céline. "Oui au futur jardin; non à seringues." *France Soir*, March 26, 2002.

Duneier, Mitchell. *Sidewalk*. New York: Farrar, Straus and Giroux, 1999.

Edelman, Marc. "Social Movements: Changing Paradigms and Forms of Politics." *Annual Review of Anthropology* (2001): 285–317.

Epstein, Beth. *Collective Terms: Race, Culture, and Community in a State-Planned City in France*. New York: Berghahn Books, 2011.

Erlanger, Steven. "Gangland Violence Divides a Paris Neighborhood." *New York Times,* September 24, 2008.

———. "Parliament Moves France Closer to a Ban on Facial Veils." *New York Times,* July 14, 2010.

Erlanger, Steven, and Maïa de la Baume. "French Ideal of Bicycle-Sharing Meets Reality." *New York Times,* October 31, 2009.

European Commission. "Urban Environment—Environment—European Commission." 2014. http://ec.europa.eu/environment/urban/aalborg.htm. Accessed 2014.

Fargue, Léon-Paul. *Le piéton de Paris.* Paris: Gallimard, 1939.

Farr, Douglas. *Sustainable Urbanism: Urban Design with Nature.* Hoboken, N.J.: Wiley, 2008.

Fassin, Didier. *Enforcing Order: An Ethnography of Urban Policing.* Cambridge: Polity, 2013.

———. "L'intervention française de la discrimination." *Revue française de science politique* 52, no. 4 (2002): 403–23.

Favre, Pierre, and Olivier Fillieule. "La manifestation comme indicateur de l'engagement politique." In *L'engagement politique: Déclin ou mutation,* ed. Pascal Perrineau, 115–39. Paris: Presses de la Fondation Nationale des Sciences Politiques, 1994.

Ferguson, James. *Expectations of Modernity: Myths and Meanings of Urban Life on the Zambian Copperbelt.* Berkeley: University of California Press, 1999.

Ferguson, James, and Akhil Gupta. "Spatializing States: Toward an Ethnography of Neoliberal Governmentality." *American Ethnologist* 29, no. 4 (2002): 981–1002.

Fernando, Mayanthi. "Exceptional Citizens: Secular Muslim Women and the Politics of Difference in France." *Social Anthropology* 17, no. 4 (2009): 379–92.

———. "Reconfiguring Freedom: Muslim Piety and the Limits of Secular Law and Public Discourse in France." *American Ethnologist* 37, no. 1 (2010): 19–35.

Fettig, Tad, dir. *Paris: Vélo Liberté.* 2008, 26 min.

Foster, George, and Robert Kemper. "Anthropological Fieldwork in Cities." In *Urban Life: Readings in the Anthropology of the City,* ed. George Gmelch and Walter Zenner, 131–45. Long Grove, Ill.: Waveland Press, 2002.

Foucault, Michel. *Discipline and Punish: The Birth of the Prison.* New York: Pantheon Books, 1977.

Fysh, Peter, and Jim Wolfreys. *The Politics of Racism in France.* New York: St. Martin's Press, 1998.

Gandy, Matthew. *Concrete and Clay: Reworking Nature in New York City.* Cambridge: MIT Press, 2002.

———. "Marginalia: Aesthetics, Ecology, and Urban Wastelands." *Annals of the Association of American Geographers* 103, no. 6 (2013): 1301–16.

Garin, Christine. "Les élus parisiens planchent sur les nouvelles règles d'urbanisme." *Le Monde*, February 1, 2005.

Gatta, Federica. "Temporality of Physical and Political Liminal Spaces in the Urban Transformations of the Greater Paris." In *Planning Times: Proceedings of the 18th International Conference on Urban Planning, Regional Development and Information Society* (2013): 879–89.

Girardet, Herbert. *Creating Sustainable Cities*. Cambridge: UIT Cambridge, 1999.

Gouvernement.fr. "Le nouveau Grand Paris: Pour une région compétitive et solidaire: Portail du gouvernement." http://www.gouvernement.fr. March 6, 2013. Accessed 2013.

Graeber, David. *Direct Action: An Ethnography*. Edinburgh: AK Press, 2009.

Graham, Mark, and Melissa Nordin. "From the Real to the Virtual: A Swedish Solution for 'Universal' Sustainable Development in Hammarby Sjöstad, Stockholm." In *Life among Planners*, ed. Jennifer Mack and Michael Herzfeld. Philadelphia: University of Pennsylvania Press. Forthcoming.

Graham, Steven, and Simon Marvin. *Splintering Urbanism: Networked Infrastructures, Technological Mobilities, and the Urban Condition*. New York: Routledge, 2001.

Gramsci, Antonio, Quintin Hoare, and Geoffrey Nowell-Smith. *Selections from the Prison Notebooks of Antonio Gramsci*. New York: International Publishers, 1972.

Haas, Tigran. *Sustainable Urbanism and Beyond: Rethinking Cities for the Future*. New York: Rizzoli, 2012.

Hannerz, Ulf. *Exploring the City: Inquiries toward an Urban Anthropology*. New York: Columbia University Press, 1980.

Harding, Alan. "Urban Regimes in a Europe of the Cities?" *European Urban and Regional Studies* 4, no. 4 (1997): 291–314.

Hardt, Michael, and Antonio Negri. *Commonwealth*. Cambridge, Mass.: Belknap Press of Harvard University Press, 2009.

Hargreaves, Alec G. *Immigration, "Race" and Ethnicity in Contemporary France*. London: Routledge, 1995.

———. *Multi-Ethnic France: Immigration, Politics, Culture and Society*. New York: Routledge, 2007.

Harms, Erik. *Saigon's Edge: On the Margins of Ho Chi Minh City*. Minneapolis: University of Minnesota Press, 2011.

Harvey, David. "The City as Body Politic." In *Wounded Cities: Deconstruction and Reconstruction in a Globalized World*, ed. Jane Schneider and Ida Susser, 25–46. New York: Berg, 2003.

———. *Justice, Nature, and the Geography of Difference*. Cambridge, Mass.: Blackwell Publishers, 1996.

————. *Paris, Capital of Modernity*. New York: Routledge, 2003.

————. *Population, Resources, and the Ideology of Science*. Worcester, Mass.: Clark University Press, 1974.

————. *Rebel Cities: From the Right to the City to the Urban Revolution*. New York: Verso, 2012.

————. *Spaces of Hope*. Berkeley: University of California Press, 2000.

Hebdige, Dick. *Subculture: The Meaning of Style*. London: Routledge, 2002.

Herzfeld, Micheal. "Shaping Cultural Space: Reflections on the Politics and Cosmology of Urbanism." In *Life among Planners*, ed. Jennifer Mack and Michael Herzfeld. Philadelphia: University of Pennsylvania Press. Forthcoming.

Hess, Charlotte, and Elinor Ostrom. *Understanding Knowledge as a Commons: From Theory to Practice*. Cambridge, Mass.: MIT Press, 2007.

Heynen, Nik, Harold Perkins, and Parama Roy. "The Political Ecology of Uneven Urban Green Space." *Urban Affairs Review* 42, no. 1 (2006): 3–25.

Heynen, Nik, Maria Kaika, and Erik Swyngedouw. *In the Nature of Cities: Urban Political Ecology and the Politics of Urban Metabolism*. London: Routledge, 2006.

Holston, James. *Insurgent Citizenship: Disjunctions of Democracy and Modernity in Brazil*. Princeton, N.J.: Princeton University Press, 2008.

————. *The Modernist City: An Anthropological Critique of Brasília*. Chicago: University of Chicago Press, 1989.

Hurin, Florence. "Fûts toxiques: Deux enterprises condamnées." *Le Parisien*, September 8, 2000.

Ingold, Tim. *Making: Anthropology, Archaeology, Art and Architecture*. New York: Routledge, 2013.

————. *Redrawing Anthropology: Materials, Movements, Lines*. Burlington, Vt.: Ashgate Publishing Company, 2011.

Iveson, Kurt. *Publics and the City*. Malden, Mass.: Blackwell, 2007.

Jacobs, Jane. *The Death and Life of Great American Cities*. New York: Random House, 1961.

Jacoby, Russell. *Picture Imperfect: Utopian Thought for an Anti-Utopian Age*. New York: Columbia University Press, 2005.

Jasanoff, Sheila, ed. *States of Knowledge: The Co-production of Science and Social Order*. London: Routledge, 2004.

Jennings, Jeremy. "Citizenship, Republicanism and Multiculturalism in Contemporary France." *British Journal of Political Science* 30, no. 4 (2000): 575–98.

Jobert, Bruno, and Bruno Théret. "France: La consécration républicaine du néolibéralisme." In *Le Tournant néo-libéral en Europe*, ed. Bruno Jobert, 21–86. Paris: L'Harmattan, 1994.

Jolé, Michèle. "Le destin festif du Canal Saint-Martin." *Pouvoirs,* no. 1 (2006): 117–30.

———. "Surveiller ou veiller sur le jardin?" *Urbanisme,* no. 343 (2005): 44–46.

Jolé, Michèle, Stéphane Tonnelat, and Andrew Newman. "Le public des jardins de Paris, entre observation et action." Report submitted to the city of Paris, Laboratoire Vie Urbaine, UMR CNRS LAVU, 2009.

Joseph, Isaac. *La ville sans qualités.* Éditions de l'Aube, 1998.

———. *L'espace du public: Les compétences du citadin:* Colloque d'arc-et-Senans, November 8–10, 1990. Paris: Plan Urbain, 1991.

Juris, Jeffrey S. "Reflections on #Occupy Everywhere: Social Media, Public Space, and Emerging Logics of Aggregation." *American Ethnologist* 39, no. 2 (2012): 259–79.

Kaika, Maria, and Erik Swyngedouw. "Cities, Natures, and the Political Imaginary." *Architectural Design* 82, no. 4 (2012): 22–27.

Kane, Stephanie C. *Where Rivers Meet the Sea: The Political Ecology of Water.* Philadelphia: Temple University Press, 2012.

Kanna, Ahmed. *Dubai, the City as Corporation.* Minneapolis: University of Minnesota Press, 2011.

Katz, Cindi. "Vagabond Capitalism and the Necessity of Social Reproduction." *Antipode* 33, no. 4 (2001): 709–28.

Klein, Kim. "Common Frame for Social Justice—Kim Klein and the Commons." http://kimkleinandthecommons.blogspot.com. Accessed 2012.

Kleinman, Julie. "The Gare du Nord: Parisian Topographies of Exchange." *Ethnologie Française* 42, no. 3 (2012): 567–76.

Kohn, Margaret. *Radical Space: Building the House of the People.* Ithaca, N.Y.: Cornell University Press, 2003.

Larkin, Brian. "The Politics and Poetics of Infrastructure." *Annual Review of Anthropology* 42 (2013): 327–43.

———. *Signal and Noise: Media, Infrastructure, and Urban Culture in Nigeria.* Durham, N.C.: Duke University Press, 2008.

Larson, Scott. *Building like Moses with Jacobs in Mind: Contemporary Planning in New York City.* Philadelphia: Temple University Press, 2013.

Latour, Bruno. *Aramis, or the Love of Technology.* Cambridge, Mass.: Harvard University Press, 1996.

———. *Politics of Nature: How to Bring the Sciences into Democracy.* Cambridge, Mass.: Harvard University Press, 2004.

———. *We Have Never Been Modern.* Cambridge, Mass.: Harvard University Press, 1993.

Lecroart, Paul. "Regenerating the Plaine Saint-Denis, 1985–2020." Paris: Institut d'Aménagement et d'Urbanisme—Île-de-France, 2008.

Lefebvre, Henri. *The Production of Space.* New York: Wiley-Blackwell, 1996.

———. "The Right to the City." In *Writings on Cities,* ed. Eleonore Kofman and Elizabeth Lebas, 62–181. Cambridge: Blackwell Publishers, 1996.

Le Gendre, Bertrand. "Pourquoi les Vélib', fétiches des bobos, sont vandalisés, par Bertrand Le Gendre." *Le Monde.fr.* June 12, 2009. Accessed 2013.

Legras, Stéphane. *Pajol: 10 ans de concertation.* Paris: Coordination Espace Pajol, 2013.

Leitner, Helga, and Eric Sheppard. "'The City Is Dead, Long Live the Net': Harnessing European Interurban Networks for a Neoliberal Agenda." *Antipode* 34, no. 3 (2002): 495–518.

Le Monde. "Heurts entre jeunes et policiers à la Gare du Nord. LeMonde.fr, March 27, 2007. Accessed 2013.

Le Parisien. "Fête du Printemps pour les Jardins d'Éole." *Le Parisien,* March 31, 2001.

———. "La drogue a vidé les Jardins d'Éole." Leparisien.fr, July 12, 2012. Accessed 2013.

———. "Les Jardins d'Éole ferment pour 'réparation.'" Leparisien.fr, March 18, 2013. Accessed 2013.

Logan, John R., and Harvey L. Molotch. *Urban Fortunes: The Political Economy of Place.* Berkeley: University of California Press, 1987.

Low, Setha M. *Behind the Gates: Life, Security, and the Pursuit of Happiness in Fortress America.* New York: Routledge, 2003.

———. *On the Plaza: The Politics of Public Space and Culture.* Austin: University of Texas Press, 2000.

———. *Theorizing the City: The New Urban Anthropology Reader.* New Brunswick, N.J.: Rutgers University Press, 1999.

Low, Setha M., and Neil Smith. *The Politics of Public Space.* New York: Routledge, 2006.

Lubin, David A., and Daniel C. Esty. "The Sustainability Imperative." *Harvard Business Review* 88, no. 5 (2010). https://hbr.org/2010/05/the-sustainability-imperative. Accessed 2013.

Lyon, David. *Surveillance Society: Monitoring Everyday Life.* Buckingham: Open University Press, 2002.

Magnon, Régine, and Catherine Mangeney. *Atlas de la santé en Île-de-France.* Paris: IAURIF (Institut d'Aménagement et d'Urbanisme de la Région d'Île-de-France), 2005.

Mairie de Paris. "Chapelle International—Paris Nord-Est." http://paris-nord-est .paris.fr. 2013. Accessed 2013.

———. "Concours de maîtrise d'œuvre pour la création d'un parc paysage Cour du Maroc à Paris 18ème arrondissement." Paris: Direction des Parcs, Jardins et Espaces Verts, 2003.

———. "Le project social—Paris Nord-Est." http://paris-nord-est.paris.fr. 2013. Accessed 2013.

———. "Les chiffres-clés du chômage à Paris—juillet 2013." Paris: Direction de l'Économie, de l'Innovation et de l'Enseignement Supérieur, August 2013.

———. "Les Vélib' et les bobos, c'est une grande histoire d'amour!" http://blog.velib. paris.fr, 2009. Accessed 2013.

———. *Plan Biodiversité de Paris*. City of Paris, 2011.

———. "Un project global—Paris Nord-Est." http://paris-nord-est.paris.fr. 2013. Accessed 2013.

———. "Vélib' fête son 6e anniversaire! Vélib' et moi le blog." http://blog.velib.paris .fr. 2013. Accessed 2013.

Marchand, Stéphane. "Après l'attentat de la rue de Tanger. Paris: Ces états qui financent les mosquées en France." *Le Figaro*, April 2, 1997.

Mariani, Manuela, and Patrick Barron. *Terrain Vague: Interstices at the Edge of the Pale*. New York: Routledge, 2013.

Massignon, Louis, and Ernest Leroux. *Annuaire du monde musulman*. Paris: Presses Universitaires de France, 1923.

McDonogh, Gary W. "Discourses of the City: Policy and Response in Post-Transitional Barcelona." *City and Society* 5, no. 1 (1991): 40–63.

———. "Learning from Barcelona: Discourse, Power and Praxis in the Sustainable City." *City and Society* 23, no. 2 (2011): 135–53.

———. "Mediterranean Reflections: Reconstructing Nature in Modern Barcelona." In *Greening the City: Urban Landscapes in the Twentieth Century*, ed. Dorothee Brantz and Sonja Dümpelmann, 57–74. Charlottesville: University of Virginia Press, 2011

McDonogh, Gary, Cindy Isenhour, and Melissa Checker. "Introduction: Sustainability in the City: Ethnographic Approaches." *City and Society* 23, no. 2 (2011): 113–16.

Meadows, Donella H. *The Limits to Growth*. London: Earth Island, 1972.

Milliot, Virginie. "Pluralistic Ambiance and Urban Socialization." Trans. Neil O'Brien. *Ambiance: Environnement sensible, architecture et espace urbain* (2013): http://am biances.revues.org/223. Accessed 2013.

Milliot, Virginie, and Stéphane Tonnelat. "Contentious Policing in Paris: The Street as a Space for Emotional Public." In *Policing Cities: Urban Securitization and Regulation in a 21st Century World*, ed. Randy Lippert and Kevin Walby. New York: Routledge, 2013.

Mitchell, Don. *The Right to the City: Social Justice and the Fight for Public Space*. New York: Guilford Press, 2003.

Mostafavi, Mohsen, and Gareth Doherty. *Ecological Urbanism*. Baden, Switzerland: Lars Müller Publishers, 2010.

Murray, Seth. "The Presence of the Past: A Historical Ecology of Basque Commons and the French State." In *Social and Ecological History of the Pyrénées: State, Market, and Landscape*, ed. Ismael Vaccaro and Oriol Beltran, 25–41. Walnut Creek, Calif.: Left Coast Press, 2010.

Myers, Garth A. *Disposable Cities: Garbage, Governance and Sustainable Development in Urban Africa*. Farnham, UK: Ashgate, 2005.

Neveu, Catherine. *Citoyenneté et espace public: Habitants, jeunes et citoyens dans une ville du Nord*. Villeneuve-d'Ascq: Presses Universitaires du Septentrion, 2003.

Newman, Andrew. "Gatekeepers of the Urban Commons? Vigilant Citizenship and Neoliberal Space in Multiethnic Paris." *Antipode* 45, no. 4 (2013): 947–64.

———. "Seeing the Republic in a Park." In *Life among Planners*, ed. Jennifer Mack and Michael Herzfeld, forthcoming. Philadelphia: University of Pennsylvania Press.

Newman, Peter, and Jeffrey R. Kenworthy. *Sustainability and Cities: Overcoming Automobile Dependence*. Washington, D.C: Island Press, 1999.

Noiriel, Gérard. *The French Melting Pot: Immigration, Citizenship, and National Identity*. Trans. Geoffroy de Laforcade. Minneapolis: University of Minnesota Press, 1996.

Nunes, Éric. "Huchon: Le Grand Paris de Sarkozy est 'un projet autoritaire.'" Le Monde.fr. March 11, 2010. Accessed 2013.

O'Connor, Martin. *Is Capitalism Sustainable? Political Economy and the Politics of Ecology*. New York: Guilford Press, 1994.

Ong, Aihwa. *Neoliberalism as Exception: Mutations in Citizenship and Sovereignty*. Durham, N.C.: Duke University Press, 2006.

Palumbo, Maria Anita. "Figures de l'habiter: Modes de négociation du pluralisme à Barbès ou de l'altérité comme condition quotidienne." *Lieux Communs Cahiers*, no. 12 (2009): 128–49.

Paquot, Thierry. "La bicyclette urbaine: Histoire et représentations." *Urbanisme*, no. 366 (May–June 2009): 45–50.

Paris sans Vidéosurveillance. "La pétition pour un Paris sans caméras de vidéosurveillance—Paris sans vidéosurveillance." http://www.paris-sans-videosurveillance .fr/. 2009. Accessed 2012.

Pearsall, Hamil. "Moving Out or Moving In? Resilience to Environmental Gentrification in New York City." *Local Environment* 17, no. 9 (2012): 1013–26.

Peet, Richard, and Michael Watts. *Liberation Ecologies: Environment, Development, Social Movements*. London: Routledge, 1996.

Perrineau, Pascal, ed. *L'engagement politique: Déclin ou mutation*. Paris: Presses de la Fondation Nationale des Sciences Politiques, 1994.

Pétonnet, Colette. "L'observation flottante: L'exemple d'un cimetière parisien." *L'Homme* 22, no. 4 (1982): 37–47.

Pinçon, Michel, and Monique Pinçon-Charlot. *Sociologie de Paris*. Paris: La Découverte, 2004.

Pinol, Jean-Luc. *Atlas historique des villes de France*. Paris: Hachette, 1996.

Prasad, Monica. "Why Is France So French? Culture, Institutions, and Neoliberalism, 1974–1981." *American Journal of Sociology* 111, no. 2 (2005): 357–407.

Quastel, Noah. "Political Ecologies of Gentrification." *Urban Geography* 30, no. 7 (2009): 694–725.

Rademacher, Anne. *Reigning the River: Urban Ecologies and Political Transformation in Kathmandu*. Durham, N.C.: Duke University Press, 2011.

Reed, Peter. *Groundswell*. New York: Museum of Modern Art, 2005.

Robbins, Paul. *Lawn People: How Grasses, Weeds, and Chemicals Make Us Who We Are*. Philadelphia: Temple University Press, 2007.

Robotham, Donald. "Anthropology and the Present Moment." *Transforming Anthropology* 19, no. 2 (2011): 154–61.

Ross, Andrew. *Bird on Fire: Lessons from the World's Least Sustainable City*. Oxford: Oxford University Press, 2011.

Ross, Kristin. *May '68 and Its Afterlives*. Chicago: University of Chicago Press, 2002.

Rotenberg, Robert L. *Landscape and Power in Vienna*. Baltimore: Johns Hopkins University Press, 1995.

Sanjek, Roger. *Gray Panthers*. Philadelphia: University of Pennsylvania Press, 2009.

Sansot, Pierre. *Jardins publics*. Paris: Payot, 1993.

Sarkozy, Nicolas. "Le Grand Paris." Presidential address at the Cité de l'Architecture et du Patrimoine, Paris, April 29, 2009. http://grandparis.over-blog.com/article-308 43350.html. Accessed 2014.

Sassen, Saskia. *The Global City: New York, London, Tokyo*. Princeton, N.J.: Princeton University Press, 1991.

Savitch, H. V. *Post-industrial Cities: Politics and Planning in New York, Paris, and London*. Princeton, N.J.: Princeton University Press, 1988.

Schmidt, Alfred. *The Concept of Nature in Marx*. New York: Verso, 2014.

Schmidt, Vivien. "French Capitalism Transformed, yet Still a Third Variety of Capitalism." *Economy and Society* 32, no. 4 (2003): 526–54.

Schneider, Jane, and Ida Susser. *Wounded Cities: Destruction and Reconstruction in a Globalized World*. Oxford: Berg, 2003.

Selby, Jennifer A. *Questioning French Secularism: Gender Politics and Islam in a Parisian Suburb*. New York: Palgrave, 2012.

Senat.fr. Projet de loi de finances pour 2013: Sécurité (gendarmerie nationale et police nationale). Senat.fr, Rapport général no. 14, November 22, 2012. Accessed 2013.

Shepard, Benjamin H., and Gregory Smithsimon. *The Beach beneath the Streets: Contesting New York City's Public Spaces*. Albany: Excelsior Editions/State University of New York Press, 2011.

Silberman, Roxanne, and Irène Fournier. Les secondes générations sur le marché du travail en France: Une pénalité ethnique ancrée dans le temps. *Revue Française de Sociologie* 47, no. 2 (2006): 243–92.

Silverstein, Paul A. *Algeria in France: Transpolitics, Race, and Nation*. Bloomington: Indiana University Press, 2004.

———. "The Context of Antisemitism and Islamophobia in France." *Patterns of Prejudice* 42, no. 1 (2008): 1–26.

Simon, Catherine. "Tour de Babel." *Le Monde*, May 25, 2007.

Simon, Patrick. "France and the Unknown Second Generation: Preliminary Results on Social Mobility." *International Migration Review* 37, no. 4 (2003): 1091–1119.

Slate.fr. "Grand Paris de droite, Grand Paris de gauche?" March 6, 2013. Accessed 2013.

Smith, Neil. "Nature as Accumulation Strategy." *Socialist Register*, no. 16 (2007): 19–41.

———. "New Globalism, New Urbanism: Gentrification as Global Urban Strategy." *Antipode* 34, no. 3 (2002): 427–50.

———. *The New Urban Frontier: Gentrification and the Revanchist City*. London: Routledge, 1996.

———. "The Production of Nature." In *FutureNatural: Nature, Science, Culture*, ed. Jon Bird, Barry Curtis, Melinda Mash, and Tim Putnam, 35–54. New York: Routledge, 1996.

———. "Remaking Scale: Competition and Cooperation in Prenational and Postnational Europe." In *Competitive European Peripheries*, ed. Heikki Eskelinen and Folke Snickars, 59–74. Berlin: Springer, 1995.

———. *Uneven Development: Nature, Capital, and the Production of Space*. New York: Blackwell, 1984.

Sokolovsky, Jay. "Civic Ecology and the Anthropology of Place: Urban Community Gardens and the Creation of Inclusionary Landscapes." *Anthropology News* 52, no. 3 (2011): 6.

Sorkin, Michael. *Variations on a Theme Park: The New American City and the End of Public Space*. New York: Hill and Wang, 1992.

Spirn, Anne W. *The Granite Garden: Urban Nature and Human Design*. New York: Basic Books, 1984.

Stanek, Lukasz. *Henri Lefebvre on Space: Architecture, Urban Research, and the Production of Theory*. Minneapolis: University of Minnesota Press, 2011.

Stoetzer, Bettina. "At the Forest Edges of the City: Nature, Race and National Belonging in Berlin." Dissertation, University of California, Santa Cruz, 2011.

Stolcke, Verena. "Talking Culture: New Boundaries, New Rhetorics of Exclusion in Europe." *Current Anthropology* 36, no. 1 (1995): 1–24.

Susser, Ida. "Global Visions and Grassroots Movements: An Anthropological Perspective." *International Journal of Urban and Regional Research* 30, no. 1 (2006): 212–18.

———. "Magical Urbanism and Rural Resistance." Leo Srole Annual Lecture, Hobart and William Smith College. Geneva, New York, March 14, 2007.

———. *Norman Street: Poverty and Politics in an Urban Neighborhood,* updated ed. Oxford: Oxford University Press, 2012.

Susser, Ida, and Stéphane Tonnelat. "Transformative Cities: The Three Urban Commons." *Focaal,* no. 66 (2013): 105–32.

Swyngedouw, Erik. "The City as a Hybrid: On Nature, Society and Cyborg Urbanization." *Capitalism Nature Socialism* 7, no. 2 (1996): 65–80.

———. "Impossible Sustainability and the Post-Political Condition." In *Making Strategies in Spatial Planning,* ed. Maria Cerreta, Grazia Concillio, and Valeria Monno, 13–40. New York: Springer, 2010.

Tassel, Fabrice. "Les expulsions de sans-papiers en forte hausse en 2012." http://www.liberation.fr, January 21, 2013. Accessed 2013.

Terrio, Susan J. *Judging Mohammed: Juvenile Delinquency, Immigration, and Exclusion at the Paris Palace of Justice.* Stanford, Calif.: Stanford University Press, 2009.

Ticktin, Miriam I. *Casualties of Care: Immigration and the Politics of Humanitarianism in France.* Berkeley: University of California Press, 2011.

Tidball, Keith G., and Marianne E. Krasny. "From Risk to Resilience: What Role for Community Greening and Civic Ecology in Cities?" In *Social Learning towards a More Sustainable World,* ed. Arjen E. J. Walls, 149–64. Wageningen, the Netherlands: Wageningen Academic Publishers, 2007.

Tonnelat, Stéphane. "Out of Frame." *Ethnography* 9, no. 3 (2008): 291–324.

———. "Paris' Parks: Between Public Service and Public Space." Paper presented at the Society for the Anthropology of North America conference, Baruch College, New York, April 22, 2006.

Tsing, Anna. *Friction: An Ethnography of Global Connection.* Princeton, N.J.: Princeton University Press, 2005.

———. "Nature in the Making." In *New Directions in Anthropology and Environment: Intersections,* ed. Carole L Crumley, 3–23. Walnut Creek, Calif.: Altamira Press, 2001.

United Nations. "United Nations Conference on Environment and Development." www.sustainabledevelopment.un.org/content/documents/Agenda21.pdf. Accessed 2013.

van Velsen, Jaap. "The Extended Case Method and Situational Analysis." In *The Craft of Social Anthropology,* ed. A. L. Epstein and Max Gluckman, 129–49. London: Tavistock, 1967.

Védrines, Ambroise. "Il y a un Vélib' à Bamako; personne ne sait comment il est arrivé là-bas." Slate Afrique.com, 2013. Accessed 2013.

VélibOfficiel. "Vélib'—interview des 'Bobos de Merde.'" Posted on http://www.you tube.com/. 2011. Accessed 2013.

Veyret, Yvette, Renaud Le Goix, Michel Lussault, and Aurélie Boissière. *Atlas des villes durables: Écologie, urbanisme, société: L'Europe est-elle un modèle?* Paris: Éditions Autrement, 2011.

Vincendon, Sibylle. "Pour Delanoë, Sarkozy n'est pas propriétaire du Grand Paris— Grand Paris et petits détours." http://grandparis.blogs.liberation.fr/. October 11, 2011. Accessed 2013.

Visser, Jelle. *Union Membership Statistics in 24 Countries.* Washington, D.C.: U.S. Department of Labor, 2006.

Wacquant, Loïc. *Deadly Symbiosis: Race and the Rise of Neoliberal Penalty.* Oxford: Blackwell, 2003.

Waters, Sarah. *Social Movements in France: Towards a New Citizenship.* Houndmills, Basingstoke, Hampshire: Palgrave Macmillan, 2003.

West, Paige. *Conservation Is Our Government Now: The Politics of Ecology in Papua New Guinea.* Durham, N.C.: Duke University Press, 2006.

White, James W. "Old Wine, Cracked Bottle? Tokyo, Paris, and the Global City Hypothesis." *Sage Urban Studies Abstracts* 26, no. 2 (1998): 451.

Whyte, William H. *The Social Life of Small Urban Spaces.* Washington, D.C.: Conservation Foundation, 1980.

Wilder, Gary. *The French Imperial Nation-State: Negritude and Colonial Humanism between the Two World Wars.* Chicago: University of Chicago Press, 2005.

Williams, Raymond. *The Country and the City.* New York: Oxford University Press, 1973.

Wolf, Eric R. *Europe and the People without History.* Berkeley: University of California Press, 1982.

———. "Ownership and Political Ecology." *Anthropological Quarterly* 45, no. 3 (1972): 201–5.

Wolff, Janet. "The Invisible Flâneuse: Women and the Literature of Modernity." *Theory, Culture and Society* 2, no. 3 (1985): 37–46.

Zukin, Sharon. *Naked City: The Death and Life of Authentic Urban Places.* Oxford: Oxford University Press, 2010.

INDEX

239

ANDREW NEWMAN is assistant professor of anthropology at Wayne State University in Detroit.